Jim R

Jim Ring was educated at Brasen
was a scholar. His biography of E
Riddle of the Sands, won the Marsh
was followed by *How the English Made the Alps*. A study of Britain's Cold War submariners, *We Come Unseen*, appeared in 2001 and won the Mountbatten prize. He is married with one daughter and one son, and lives on the north Norfolk coast.

Also by Jim Ring

Erskine Childers

How the English Made the Alps

We Come Unseen

Riviera

The Rise and Rise of the Côte d'Azur

JIM RING

JOHN MURRAY

For Ashmole

First published in Great Britain in 2004 by John Murray (Publishers)
A division of Hodder Headline

Paperback edition 2005

1 3 5 7 9 10 8 6 4 2

A CIP catalogue record for this title is available from the British Library

ISBN 0 7195 5696 1

Typeset in Monotype Bembo by Servis Filmsetting Ltd, Manchester

Printed and bound by Clays Ltd, St Ives plc

Hodder Headline policy is to use papers that are natural, renewable and recyclable products and made from wood grown in sustainable forests. The logging and manufacturing processes are expected to conform to the environmental regulations of the country of origin.

John Murray (Publishers)
338 Euston Road
London NW1 3BH

'What do you do with a place that is beautiful? Destroy it.'

Claus von Bulow

The South of France
DRÔ
Montélimar
ARDÊCHE
LOZÈRE
AVEYRON
Alès
Orange
Millau
VAUC
GARD
R. Rhône
Avignon
Nîmes
Arles
Montpellier
BOUCHES
HERAULT
Béziers
Narbonne
GOLFE DU LION
Carcassonne
AUDE
MEDITERR
Perpignan
PYRÉNÉES
ORIENTALES
V
Draguignan
Figueras
R. Argens
N
N
SPAIN
Grimaud
St Maxime
Gerona
St Tropez
Cavalaire-sur-Mer
0 10 20 30 40 50 miles
0 10 20 30 40 50 km

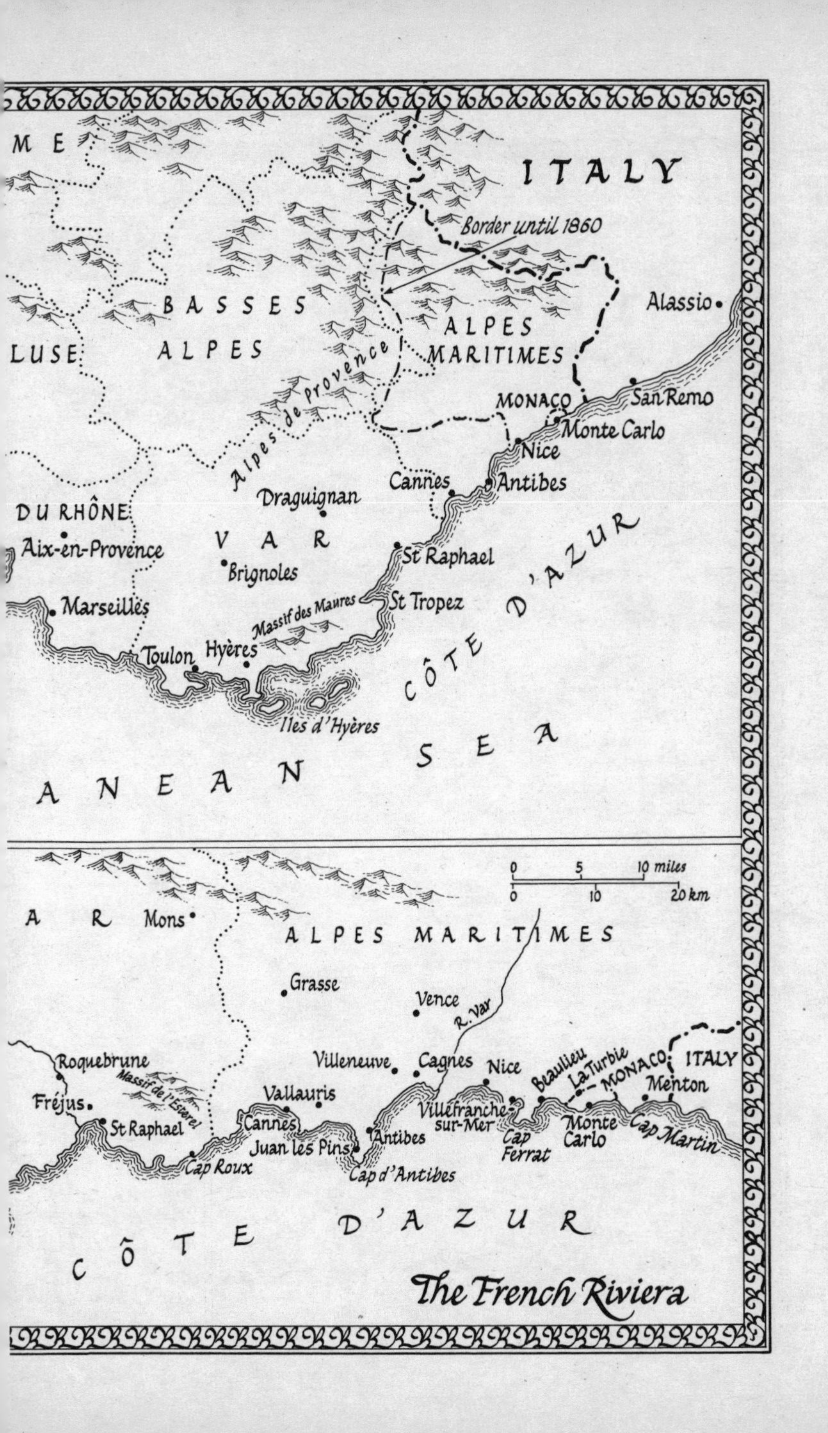
ITALY
Border until 1860
BASSES ALPES
ALPES MARITIMES
Alassio
LUSE
Alpes de Provence
MONACO
San Remo
Monte Carlo
Nice
Cannes
Antibes
Draguignan
DU RHÔNE
VAR
Aix-en-Provence
Brignoles
St Raphael
CÔTE D'AZUR
Massif des Maures
St Tropez
Marseilles
Toulon
Hyères
Iles d'Hyères
ANEAN SEA
0 5 10 miles
0 10 20 km
AR
Mons
ALPES MARITIMES
Grasse
Vence
R. Var
Roquebrune
Massif de l'Esterel
Villeneuve
Cagnes
Nice
Beaulieu
La Turbie
MONACO
ITALY
Menton
Fréjus
Vallauris
St Raphael
Cannes
Villefranche-sur-Mer
Cap Ferrat
Monte Carlo
Cap Martin
Antibes
Juan les Pins
Cap Roux
Cap d'Antibes
CÔTE D'AZUR
The French Riviera

Contents

Illustrations

Section 1

Section 2

Foreword

When I first visited the Riviera as an undergraduate twenty-five years ago, I was aghast.

I had little enough experience of the Continent, let alone gone further afield. My parents were both London doctors who rarely allowed themselves a week's holiday a year. It was not spent abroad – partly because they had little truck with foreigners, and also because it was just before the time when the British made it their habit to holiday beyond their own shores. The 'jet-set', those who travelled by the pioneering de Havilland Comet and the Boeing 707, were celebrities – the actors Richard Burton and Elizabeth Taylor, the Beatles on their way out to Shea Stadium, the racing driver Jackie Stewart, Presidents Khrushchev and Lyndon Johnson. We were not.

As a consequence, destinations like St Moritz, Acapulco, Barbados, Capri, Florence and Mustique had an infinite romance and allure, Shangri-las of unattainable luxury, sophistication, glamour, culture, exoticism and romance. Brought up as I was in Bexley, Sidcup, Redhill and Croydon, they might have been Prospero's enchanted island.

The jewel in the crown of my imagination was the Côte d'Azur. Largely ignorant of French history, manners, achievements and people, I took France at its own estimate as the byword for Continental – no, global – sophistication, culture and taste. It was not long after President de Gaulle's refusal to admit the United Kingdom into what was then the European Common Market.

Paris was the capital of the world's imagination, art, beauty, women and, of course, cuisine. No wine other than French *was* wine. As for the South – the Riviera, the Côte d'Azur – it was the *ne plus ultra* of the world's resorts: the golden chain of Monaco, Nice, Antibes, Juan-les-Pins, St Raphael and St Tropez was a Promised Land of warmth, natural beauty, hospitable people and, presumably, jolly good five-star hotels like the Hilton.

So when I eventually visited it in 1978 I was surprised by the agglomeration of tower blocks, dilapidated Edwardian hotels, estate agencies, fast-food restaurants and shopping centres that I discovered littering the hundred-mile stretch of pebble-stone beaches from Hyères to Menton and the Italian frontier. Surprised, too, by a coast that seemed little more than a strip of polluted sea, bordered by a few yards of burning human flesh, a railway and an autoroute. Surprised by the French who – as I might have guessed from de Gaulle – were Anglophobe, choosing to remember Napoleon, Trafalgar and Waterloo rather than their liberation at British and American hands in two world wars.

I was not to return to the Riviera for almost twenty years.

I was then working on a book about the contribution made by the English to the development of the Alps. Without the mountaineer Edward Whymper, the travel agent Thomas Cook, the pioneer skiers Arthur Conan Doyle and Arnold Lunn, I argued, the range today would have been little better than the East Anglian fens. Research on this took me first to the alpine resorts that, until 1939, had been virtually English enclaves: places like Wengen, Mürren, Kandersteg and Zermatt. Then I visited two resorts created by English entrepreneurs after the Second World War: Colonel Robert Lindsay's Méribel in the Haute Savoie and Peter Boumphrey's Isola 2000 in the Alpes Maritimes, high above Nice. As the post-war French high-altitude resorts, like Flaine, Courchevel and Val d'Isère, represented some of the worst acts of architectural vandalism ever perpetrated in the Alps, I wanted to see if the English had managed any better. As I discovered in the course of my 1997 trip, they had not.

From Isola I drove down into Nice. On this occasion my expectations of the city were low, and not much about it surprised me. True, its setting between the Alpes Maritimes and the azure sea was incomparable, and the labyrinthine old town had a vitality, character and pleasing squalor of its own, a sort of Soho-en-Mer. But other than that and the weather, what with its stony beach and *belle époque* hotels, it was reminiscent of Brighton. Two things surprised me, though: first, the people – the concierge in my hotel said that the Riviera attracted more than eight million visitors each year and, as far as I could see, they were all in Nice – and second, that the palm-fringed motorway along the front was named Promenade des Anglais. The English made the Alps: had they made the Riviera too?

I had a book to finish and I cannot say I troubled myself much with the question then. In due course, though, the paradoxes of the coast began to interest me. As cursory research suggested – not least in Patrick Howarth's *When the Riviera Was Ours* – it was indeed foreign tourists rather than the French who had developed the coast. The English were prominent among them, subsequently the Russians and the Americans. The locals did not reclaim their own coast until after the Second World War. As for the huge popularity of a destination that by any rational estimate was decades past its sell-by date, grossly polluted and spoiled, that was a puzzle and the second paradox. What was it about the Côte d'Azur that made it a Shangri-la?

Of the Alps, Arnold Lunn wrote: 'Men lifted up their eyes to the hills to discover the spiritual values which were clouded by the smoke and grime of the industrial revolution.' It was difficult to imagine that Victorian Englishmen would have felt the same about the Riviera. What had attracted them to the coast? What had they done to develop it? And what continues to attract people from all over the world to it in such numbers?

In trying to answer these questions I have not attempted to write a comprehensive social – or, indeed, Social – history of the coast. Rather, I have drawn together a series of incidents and a collection of people who seemed emblematic, illustrative or symptomatic of the way in which the Côte d' Azur developed, as well as being of particular interest to a right-thinking English audience.

I thought it a curious, entertaining and rather salutary story.

Jim Ring, Burnham Overy Staithe
January 2004

Prologue:
The Blue Train

London's great railway termini are our gates to the glorious and unknown, through which we pass into adventure and sunshine. Or so E. M. Forster thought during the infancy of air travel and in the days when people still took holidays in Britain. In Paddington all Cornwall was latent; from the inclines of Liverpool Street lay fenlands and the Norfolk Broads; Scotland was beyond the pylons of Euston; Wessex behind the poised chaos of Waterloo. But through stolid Victoria lay a land of infinitely greater promise: that of the snow-capped mountains, blue seas and palm trees of the Riviera – or, if you had the misfortune to be French, the Côte d'Azur.

The novelist Evelyn Waugh found plenty of reasons to make such an escape from London in February 1929. In *Labels*, his journal of a Mediterranean voyage, he wrote that 'almost every cause was present which can contribute to human discontent'. The government was about to fall, the introduction of talking pictures at the expense of silent cinema had set back twenty years the most vital art form of the twentieth century, and there was not even a good murder case. Above all, though, 'It was intolerably cold. People shrank, in those days, from the icy contact of a cocktail glass, like the Duchess of Malfi from the dead hand, and crept stiff as automata from their draughty taxis into the nearest tube railway station, where they stood, pressed together for warmth, coughing and sneezing among the evening papers.' Waugh, with an enthusiasm for speed and modernity that was soon to abate, flew from Croydon to Paris. Commercial air services were still a novelty. Most travellers to the

Riviera took the morning boat train from Victoria, out through the grey suburbs of Battersea and Dulwich, past the hunched winter landscape of Kent to Dover. Then they hazarded their stomachs on the steel grey seas to Calais. It was there that their adventures began, for at the Gare Maritime the Blue Train awaited them.

The Paris–Lyon–Mediterranée railway had reached the Riviera in the 1860s. At a stroke, it transformed a journey that had taken twelve days from Paris into one of thirty hours. 'Railways,' wrote one of the early advocates of the Riviera, Dr J. Henry Bennet, 'have all but annihilated space … A traveller may leave the London Bridge Station at 7.40 on a Monday morning, by mail train for Paris, and be at Nice or Menton for supper the following day.' It was miraculous, and even in the early days standards of comfort, as well as speed, on these expresses were high. *Coupe-lits* were compartments with four seats, three of which were convertible into beds. The fourth concealed a closet, characterised by Dr Edward Sparks as 'well trapped'. Parties could hire private carriages with separate sitting-, smoking- and bedrooms. Proper sleeping cars, the invention of the American George Pullman, appeared in 1877 in the form of *wagons-lits* running from Paris. In 1883 the service was extended to Calais, while 1893 saw the inauguration of the weekly Mediterranean Express, composed entirely of sleeping and dining cars, as though there was nothing else in life to do. It ran on Thursdays throughout the traditional Riviera season from December to April, and connected with the boat train from London.

There were various minor improvements in comfort and speed in the years until 1914 and the outbreak of the First World War, but the train introduced on 8 December 1922, the Blue Train, represented the apotheosis of railway travel. The thirty-foot, four-wheel carriages that had jolted, shaken, rattled and rolled along the tracks were replaced with smooth double-bogied cigar tubes, almost twice as long as their predecessors – much the same as those used today. Rather than packing the passengers in like ninepins, each carriage accommodated only ten sleepers and had its own attendant. The dining car, with its movable scenery, upstaged Maxim's, the Café Royal, Simpson's and the Savoy. Standards of craftsmanship and joinery made the carriages seem a creation of the cabinet-maker rather than the railway works. The teak ones on the Paris–Lyon–Mediterranée had generally been varnished brown. Uniquely on the French railways, the new steel carriages were painted blue, picked out with gold. To the official title of the Calais–Mediterranean Express was soon added the colloquialism that even an Englishman could understand: Le Train Bleu. It sounded much better than *train brun*.

The Blue Train built its reputation not simply on its physical entity but on its clientele and the destinations it served. The accommodation was exclusively first class and patronised principally by the famous – or so the Paris-Lyon-Mediterranée publicity would suggest. Royalty was represented by the Prince of Wales, subsequently King Edward VIII and – less happily – the Duke of Windsor, who had his own private carriage attached to the train; the big screen by Charlie Chaplin, at the height of his fame; glamour by the gamine couturier Coco Chanel, who designed the costumes for Sergei Diaghilev's ballet inspired by the express, so named, and premièred in Monte Carlo in 1924. There was the tennis player Fred Perry, who won both Wimbledon and the United States Open singles championships three times. Winston Churchill was so frequent a traveller that he might have deserved a discount, if such a thing had existed. Agatha Christie came to research *The Mystery of the Blue Train*. The Duke of Westminster, the richest man in Britain, travelled on it to meet his yacht at Cannes, the four-masted *Flying Cloud*. James Gordon Bennett, the American newspaper magnate, once tipped the *conducteur* twenty thousand francs. During the height of the season the service was grossly oversubscribed, and it became a privilege – albeit one that could be bought – to procure a seat and a berth. No wonder some called it the millionaires' train.

At 1 p.m. sharp, with all the ceremony of an ocean liner, the express would draw out of the grey windswept Gare Maritime and was soon thundering along the fast line to Amiens. Dusk would already be falling at the Gare du Nord in Paris, where a few passengers alighted. Then, the train took the *ceintre* line round the eastern side of the capital to the Gare de Lyon, where it was coupled to more carriages. It was early evening when it pulled out to begin the long haul to Dijon, Châlons and Lyon, with cocktails and dinner ahead of the passengers. So far did the dining car aspire to *haute cuisine* that the feast served to Charles Ryder and Rex Mottram in Evelyn Waugh's *Brideshead Revisited* might well have been on the menu: soup of *oseille*, sole in white wine sauce, *caneton à la presse*, and lemon soufflé, all washed down with a 1906 Montrachet and, to accompany the duck, a 1904 Clos de Bère. Diners ate to the muffled roar and steady beat of the train plunging south, rain and sleet slashing the windows. Brandy followed, then bed in the exquisite miniature cabins of the sleeping car.

To draw up the blind the following morning was to experience deliverance. The spectral cold, the gloom, the damp, the fog, the grey had vanished, replaced by a sunlit world of terracotta roofs, white houses, blue Mediterranean bays, high green hills with a glint of alpine snow, and vegetation reminiscent of the tropics – mimosa and eucalyptus, Mexican yucca, bougainvillaea and palm trees. Here, after the English winter, was the light, warmth and vitality of what the Victorians had discovered to be the best climate in Europe. 'It was like passing from winter to summer,' wrote the feminist and philanthropist Frances Power Cobbe in 1864. 'We feel that we have left behind the atmosphere of black frosts, moral and physical, and may expand ourselves happily in a much milder medium.' Yet, as Cobbe implied, the climate was only the most obvious attraction of the South. For the Victorians and their successors the Riviera was also a realm of peace, freedom, self-indulgence and self-expression, a glorious escape from the ethical and social irons of the North.

The train that brought them to such a promised land reached the coast at Marseille, the ancient Greek port at the western end of the

Riviera. There it turned east and headed towards the principal resorts of the seaboard: St Raphael, Juan-les-Pins, Antibes, Cannes, Nice, Monaco. These were the stations served by the train *en route* to its terminus at Menton, the eastern extent of the French littoral, beyond which lay Italy and its own, inferior riviera. By Evelyn Waugh's time these places had become synonymous with glamour, exclusivity, luxury, beauty and pleasure. For Waugh, writing much later in the persona of his *alter ego* Gilbert Pinfold, it was a land of lost content: 'The sea might have been any sea by the look of it, but he knew it to be that splendid enclosure that held all the world's history and half the happiest memories of his own life.' No wonder that a favourite description of Le Train Bleu was 'Train of Paradise'.

The Riviera was the world's first major tourist destination. Ever since its 'discovery' in 1834 by the former Lord Chancellor, Lord Brougham, it had been developed – largely by the British. Its capital, Nice, soon became the fastest growing town in Europe. The arrival of the railway turned a trickle of winter visitors into a torrent. By the turn of the century Nice had grown from a pre-revolutionary city of 12,000 to one ten times that size. With the people came roads, villas, hotels, *pensions*, restaurants, tennis courts, dust, sewage, rubbish, noise and the motor-car. The coast's traditional sources of income had been derived from fishing and olive oil, the perfume industry in Grasse, the oranges and lemons of Menton, the cork trees of the Esterels and the great salt pans at Hyères, but soon gave way to the provision of services of almost every sort imaginable to winter visitors. By the time Waugh stepped off his train in Monaco in late February 1929, the remote, penurious, sun-drenched winter coast where Brougham and his English contemporaries had sought warmth was fast disappearing. At Monaco, Waugh hated 'the newness and neatness of the buildings; the absolute denial of poverty and suffering in this place, where sickness is represented by fashionable invalids and industry by hotel servants, and the peasants in traditional costume come into town to witness in free seats the theatre ballets of *Le Pas d'acier* and

Mercure. All these things make up a Principality about as real as a pavilion at an International Exhibition.' Waugh's contemporary and – periodically – friend, the critic Cyril Connolly, pronounced that 'Nice is never worthy of the Blue Train.'

Indeed, 1929 was a turning-point for the coast, arguably its crux. Behind it lay a century of development, which had culminated in the pre-war *belle époque*, when from December to April the Riviera was the most fashionable destination on earth. The years since the war had seen the beginnings of a summer season, pioneered principally by Americans. There were few signs yet, though, that it might ever rival winter. Immediately ahead lay the Wall Street crash of November 1929, which would devastate the world's capitalist economies and cut a swathe through the Riviera tourist industry. Soon the socialist Front Populaire would introduce paid holidays – *congés payés* – for the French workforce and large numbers of French – of a class hitherto rarely seen in the South other than as local peasants and *vendeuses*, cabbies, maids, waiters, washerwomen and footmen – would pour in by train. Despite those declarations of equality and fraternity, the French *bourgeoisie* thought this deplorable: 'In opening the way to the red trains,' they said, 'we close it to the famous Blue Train.' The rise of Fascism would cast a further shadow that deepened as the decade drew on. Mussolini's Italy bordered the coast to the east, Hitler's Germany lay further to the north. Even from the windows of the Blue Train, the prospects looked uncertain.

'There was gold on the Côte d'Azur', wrote the biographer of François Blanc, the genius behind Monte Carlo, 'and everybody hoped to have a share in it.' Yet the story of the Riviera's rise is about more than greed. It is the story of those people, many famous, some gifted, who sought warmth, fun, health, peace, escape, sex, leisure, companionship, wealth, artistic inspiration and, perhaps above all, happiness on a coast that seemed to promise all those things. It is the story of the search for earthly paradise.

PART ONE

I

Augustans on the Riviera

> 'The ruins of trophies, aqueducts, triumphal arches and public monuments, are proud testimonies of the enlightened policy and gigantic resources of the victors, while their present condition must necessarily awaken melancholy reflections on the fragility of human labours, and on the inevitable ravages which time makes on the architect, as well as his works.'
>
> J. Bunnell Davis, *The Ancient and Modern History of Nice*

1

The conspirators gathered early on the morning of 15 March, 44 BC. Their leaders Gaius Cassius and Marcus Brutus were among them – Brutus, by some accounts, Caesar's son by Servilia, one of his favourite mistresses. It was said that the augur Spurinna had warned Caesar to beware the Ides of March; that at dinner the night before, when asked what sort of death he would prefer, the *dictator perpetuus* had replied, 'A sudden one.' This all seemed propitious. The assassination was to be attempted at the Theatre of Pompey, behind the Campo dei Fiori, where the Senate was meeting. The conspirators, senators all, armed themselves with daggers and set off for the theatre.

Caesar, on his way there that morning, had encountered Spurinna, to whom he remarked lightly that the Ides of March had come. Spurinna retorted: 'Aye, Caesar, but not gone.' Before Caesar had gone many steps further, a scroll was thrust into his hand disclosing the conspiracy. He did not give it a glance.

As the ruler of the known world entered the assembly room in the theatre, the conspirators crowded round him mouthing requests. Publius Servilius Casca unsheathed his dagger, and struck the first blow from behind. His fellow murderers crowded round, leaving Caesar facing a circle of daggers. He realised that his time had come. On seeing Brutus among the assassins, he said, in Greek, 'And you, too, my son?' Then he pulled his toga over his head, offering no resistance to the attack.

Seconds later he lay dead at the foot of Pompey's statue, in a slowly widening pool of blood.

Gaius Octavius Thurinus took control of the Roman Empire, and in so doing became the father of the Côte d'Azur.

Octavius, subsequently known as Augustus, was Julius Caesar's great-nephew, the son of his niece. Caesar, having no children himself, had taken a fancy to the boy and appointed him his heir. This set Rome talking about catamites – Caesar's bisexuality being known to all. When he was assassinated, Augustus was barely eighteen and his legitimacy as the new emperor was soon questioned; opponents rallied round Caesar's old companion in arms, Mark Antony. He had succeeded Caesar as Queen Cleopatra's lover, and aspired to do the same with his empire. Augustus was confirmed as emperor only when he had defeated the combined fleets of Antony and Cleopatra at the battle of Actium in 31 BC.

Thereafter, he came into his own. He was short and plagued with chronic ill-health. Careless of his personal appearance, he was so impatient when having his hair cut that he would have three barbers snipping away simultaneously. Suetonius, his first biographer, admitted, 'Not even his friends would deny that he often committed adultery.' But his reasoning was unimpeachable: 'He wanted to discover what his enemies were at by getting intimate with their wives and daughters.' He had a taste for virgins, which he retained until old age, and his wife Livia acted as his procuress. He was also a fine general, an astute politician and – unlike several of his notorious successors – took seriously his duties to the empire and its peoples. It was under Augustus that the doors of the temple of the two-headed god Janus were often closed – they were open in times of war – and peace proclaimed. When he came to power Rome was built of brick, but he left it clothed in marble. He promoted colonisation, reviewed the system of provincial administration, and reinforced frontiers. He put his empire in as much order as it had ever been, presiding over what has come down to us as the Augustan age, a byword for peace and plenty.

The backbone of Augustus's empire was its system of roads, of which there were eventually 54,000 miles. The Greeks had not fully appreciated their value as a means of communication with, and control of, far-flung outposts. In 312 BC Appius extracted funds from the Senate to inaugurate the Roman system: the roads had to be sufficiently robust to carry ox-carts weighing up to 1200 pounds, so a trough was excavated to a depth of three feet, filled with rubble and topped with stones that fitted together so well that a knife blade could not have been slipped between them. The first such paved road, the Appian Way, ran 132 miles from Rome south-east to Capua. It was followed by four more, the Via Flaminia, the Via Valerra, the Via Latina, and the Via Aurelia. Work started on the via Aurelia in 241 BC: it ran north-west from Rome straight up the coast to Genoa, the northernmost point of the Ligurian Sea. In the first century BC it was gradually extended until it reached the foothills of the Alpes Maritimes, a few miles to the east of the settlement that is now Nice.

Augustus was a military strategist who understood the contribution that rapid communications with southern Gaul and the Iberian peninsula could make in unifying his empire. When he came to power in 31 BC he was determined to force the road further round the coastal strip running from Italy to the Pyrenees, and into the Gallo-Roman Provincia, later known as Provence. Here, though, the route was blocked both by the Alps and by their warlike indigenous inhabitants, the Ligurians. According to the Roman historian Livy, there was

> everything to put soldiers on their mettle: positions to scale in themselves difficult enough, without having to oust a force that is already in possession; hard marching through defiles lending themselves to constant surprises, an enemy extremely dashing and light-footed, rendering every spot and hour insecure; wearisome and perilous blockadings of fortified strongholds in a country barren of resources and yielding no plunder worth mentioning, with no camp followers and no long line of beasts of burden; no hope but in cold steel and individual pluck.

Between 15 and 14 BC Augustus's forces conquered the Ligurians in a series of bitter skirmishes, so opening up a secure road into Provincia and Gaul. In 12 BC the Senate voted to celebrate this with one of the greatest monuments in the Roman world: the Tropaea Augusti (Trophy of Augustus) was built on the crest of the 1300-metre pass that marked the boundary between Italy and Gaul. Set in a walled enclosure, it was a magnificent tower some 160 feet high, clad in dazzling white Carrara marble, surmounted by a heroic statue of Augustus. Twenty-four Doric columns carried statues of the Imperial Family, and on the west face of the rectangular podium were inscribed the names of the forty-five conquered tribes. Today, its remains standing close to the village of La Turbie, the name a corruption of Tropaea.

The defeat of the Ligurians meant that Augustus could extend the road further west along the coastal strip now called the French Riviera. From the pass, the road looked down on what the Romans called Monoeci (Monaco). (A Victorian doctor described this settlement as 'a fashionable health resort ... the Condamine, Monte Carlo, Roquebrune and Cap Martin were dotted with elegant Roman villas.') From there the road plunged down towards a fine natural harbour, the Baie des Anges. Five hundred years previously, the Greeks of Massalia (Marseille) had landed there, conquered the defending Ligurian tribes, and founded a city on the waterfront. They called it Nike (Nice), after the Greek goddess of victory. Later, the Romans established an adjoining community called

Cemenelum (Cimiez) on the hills above the waterfront. It boasted an amphitheatre, baths, aqueducts and some fine houses, and became the capital of the Roman province of Alpes-Maritimes, and at its height in the second century AD supported a population of 20,000.

The road continued west from Cemenelum, halted on the banks of the river Varus (Var), and continued on the far side to Antipolis (Antibes). Originally another Greek colony, this seems to have meant the 'city opposite' – across the bay from Nice. Antipolis had appealed for Roman help against the Ligurian tribes as early as 154 BC, and by Augustan times was Romanized: writers like Martial and Pliny celebrated it as a tuna-fishing port. Then, as the Alpes Maritimes began their retreat, the land opened up and was relatively flat until the river Siagne, some ten miles west. The road continued easily down the coast towards Neapolis (La Napoule). In Roman times this was Ad Horrea – at the granary – suggestive of a grain port. Here the road encountered the eastern massif of the Esterels, the extraordinary range of volcanic peaks composed of red porphyry, described by a Victorian clergyman as 'flame-red crags shooting out of a sea the colour of a peacock's neck'. Today the major road turns due west, but the via Aurelia followed the coast to Forum Julii (Fréjus). This was the port founded by Caesar, and to which Augustus despatched Antony and Cleopatra's captured fleet of three hundred galleys after the battle of Actium. In Augustan times it grew rapidly – the road appears to date from 3 BC – until it was much the same size as the town today. It was here, at Forum Julii, that the via Aurelia, long a companion of the coast, finally turned away from the sea and headed west towards the great Roman centres of Aix and Arles, leaving the Massif des Maures to the south. Another twenty-five miles south-west lay what was originally the Greek port of Olbia, which the Romans renamed Hyeres Almanare. Beyond lay the Greco-Roman port of Telo Martius (Toulon), then the western end of the Riviera, marked by Marseille and the mouth of the Rhône.

When it was completed, Augustus's road – sometimes called the Via Julia Augusta – linked a series of semi-independent and largely self-sufficient communities along the coast, and permitted a level of trade between them hitherto limited by the uncertainties of sea communication. At the same time, by allowing the rapid movement of military forces, the areas through which the road passed could be effectively policed against barbarian hordes. It also enabled the Riviera to be reached conveniently from Rome: as one of the imperial post roads, travellers would find on the via Aurelia fresh relays of horses once every ten or twelve Roman miles and overnight accommodation at twenty – the distance normally covered in a day. The road brought the order, stability and prosperity of Rome to the coast; it conferred and symbolised civilisation. As a consequence, in Augustan times Romans settled on the Riviera in large numbers and on the widening plains to the west of Nike. There was more than colonisation, though; there was also tourism.

In the summer, the metropolis of ancient Rome became too hot, and too subject to epidemics and malaria, for the rich to wish to remain. With Augustus came the sustained peace, prosperity and ease of movement that encourages travelling for pleasure. In the great days of the empire, guidebooks and travel itineraries found a ready market. Plutarch spoke of 'globe-trotters who spend the best part of their lives in inns and boats'. In the summer many Romans fled south to the Bay of Naples – Julius Caesar and Mark Antony had been among the first to do so. By the first century AD, the northern coast of the bay, and in particular the island of Capri and the resorts of Cumae, Misenum and Baiae, had established itself as something recognisable on today's Riviera: of Baiae, the scholar Varro complained that 'unmarried women are common property, old men behave like young boys, and lots of young boys like young girls'. Seneca was so appalled by what he saw that he left the day after his arrival, complaining that it was almost as if 'the location itself demanded vice'. To the north of Rome, at Monoeci, Cemenelum, Antipolis, Forum Julii and Hyeres Almanare, the

Victorians also found evidence of such revels, of travellers who came and stayed for pleasures that later became traditional in these parts. A stable, civilised Riviera, with good communications, a dramatic combination of sky, mountains and sea, and an unrivalled climate was established under the auspices of Augustus almost two thousand years ago.

In 1873, C. B. Black sang the praises of the view from La Turbie in his guide to the coast – a prospect that can have scarcely changed since Augustus came to inspect the great symbol of his achievement at about the time of the birth of Christ: 'The whole coastline lies before us . . . as far as the hills above San Remo, headland after headland running out into blue water, white little towns nestling in the depths of sunny bays or clinging to the brown hillsides, villas peeping from the dark olive masses, sails gleaming against the purple sea.'

The *Pax Romana* ensured an extended holiday on the Riviera that lasted until the collapse of the Western Empire in the fifth century AD.

The Dark Ages on the coast were dominated by the barbarian hordes of Visigoths, Ostrogoths, Burgundians and Vandals. In the eighth century the Saracens arrived, and with them the barely accessible inland settlements built by those fleeing the coast from the raiders. These were the *villages perchés*, like Peillon, Gorbio, Castellar and Utelle. Two hundred years later the Saracens were expelled by Guillaume le Libérateur. By the middle of the thirteenth century – the age of the troubadours – the region had achieved a measure of political coherence as the Compte de Provence. In 1481, it was united with France, and in 1539 French was decreed the region's administrative language. By the eighteenth century, a clear cultural and economic identity was being forged. Ultimately, under Napoleon, this would be codified as the *département* of Provence, the region that, with the *départemen*t Alpes-Maritimes on the east side of the river Var, governed the coast that is now called the French Riviera.

2

It was testament to the integrity of Roman construction and the skill of its craftsmanship that Augustus's Trophy at La Turbie long survived the collapse of the empire whose achievement it symbolised. As the Dark Ages gave way to the Middle Ages, it saw other uses. In Saracen times it was a fort, in the Renaissance a castle keep and watchtower. It survived until the Enlightenment and the arrival of modern civilisation: at the instigation of the Prince of Monaco, in 1705 Maréchal de la Feuillade set about it with gunpowder and its stones were used to build the village and church at La Turbie. When the first modern travellers appeared in the aftermath of the Seven Years War in 1763, they saw little more than the Trophy's foundations. They were fascinated, though, by this ruined emblem of imperial Rome, because they saw their country as Rome's successor. Insular, presumptuous, ignorant of foreign languages, arrogant and, above all, rich, they were, of course, English.

Englishmen had first compared themselves with the Augustans during the reign of Queen Anne. The establishment of a constitutional monarchy and parliamentary democracy, the Union of England and Scotland, Marlborough's victories over the Spanish and French – and their own genius – made it a natural analogy, which was reinforced as the eighteenth century continued with the growth of the British Empire. The idea encouraged wealthy Englishmen to visit the countries where the ancient civilisations had flourished in the Mediterranean basin. The journey, which typically took young men completing their education through France and the Alps to Italy over a period of up to three years, became known as the Grand Tour. It was supposedly edifying, but the economist Adam Smith complained that the tourist 'commonly returns more conceited, more unprincipled, more dissipated and more incapable of any serious application either to study or business, than he could have well become in so short a time had he lived at home'. Despite, or perhaps because of, this, the travellers grew steadily in numbers until war broke out with France in 1756. Afterwards, the English returned in such unprecedented numbers that a contemporary wrote, 'Where one Englishman travelled in the reign of the first two Georges, ten now go on a grand tour. Indeed at such a pitch is the spirit of travelling that there is scarce a citizen of large fortune but takes a flying view of France, Italy and Germany.'

Interest in the heritage of ancient Rome had been stimulated in 1763 by the beginning of the excavations at Pompeii, where the eruption of Mount Vesuvius in AD 79 had preserved much of the city's daily life under a shroud of ashes, and was galvanised in 1776 by publication of the first volume of Edward Gibbon's *Decline and Fall of the Roman Empire.* Like Charles Darwin's *The Origin of Species*, Oswald Spengler's *Decline of the West*, and Shere Hite's *The Hite Report*, it was a book that informed the thinking of a generation. As the British Empire grew in the early years of the nineteenth century, the comparison between the glories of the Roman Empire under Augustus and contemporary England seemed increasingly evident. Visiting Rome in 1858, Lady Eastlake, wife of the president of the Royal Academy, wrote, 'I felt proud that my nation was more truly the descendant of that matchless race than any other in the world.' A character in *Venetia*, by Benjamin Disraeli, remarks, 'These shores have yielded us our religion, our arts, our literature, and our laws. If all that we have gained from the Mediterranean was erased from the memory of man, we should be savages.' The peace and prosperity of the Augustan age and that of Victorian England were linked in the phrase *Pax Britannica.* The English were the new Augustans.

If Italy was the principal attraction for Grand Tourists, the Riviera was visited because it was one of the routes south. It was more direct, of course, to cross the main alpine chain at one of the established high passes, the St Bernard, the Mont Cenis or the Brenner, but that was a challenge in itself. The passes were only free of snow for three or four months of the year, and passage was rarely comfortable and frequently dangerous. One alternative was to take a boat down the Rhône from Lyon to Marseille, and then a coastal vessel to Genoa, which would call at Nice *en route*. Alternatively there was an overland route via Fréjus over the Esterels.

Yet the Riviera – at first, as James Pope-Hennessy put it, 'a rather uncomfortable corridor to Italy' – was so rich in Roman remains that in the eighteenth century it gradually became an object of interest in its own right. Many of the earliest modern visitors came to La Turbie, then marvelled in Cimiez and Fréjus at the crumbling aqueducts, amphitheatres, temples and baths. They were fascinated by these tokens of great civilisation and by its fate. As one visitor to Nice in 1803 wrote:

> Let the mind's eye extend itself to the antique walls of Cimiez, meditate on the ample edifices and superb temples that adorned that once famed city. Be they the tombs which contain the ashes of heroic virtue, honoured worth, and modest beauty, incentives to solemn admiration and exemplary patriotism! Let the remains of those lofty structures, that once ravished the human eye, that inspired the citizen with love of his country, which the foe envied, and the savage ruined, receive at least the tribute of compassion for their honours lost.

History, though, was not the only attraction. Although meteorologists describe the British climate as mild, temperate, variable and wet, some deplored it. In *As You Like It*, Shakespeare complains of 'the icy fang, and churlish chiding of the winter's wind'. Dickens, particularly in *Bleak House* and *Hard Times*, made much of the sapping claustrophobia of British weather: in the late eighteenth and nineteenth centuries, the furnaces of the industrial revolution further darkened the pervading gloom of the climate. Visiting the country in 1849, the American poet and essayist Ralph Waldo Emerson found much to admire, declaring 'England ... the best of actual nations', London 'the epitome of our times, and the Rome of today'. He complained, though, of the ash-coloured sky, the constant rain, and that night and day are too nearly of one colour. It strains the eyes to read and to write. Add the coal-smoke. In the manufacturing towns the fine soot or *blacks* darken the day and give white sheep the colour of black sheep, discolour human saliva, contaminate the air, poison many plants, and corrode the monuments and buildings ... The London fog aggravates the distempers of the sky, and sometimes justifies the epigram on the climate by an English wit – 'on a fine day, looking up a chimney; on a foul day, looking down one'. A gentleman in Liverpool told me he could do without a fire in his parlour about one day a year.

3

The novelist Tobias Smollett was among the first of those in modern times determined to escape. A notoriously difficult and surly man, he was regarded by his contemporaries as highly as Charles Dickens seventy-five years later, one of the great mirrors of his age.

Born in Dumbartonshire in 1721, Smollett qualified as a doctor at the University of Glasgow, and sailed as surgeon's mate in the Spanish war of 1741. He made his name with two picaresque novels, *Roderick Random* (1748) and *Peregrine Pickle* (1741), then turned to editing the *Critical Review* – until he was tried for libel, imprisoned for three months and fined £100. He had called Sir Charles Knowles 'an admiral without conduct, an engineer without knowledge, an officer without resolution, and a man without veracity'. In 1763, his health uncertain – he suffered from various chest complaints – he hired a barque at Folkestone and set sail for France. A chance encounter with a fellow Scot, General James Patterson, made him decide to visit Nice: 'The general talks so favourably of the climate of Nice, with respect to disorders of the breast, that I am now determined to go thither.' In the company of his wife, two girls she was looking after, and a servant, he took the sort of leisurely course south that French roads and the carriages that laboured over them permitted. In November the party arrived in Nice, an Italianate settlement then ruled by the Kingdom of Sardinia. It nestled on a grassy plain between the Alps and the sea, 'a little town, hardly a mile in circumference, said to contain 12,000', Smollett wrote. He rented a house, pottered about, enjoyed the view, and even indulged in the English vogue for sea-bathing – much to the astonishment of the locals. More importantly, he recorded his impressions of the journey and his destination in letters home, published in 1765 as *Travels in France and Italy*. The book showed him as, at best, a dyspeptic traveller, yet it proved the first of almost a hundred and fifty years of literary dispatches in dozens of languages that sent travellers and tourists hurrying to the Riviera.

But Smollett's book and other early modern travelogue might prompt one to wonder why they bothered – Smollett, setting the fashion for the Englishman (or Scot) abroad, found fault with almost everything he saw. In Nice, the shopkeepers were 'generally poor, greedy, over-reaching'; the place was 'devoid of taste and literature. Here are no tolerable pictures, busts, statues, nor edifices: the very ornaments of the churches are wretchedly conceived, and worse executed.' The local brand of Roman Catholicism seemed to have bred merely 'superstition that reigns under the darkest shades of ignorance and prejudice'. Rather than work, the populace chose 'to starve at home, to lounge about on the ramparts, bask themselves in the sun, or play at bowls in the streets from morning to night'.

Arthur Young, too, thought the coast had been 'praised beyond its merit'. He was a Suffolk farmer with a passion for travel that was at least partly explained by the deficiencies in his wife Martha Allen's personality. Young was vivacious, high-spirited and something of a dandy; he was also an excellent observer, the possessor of a fine, rational mind and a prose style that placed him among the greatest writers on agriculture. 'He carried into agriculture,' wrote the critic Leslie Stephen, 'the spirit which we generally associate with the great revolution of manufacturers.'

Young visited the Riviera at the time of the French revolution, some fifteen years after Smollett. Unlike his Augustan predecessors, who enjoyed the convenience of the via Augusta, he was much tried by the difficulties of travel along the coast. 'And will it be believed,' he thundered, 'that from Marseille with 100,000 souls, and Toulon with 30,000, lying in the great road to Antibes, Nice and Italy, there is no regular carriage or voiture? To a person accustomed to the infinity of machines that fly about England, in all directions, this must appear hardly credible.' From Toulon he was obliged to take a barque to Cavalero, a small port south across the peninsula from St Tropez. This, which he expected to be a small town, 'consists only of three houses, and a more wretched place is not to be imagined. They spread a mattress on a stone floor for me, for bed they had none; after starving all day, they had nothing but stale eggs, hard bread, and worse wine; and as to mules which were to take me to Fréjus, there was neither horse, ass nor mule in the place.' He was obliged to walk to Esterels. Here there were post-horses, but no butter. 'At all the villages, since Toulon, at Fréjus, Estrelles [sic], I asked for milk, but no such thing is to be had, not even of goats or sheep; the cows are all kept higher on the mountains; and as to butter the landlord at Estrelles told me, it was a contraband commodity that came from Nice.'

A few years later, after the Peace of Amiens had been signed in 1802, a doctor called John Bunnell Davis took a similarly critical view of the coast. In *The Ancient and Modern History of Nice* he complained: 'The difficulties with which travelling is attended in the southern parts of France, and the general want of comfortable bedding are circumstances that render it prudent for a delicate person to take a bed and blankets with him.' Of Hyères, he wrote: 'It will not be easy to find a town more beautifully situated, nor worse built than Hyères. Its foundation is on a craggy rock; the streets very narrow, and so rugged as to be almost impracticable in wet weather. The houses are mean, dirty and crowded.' A contemporary Frenchman, the Abbé Dupaty, whose *Travels Through Italy* was translated by 'An English Gentleman', found Monaco

> filled with three fishing boats and a Dutch vessel … two or three streets of perpendicular rocks; eight hundred wretches dying of hunger; a decayed castle; a battalion of French troops; a few orange, olive and mulberry trees, scattered over a few acres of land, themselves scattered over rocks; such is, pretty nearly, the picture of Monaco … all here is poverty and wretchedness in the extreme.

The civilised world created by the Romans along the artery of the via Aurelia had all but disappeared. After seventeen hundred years of progress all that was left were a few isolated villages, paupered in all but sunshine.

4

For the English, though, the sunshine was the main point – or, at least, the most obvious one. Davis talked about the 'climate celebrated for its temperature'. Young, 'worried' by his landlord with a list of the English who passed the winter in Hyères, mused that the winter climate must be good – 'if they do not feel the *vent de bize*.' This was the northerly winter wind, nowadays called the *mistral*, which swept down the Rhône valley with such force that it once overturned a horse and carriage into the harbour at Marseille. Dupaty noted the English colony established in Nice for winter visitors and remarked that during the season – winter – the town was a 'sort of hot-house for those of delicate constitutions'. According to Davis, the temperature in November averaged fifty-five degrees Fahrenheit, fell to forty-six in December, then levelled off at forty-seven the following month. By February it had risen to fifty, by April to fifty-nine. Meanwhile, if November boasted only seventeen fine days, both January and March had twenty-three. What a comparison it made with the north, where between November and March the temperature hovered around freezing, and the skies were invariably overcast. Adolphe Smith remarked in his guidebook *The Garden of Hyères* that sometimes the severity of the weather in London was such that 'it assumed the proportions of a public disaster'.

At the same time Young, never one to give credit even when it was due, conceded reluctantly the exoticism of the vegetation: on the road to Hyères 'the ... singular features are the orange and lemon trees; they here thrive in the open air, are of great size, and render every garden interesting to those that travel to the south'. Grasse, a dozen miles north of Cannes and picturesquely situated on the slopes of Mont Roquevignon, provided 'luxuriant lavender, rosemary, bergamot, oranges, together with rose and tuberoses produced for perfumes'. 'Half Europe,' he averred, 'is supplied with essences hence.'

Smollett, too, celebrated the plain of Nice, which displayed

> nothing but gardens full of green trees, loaded with oranges, lemons, citrons, and bergamots, which make a delightful appearance. If you examine them more nearly, you will find plantations of green peas ready to gather; all sorts of roses, carnations, ranunculuses, anemones, and daffodils blowing in full glory, with such beauty, vigour and perfume as no flower in England ever exhibited.

Similarly, Davis, for all his complaints about Hyères, wrote that 'the view of the surrounding countryside makes amends for all these imperfections. For the eminence on which the town is built, a gradual slope extending three miles to the sea. All this space is one luxuriant wood of orange trees. Noble hills shelter the town from the north, and on the south the view is terminated by the isles of Hyères, a few miles out to sea.'

It was this potent combination of a history associated with empire, the exoticism of luxuriant flora, the dazzling combination of peacock sky, mountains and limpid sea, and the welcoming winter climate that led many eighteenth-century English travellers to see the coast as another Eden. Looking down on Nice from its ramparts, even Smollett declared that he could 'scarce help thinking himself inchanted'. To Davis, caught up in the romanticism of an age that was beginning to understand the horrors of urbanisation and delight in the – theoretical – purity of the peasant life, even the Niçois locals seemed to have stepped out of Arcady: 'Their lives are regulated by the movement of the stars by night and the sun by day. Neither clocks, sun-dials nor barometers of any description mar their innocence.' Having secretly observed their dances and country rituals, he exclaimed, 'What a lovely image of happiness, of social concord, and virtue, these contented swains afford us!'

For its first modern visitors, exiles from the grey, windswept British Isles, the French Riviera was the Kingdom of Cockayne.

2

'I was only happy once, that was at Hyères'

> 'Pendant que j'étais a l'hôtel d'York, une chaise de poste arriva. Un instant après, l'aubergiste entra dans ma chambre. Qu'est-ce que vos nouveaux venus? lui demandais-je. "Ce sont de certains Anglais, mais je ne saurias dire s'ils sont Français ou Allemands."'
>
> Alexandre Dumas, *Impressions de Voyages*

1

Europe having been closed to most foreign visitors during the Napoleonic wars, it was not until a few years later that the Continent was once again open to English travellers – or at least to those with large purses and a similarly ample provision of patience and time. Then, Marguerite Gardiner, the Countess of Blessington, joined adventurers like Byron, Keats, Shelley and Wordsworth. Her first husband had been Captain Maurice St Leger Farmer, a madman and drunkard who was 'killed during a drunken orgie [sic] by falling from a window in the King's Bench prison'. Her second was a happier choice: he was Viscount Mountjoy, who lavished riches and treats on his wife. On 22 August 1822 the couple and their retinue set out on a Continental tour that was to take them to Genoa and Naples. In the leisurely manner of those days, it was not until the spring of 1823 that they reached Nice where the Countess met

> some fair English girl with the bright hectic tinge on her delicate cheek, and the lustrous eyes which betoken the presence of that

> most perfidious and fatal of all diseases, consumption, mounted on a pony, led by a father, a brother, or one who hoped to stand in a more tender relation to her. I tremble when I see the warm cloak in which she is enveloped, swept by the rude wind from her shrinking shoulders, and hear that fearful cough which shakes her tortured chest. A few weeks, and such invalids (and alas, there are many) are seen no more.

If at first the English had principally sought warmth on the Riviera, in the early nineteenth century many came for the sake of their health.

The man behind this development was Dr John Brown. A Scot born in 1735 to a Berwickshire farm labourer, he was a short, thick-set figure with a remarkable memory. He excelled at his local school, and soon found himself studying medicine in Edinburgh. There, and in the course of his subsequent practice as a physician, he developed his medical theories. These were that the phenomena of life were dependent on stimulus, and that diseases fell into one of two categories: those caused by the absence of stimulus, the *asthenic*, and those caused by too much, the *sthenic*. The remedies he prescribed were, respectively, alcohol and opium. He became addicted to both. As it happened, these panaceas were readily available in the Mediterranean – opium particularly in Marseille, where it was imported in large quantities from Algiers. Additionally, Brown and his contemporaries regarded the Mediterranean climate as offering a considerable variety of tonic and sedative environments. This meant that a patient could be despatched to live for a time in a resort chosen according to the disease from which he or she suffered, a treatment dubbed climato-therapy. The so-called 'Brunonian theory' came to dominate European medical thought in the last quarter of the eighteenth century, and the entire Mediterranean coast became something of a winter health resort for sufferers from all sorts of diseases. Not least of these was tuberculosis, which in England was then killing one in six.

Brown's ideas were discredited in the years after his death in 1788

– the medical historian E. H. Garrison later claimed that they 'destroyed more people than the French Revolution and the Napoleonic wars combined'. Yet with the discovery that bacteria caused tuberculosis still a century away, the medical profession in the early nineteenth century could do no more than try to isolate the conditions under which the disease was likely to develop, and remove the patient from them. As this often meant sending patients south, away from the damp and cold of England – notably from the established spa towns like Bath and Cheltenham – the Riviera continued to be prescribed for sufferers from consumption. Davis's *The Ancient and Modern History of Nice* was one of the first guides to advocate the ambient advantages of its Mediterranean climate for chest diseases in general and tuberculosis in particular. In 1804, he wrote, 'Who can for a moment doubt but that health is more likely to return when the path to its acquisition is strewn with flowers; when the painful burden that overwhelms the soul is alleviated by agreeable occupations, and when anxiety is exchanged for patience and resignation?' Soon the French historian Paul Gonnet noted that the doctor was sending 'to our shores a colony of pale and listless English women and listless sons of nobility near death'.

During the Napoleonic Wars, with the Continental resorts inaccessible, English invalids escaped the worst of the winter in places like Madeira and Lisbon. After Waterloo, resorts as widespread as Pisa, Rome, Naples, Malta, Málaga and Algiers vied with the Riviera for the invalids' money. Soon, a series of books had joined Davis's, comparing and contrasting the advantages of the various 'Mediterranean health resorts'. These included James Clark's *The Sanative Influence of Climate*, Charles Williams's *The Climate of the South of France, and its Varieties most suitable for Invalids*, William Marcet's *On the Mediterranean Coast of the South of France in its Medical Aspect*, and J. A. Lindsay's *The Climate Treatment for Consumption*. The upshot of this was that by the 1830s Nice and the South of France were firmly established as the destination for a winter health cure, if not quite the Englishman's grave.

2

With Nice developing as the *fons et origo* of what was now beginning to be called the Riviera, interest in the coastal strip to the west of the Var remained limited. As Arthur Young had recorded, a few English families had wintered in Hyères during pre-revolutionary times. A number returned after the Congress of Vienna in 1814, and established a substantial English colony in the most southerly of the coast's resorts. St Tropez, though, was nothing more than a fishing-port. According to Murray's *Handbook* of 1847, a guide based on travels dating back to 1830, Fréjus was a 'small, dirty town', and its neighbour St Raphael little more than its fishing-port; Juan-les-Pins was scarcely on the map. Antibes, on the border between France and Sardinia, the island state that then ruled the environs of Nice, had most of the conventional disadvantages of a border town. It was ramshackle, full of dubious characters, a garrison of disorderly soldiers – in fact, it was a hotbed of vice. Yet change was at hand, in the form of one of the now forgotten eminences of the Victorian age.

In 1830 Henry Peter Brougham took his seat in the House of Lords as First Baron Brougham and Vaux, and was simultaneously appointed Lord Chancellor. A Scot by birth and a lawyer by training, he had entered Parliament in 1810. Almost at once, he championed an Act outlawing one of the greatest injustices of the age: the slave trade. Learned, passionate and superbly eloquent, he became known as one of the greatest advocates of the day. His most extraordinary achievement was the successful defence of the Queen, Caroline of Brunswick, against a charge of adultery trumped up by her husband George IV. Brougham was one of the leading lights behind the foundation of London University and the Society for the Diffusion of Useful Knowledge. Then, in the years up to 1832, he was one of the principal forces behind the Reform Act, a critical stage on the way to universal suffrage. The economist and journalist Walter Bagehot, best known for his deification of the monarchy, wrote of him, 'There is a glance in some men's eyes which seems to me to say, "Beware, I am dangerous: *Noli me tangere*": Lord Brougham's face has this. A mischievous excitability is the most obvious expression of it. If he were a horse, no one would buy him; with that eye no one could answer for his temper.'

In 1834 Brougham left office with the Whigs, never to return. His brother had just died and he was exhausted from years of overwork. In the autumn he got into his six-horse carriage and fled across the Channel with his sickly daughter Eleonor. He headed for Genoa, his ultimate destination Rome. It was both his misfortune and fortune that cholera had broken out in Marseille. Soon an epidemic was declared, and by the time the party reached Antibes the Sardinian government had declared a *cordon sanitaire*. To prevent the spread of the disease eastwards towards Nice, no travellers from the west were permitted to cross the Var. This was not the reception Brougham had anticipated: he was used to getting his own way, and, as the historian Macaulay said, 'There is no other man whose entrance into any town would be so certain to be greeted with huzzaing.' Yet although Brougham huffed and puffed, the border guard stood firm.

History is made on such incidents. On 28 December 1834 the party was obliged to retrace its steps to Antibes. Thwarted in an attempt to rent a house once used by Napoleon – the French objected to its occupation by an Englishman – he retreated to the Hôtel de la Poste in Cannes. Situated on the apex of the bay, looking out to the Îles de Lérins, sheltered by high ground to the west, north and south, Cannes was then a fishing-village of no more than three hundred inhabitants, with two streets of the most humble Provençal houses. Brougham was enchanted by the winter warmth, the light and the scenery. He also enjoyed the local *bouillabaisse*, and even the region's thin wines. Within a week he had bought a plot of land on the Fréjus road, with a view to establishing Cannes as his second home. Between 1835 and 1839 he had a villa built there, the

Italianate Château Eleonor Louise, where he wintered for the remainder of his life. There he enjoyed 'the delightful climate of Provence, its clear sky and refreshing breezes, while the deep blue waters of the Mediterranean lay stretched before us; the orange groves and cassia plantations perfumed the air around us, and the forests behind, crowned with pines and evergreen oaks, and ending in the Alps, protected us by their eternal granite, from the cold winds of the north.'

Then, in a phenomenon that repeated itself to the extent that it became a critical factor in the development of the coast, Brougham himself became an attraction. His fame and his endorsement of the village put Cannes on the map, in much the same way that the Prince Regent's patronage had popularised Brighton. Soon others among the great and the good of Victorian England had established homes in what would become one of the first serious rivals to Nice. 'At some time or other,' wrote Brougham's biographer G. T. Garratt, 'everyone of importance seems to have drifted down to see him in the South of France.'

Brougham was nothing if not a puller of strings. After he had settled himself in Cannes, he used his friendship with King Louis-Philippe – restored to the monarchy after the 1830 revolution – to have Cannes improved. The local roads were so poor that the best way to reach the town was by sea. The bay, though fine when the wind was northerly, was impossible for coastal vessels to use when it was blowing from the south. Cannes needed an artificial harbour: not only would this enable Brougham and his friends to reach their private paradise more conveniently, it would also allow the produce from Grasse to be exported far more easily and cheaply than carting it overland to Marseille. Brougham persuaded Louis-Philippe to put up nearly two million francs for a breakwater on the west side of the bay, and work started in 1838. In 1847 Murray's *Handbook* described Cannes as a 'neat and cheerful small town'. Courtesy of Brougham, Cannes had arrived. Soon, guidebooks would be referring to it as the 'Mediterranean Cowes'.

3

If all this smelt of colonisation, the anglicisation of the coast became marked after the revolution of 1848 that brought Napoleon III to power. In some respects it had begun less with Brougham than with the Reverend Lewis Way, an English clergyman. He was a man of some charisma and force of character who took the view that 'It is the duty of our favoured land to revive its character as "defender of the faith" even in foreign lands.' France, with its predominantly Catholic population, was certainly sufficiently benighted, and Way was one of the first to preach in the new Anglican church in Nice in 1822 – built to minister to the spiritual needs of the English winter residents, or *hivernants*. That year a terrible frost destroyed many of the orange trees in the orchards that then surrounded the town, throwing large numbers of local people out of work. Way induced the British residents of Nice to pay the unemployed to turn their hands to the construction of a walkway on the sea front, to the west of the mouth of the Paillon river. It was gradually extended, and in due course became generally known as the Promenade des Anglais.

Another manifestation of colonisation was housing. The Frenchman Auguste de la Lande noted as early as 1787 that in Nice the abundance of English visitors 'has stirred the locals to construct and furnish numerous houses aimed especially at the foreigners'. Much of this development occurred in the Croix-de-Marbre district, across the Paillon river from the old town. Soon the English, with their gift for names, had dubbed it Newborough. In 1826 the American Nathaniel Carter admired 'long ranges of neat white houses, with Venetian blinds and uniformly surrounded by gardens'. In Cannes, Brougham's villa was the first of many. One of his friends, Thomas Robinson Woolfield, became the village's first *de facto* estate agent: he acquired building plots from the locals and sold them on to aristocratic English acquaintances. In 1855 he built an Anglican church on his own property in the village.

Not content with these adornments to the landscape, Brougham himself led the way in importing turf from England to create an 'English country garden' – although the summer temperatures meant it had to be replaced every year. At the Villa Victoria Woolfield introduced flora to the coast that eventually came to be regarded as typical of the region and thought by many to be indigenous: gooseberry, sweet potato, eucalyptus and acacia. Soon mimosa and – notably at Hyères – the palm tree joined them. These trees seem to have been introduced originally to Hyères and other parts of the coast by the Moors, whose favourites they were. In the first third of the nineteenth century they were planted in such numbers at Hyères that the settlement began to style itself Hyères les Palmiers. Adolphe Smith later commented in his *The Garden of Hyères*:

> Most periods have had to travel hundreds of miles further south in order to experience a transition similar to that which the comparatively short journey to Hyeres will enable us to enjoy. It is difficult to believe that in France, while still within the pale of advanced civilisation, we can live in a semi-tropical climate surrounded by all the marvels of vegetation which are generally associated with distant colonies and semi-barbaric countries.

Then there was the food. The reputation France now enjoys as the home of fine cuisine was forged largely in the late nineteenth and early twentieth centuries. In the eighteenth century, English visitors to France deplored the local fare and, as far as possible, imposed the delicacies of English cuisine on the French. In Nice, on 20 September 1789, Arthur Young found himself dining on roast beef, plum pudding, and porter, which made him 'drop for a moment the idea of the formidable distance that separated me from England'. The physician Edward Rigby, visiting the town that year, was treated to a dinner *tout à l'anglaise*. Seventy years later, of the situation in Menton at the eastern end of the coast, Dr J. Henry Bennet recorded:

> As I have been told by Menton hotel keepers, the dinners we positively require and exact every day at the hotels and 'pensions' are to them festive dinners, which they never dream of unless to welcome friends for a marriage or a baptism. To provide this high standard of food, to many hundred strangers, the country had to be ransacked for a hundred miles around.

The travel writer Augustus Hare, like Bennet one of the earliest English *hivernants* in Menton, wintered there from November 1860 to May 1861. In *Winter at Mentone*, he explained that he found the cuisine satisfactory only after his dinner 'had been stripped of its oil and garlic, and has had some extra cooking bestowed on it'.

Given that for the majority of the early English visitors the Riviera was a series of health resorts, and that the British were pioneers in public-health initiatives necessitated by the rapid growth of the urban environment, sanitation was another aspect of early English colonisation. The French, of course, were well known to be careless and deficient in such matters. Smollett remarked that their personal habits would be regarded as 'detestable even in the capital of North Britain'. The outbreak of cholera in Marseille that had sent Brougham to Cannes underscored such perceptions, although the causes of the disease beyond its general association with dirt and squalor were not finally identified for half a century. Of Hyères, Adolphe Smith warned of the 'more or less contaminated water of the wells which, as usual, are dug dangerously near to the cesspool or manure heaps'. As late as 1892 Murray's *Handbook* for the Riviera declared that 'some of the most important essentials to *sanitary comfort* and *personal decency* ... are utterly disregarded, and evince a state of degradation not to be expected in a civilised country, and highly discreditable to French manners and habits'.

In the interval, though, the English pressurised local authorities into making improvements. A British company was contracted to attend to the water supply at Cannes, and according to Murray, drainage was made more efficient by the implementation of 'Captain

D. Galton's plans and suggestions'. In Hyères, the proprietors of some of the better hotels were seeking to upgrade. It was true that, as Smith put it, 'With respect to the sanitary condition ... it would scarcely be fair, now that the town is in a state of transition, to describe the old state of affairs,' but he singled out for praise the Hôtel de l'Hermitage, where 'the soil is removed every twenty-four hours so that no time is allowed for the process of fermentation to set in. Here, also, the tank for the supply of drinking water is separate from that which supplies the means of flushing the house drains.' Even so, he cautioned, 'It would be well that each visitor should see the drains of the house he may rent; should make lavish use, on the least provocation, of *Sporokoton*, or some other equally powerful combination of disinfecting and deodorising chemicals.'

Finally, there was the English language itself. The smaller communities along the coast had been isolated since the collapse of the Roman Empire and the local *patois* had developed to such an extent that variations in vocabulary and diction were found within a few miles. Murray claimed that the locals' dialect was 'unintelligible, even to themselves'. Moreover, in Nice and beyond to the east the influence of Italian was profound. John Bunnell Davis noted that the *patois* differed even between Menton and Monaco, which were a mere dozen miles apart: each was composed of a mixture of Provence, Ligurian and Piedmont, but in different proportions. All in all, then, there was little point in the visitors bothering to learn the local language. The natives would have to learn theirs – and not only that: their own language became gradually tainted with English. The Riviera pioneered Franglais. The high life that the English enjoyed on the coast became 'hig-lif'. As British sports insinuated themselves along the coast in the second half of the nineteenth century, a French golfer began taking 'son putter sur le green'. Washerwomen advertised their talents with 'le pull-cardigan'. Later there were English-language newspapers, most prominently the *Menton and Monte Carlo News*.

This all meant that by the late 1850s the English had definitively arrived, and that much of the coast was on its way to becoming virtually an English *dependence*. The novelist Henry Rider Haggard noted wryly, 'English folk would celebrate book teas and play golf or any other accustomed game upon the brink of the Styx. Perhaps that is why they remain a ruling race, for to do this it is necessary to preserve the habits and traditions of the fatherland, refusing persistently to allow them to be overwhelmed by those of any surrounding people.'

4

If a duly anglicised Cannes was the creation of Henry Brougham, Menton was the child of Dr James Henry Bennet. Cannes, though, was for the living. Menton, situated at the eastern extreme of the Riviera, was for the dying.

Further north than New York, Menton's climate was claimed, with some justice, to be the best on the Riviera, and related to its location at the foot of the Alpes Maritimes, perched on a narrow ledge of land that dropped almost at once into the Ligurian Sea. The rocky amphitheatre that rose behind the town sheltered it almost completely from the cold northerly winds that affect the coast to the west. This created a sub-tropical greenhouse on a latitude at which it should not exist. In 1860, Augustus Hare recorded that during his stay, 'Throughout the winter we seldom wanted a fire, except on wet days, or in the evening, and in January it was often hot enough to breakfast at nine o'clock with windows open to the ground.' Until Bennet arrived, the village subsisted on the lemons that flourished in this climate.

Bennet was born in 1816 to a Manchester textile manufacturer at the forefront of turning Britain into the first industrial society. The young Bennet studied medicine in Paris, then set up as a practitioner in London. In his forties he developed tuberculosis. The prognosis seemed hopeless so he closed his practice and made for the restorative southern French coast. Twenty or thirty years previously he might have fled to Nice. By the 1850s, though, Nice was a substantial town with a foreign colony of some seven thousand, and would soon become the fastest growing city in Europe. Bennet wrote that 'More than half of the northerners who crowd there in the winter are cured invalids of former days ... and they are also specimens of the more restless of our countrymen and women, who, after wandering all over Europe for years, settle down at last to winter at Nice, on account of its social attractions.' By contrast, the Menton that he discovered in 1859 was 'a quiet little Italian town on the sunny shore of the Riviera, with two or three small hotels, and half dozen recently erected villas'. There, contrary to his expectations, 'under a genial sky, freed from the anxieties and labours of a former life', he rallied.

This was a miracle that clearly needed promulgating, and a book was soon in hand. *Winter and Spring on the Shores of the Mediterranean* appeared in 1861, and was soon running to fresh editions, then translations. Inevitably English tuberculosis sufferers flocked to Menton. This had several consequences. First, many of the invalids availed themselves of Dr Bennet's professional services, and he built up a lucrative practice in what became his permanent winter home. Second, the village developed to meet the needs of the visitors, and the lemons took a back seat. By 1875, Bennet could describe Menton as 'a well-known and frequented winter resort, with thirty hotels, four times that number of villas, and a mixed foreign population of above sixteen hundred'. Third, Menton became synonymous with death. Despite the example of Dr Bennet himself, its climate could scarcely cure the incurable. One of his contemporaries, Dr James Johnson, pointed out in *Change of Air* that he had 'lived too long, and seen too much, not to know the errors of discrimination and the fallacies of hope that send pulmonary invalids from the gloomy skies but comfortable abodes of England to lands where comfort is unknown, even by name, and whose atmosphere cannot work miracles, whatever their saints may do'. Similarly, in

Wanderings in Search of Health, Dr Coupland Taylor wrote of patients dying 'almost immediately after their arrival, not having sufficient strength even to survive the fatigues of the journey or voyage'. Alongside the hotels and sanatoria, it soon became necessary to establish a cemetery. The illustrator Aubrey Beardsley died of tuberculosis at Menton at the age of twenty-six, and was buried there. So, too, was the founder of rugby football, William Webb Ellis. James Bennet, however, lived on for another thirty-two years after he had arrived as a hopeless case.

5

Most famous of all of the early Riviera invalids was the Scottish poet and novelist Robert Louis Stevenson. Aged twenty-four, he was diagnosed as at risk of tuberculosis and despatched by his doctor Sir Andrew Clark to Menton in the autumn of 1873. He read George Sand, visited Monte Carlo, and made the recovery chronicled in his 1874 essay 'Ordered South'. Ten years later he was married to the American Fanny Van de Grift, had published *Travels with a Donkey in the Cevennes*, and was on the brink of the fame that *Treasure Island* would bring. By now, though, his tuberculosis was sufficiently established to force him to spend a winter taking the Alpine cure in Davos, high in eastern Switzerland. Neither Stevenson nor his wife enjoyed the sterility of a large village that had been turned into a sanatorium, and in the autumn of 1882 they welcomed Sir Andrew's advice to return to the South of France.

At first they settled in the Campagne Delfi at St Marcel, some five miles from Marseille. This was a disaster: Stevenson was constantly ill and suffered several tubercular haemorrhages. Then, at the end of the year, the village was struck by a fever. The writer fled for Nice, and eventually he and his wife found a villa to rent just above Hyères, now second only to Menton as a resort for the

English. The villa was on the hillside that led up to the remains of the ruined medieval castle. Chalet La Solitude commanded views across the plain of Hyères to the Îles d'Or. It was no more than a cottage, but for Stevenson it was 'the loveliest spot in the Universe', its garden 'like a fairy-story and a view like a classical landscape'. By night, too, the villa was exquisite: 'When the moon is out, that garden, the arbour, the flight of stairs that mount the artificial hillock, the plumed blue gum-trees that hang trembling, become the very skirts of paradise.'

It was at La Solitude in May the following year that Stevenson heard from his publishers, Cassell, about the sale of the book-rights to *Treasure Island*. 'How much do you suppose?' he wrote to his mother. 'I believe it would be an excellent jest to keep the answer till my next letter. For two cents I would do so. Shall I? Anyway I'll turn the page first. No – well, a hundred pounds, all alive, O! A hundred jingling, tingling, golden, minted quid. Is not this wonderful?' It was also at La Solitude that he composed many of the poems that comprise *A Child's Garden of Verses*. He had begun them on a summer visit to the Scottish Highlands in 1881, when he completed fourteen or fifteen lyrics. During his stay at La Solitude he tripled that number. A few were published in 1884, and the complete volume appeared in 1885, after his departure from Hyères. 'Travels' is the poem perhaps most reminiscent of the coast:

> I should like to rise and go
> Where the golden apples grow;
> Where below another sky
> Parrot islands anchored lie
> And, watched by cockatoos and goats,
> Lonely Crusoes building boats...

Along with Smollett's book on the pleasures of Nice, the writings of Stevenson mark the beginning of the coast's role as a cradle for the arts. It was a place with a climate and an ambience to inspire.

'Happy,' wrote Stevenson in Samoa towards the end of his life when he was dying of tuberculosis. 'I was only happy once, that was at Hyères; it came to end for a variety of reasons, decline in health, change of place, increase of money, age with his stealing steps; since then, as before then, I know not what it means.'

3

François Blanc and the Iron Horse

'I want – I want somehow to get away with you to a world where words like that – categories like that won't exist. Where we shall simply be two human beings who love each other.'
'Oh my dear – where is that country? Have you ever been there? I know some who've tried to find it; and believe me, they all got out by mistake at some wayside station: at places like Boulogne, or Pisa or Monte Carlo – and it wasn't at all different from the old world they'd left, but only rather smaller and dingier and more promiscuous.'

Edith Wharton, *The Age of Innocence*

1

'"How did you get over the precipices?"' said the travel writer Augustus Hare, 'is generally the first question asked of anyone who arrives at Mentone.' In his own case, he went on to explain, 'it was a real subject of congratulation, that we arrived with unbroken necks, for the hour, the weather, and the driver alike had been favourable to an accident'. This suggests all too accurately the state of the roads on the Riviera as late as 1860, when Hare had wintered in Menton; and it was a state that had existed virtually since the decline and fall of the Roman Empire fourteen hundred years previously and the gradual destruction of its road system.

This was not entirely for want of trying by the French. As early as 1664 Louis XIV had provided grants for a series of *pavés du roi.*

An École des Ports et Chaussées – a sort of highways authority – was established in the middle of the eighteenth century, and in 1775 Pierre Tresaguet became its inspector general. From Nevers on the Loire, he pioneered road improvement with large stones laid on a firm foundation, then progressively smaller ones towards the top, an approach subsequently adopted in Britain by Thomas Telford and John McAdam. Napoleon built on his work. In March 1796 he had arrived in Nice as an inexperienced young general at the beginning of the campaign that would see his conquest of Italy and the establishment of his reputation as a military genius. At first, though, he faced almost precisely the same issues as Augustus when he had been subduing the alpine tribes and uniting Rome with Gaul: the barrier of the Alpes Maritimes that lay on the direct coastal route between France and Italy. Six years later, in the aftermath of the Peace of Amiens, Napoleon, appreciating the critical importance of road communications in binding his new empire, planned a series of fourteen strategic highways radiating from Paris.

With his experience in the Italian campaign, the South of France also attracted his attention. There he planned to build the southernmost strategic highway, close to where the via Aurelia had once run. Starting at Nice, it would drive eastwards round the coast to San Remo on the Italian riviera, more often than not forming a ledge chiselled into the mountainside high above the sea. It was this that inspired its name: the Grande Corniche – Great Ledge. Begun in 1803, the huge project was occasionally pursued with such conviction that an army of two thousand men was at work. The road eventually reached San Remo in 1814. In 1823 when the Countess of Blessington swept along the Corniche in her carriage, two years after Napoleon's death, she could declare that it 'leaves the indelible mark of *him* who planned it; boldly designed, and solidly executed, with a disregard for difficulties'. Nevertheless, in places the road was winding and tortuous, and irregularly maintained. In November 1859, Augustus Hare's *diligence* was obliged to make its way over the tree roots and boulders that had fallen down the steep hillside to lie on the road.

As Lord Brougham had discovered, the coast to the west of Nice was even less exposed to the advantages and disadvantages of modern road communications. The route to the Iberian peninsula was as interesting to Napoleon as it had been centuries previously to Rome. From 1808 his brother Joseph ruled Spain. Insurrections against him began virtually on the day of his coronation in Madrid, and continued until his defeat by Wellington at Vitoria in June 1813. French military support was essential, and at one time more than 300,000 troops were stationed in Spain. France shared a long and relatively porous border with the Iberian peninsula that followed the base of the Pyrenees from the Atlantic to the Mediterranean. For the Romans, the via Aurelia running from Genoa to the eastern Pyrenees was a vital artery. To Napoleon, however, any such road was a capillary, and an insignificant one at that. The Riviera of Smollett and Brougham was no more than a series of mutually inaccessible fishing villages, Nice, and the little principality of Monaco.

Until the coming of the railways, communications were maintained largely by sea. The Romans used *feluccas*, small wooden, carvel-built vessels, between twenty-five and fifty feet long. Powered either by sail or oar, they were used all over the Mediterranean for transport and trading. It was a descendant of such a craft – and not a very distant one – that Arthur Young was obliged to take on his journey east from Toulon in 1789, in the absence of a 'suitable diligence or voiture'. As he had been promised, the voyage provided him with splendid views of the coast, 'the finest object in all Provence'. As he left Toulon, he noted that 'the town, the shipping, the high mountain, which rises immediately above it, the hills, covered with plantations, and spread everywhere with *bastides*, unite to form a striking *coup d'oeil*'.

Yet whatever its aesthetic advantages, sea travel was slow, susceptible to contrary winds and storms, periodically unpleasant, occasionally dangerous. Antibes to Genoa was something like ninety miles. It might take a day with a favourable easterly or southerly wind, three times as long under oars – even longer if the captain stuck to the coastline to avoid the worst of the seas. There were also pirates. In the seventeenth century they had plagued the coast, while Barbary and Corsair marauders were active as late as 1815. In 1780 the party of Madame de Genlis spent ten days in Antibes waiting for a favourable wind, then found themselves escorted by soldiers in another *felucca* 'to assure our safety from pirates', which 'thrilled the romantic imagination' of the author.

Travel by water to the South of France and along the Riviera was improved rather than revolutionised by the advent of steam. James Watt's steam engine, introduced when Smollett was visiting Nice in the 1760s, paved the way for the first cross-Channel steamer service in 1820. From Calais travellers had usually broken the route south by road by taking a boat down the Rhône, typically from Lyon to Avignon, occasionally as far as Marseille. After the introduction of steam, the artist William Boxall wrote of this inland voyage, 'The Rhône is so rapid that the boat performs in one day what it takes by diligence two days and two nights.' Then, in April 1832, a visitor to Nice spotted 'an American ship which travels without sail and by means of fire'. By comparison with the *feluccas* plying the coast, it had consummate advantages. 'It goes in any wind and even against the wind, and at great speed.' Soon it was possible for English travellers to take a packet boat from Southampton to Marseille, then along the coast to Nice.

Sea travel in the Mediterranean, though, even by paddle-steamer, remained slow and by no means invariably congenial. On a passage from Genoa to Naples in 1853, Charles Dickens found the overcrowding such that 'The scene on board beggars description. Ladies on the tables; gentlemen under the tables, bedroom appliances not usually beheld in public airing themselves in positions where soup tureens had been lately developing themselves; and ladies and gentlemen lying indiscriminately on the open deck, arranged like spoons on a sideboard.' There was also, as usual, trouble with the

French. At about the same time, aboard one of the French government Messageries Impériales vessels, the Rev. John Aiton noted:

> English passengers are insulted by Frenchmen and rendered as uncomfortable as possible by the authorities on board. They are cheated on every hand and a different rate of charge [is] brought against them. They are scarcely permitted to walk the deck, far less to take up any position so as to take a view for a minute or two, and as to a Frenchman lending an English voyager a spyglass, or telling him the name of an island, he would rather spit on his face.

At least the pirates had gone.

2

'If God had intended us to fly,' remarked the British lyricist and entertainer Michael Flanders, 'he would never have given us the railways.'

Although not necessarily antediluvian, railways had certainly existed as long ago as the sixteenth century when they were used in German and English mines to facilitate the movement of heavy trucks. Horses, mules or men provided the motive power. Its sheer size meant that the early steam engine was used in ships; a smaller model lay behind the invention of the steam locomotive by Richard Trevithick, son of a mine manager. By 1803 his New Castle was at work, which, in its turn, inspired George Stephenson, designer of the Rocket and engineer of the Stockton–Darlington and Liverpool– Manchester railways. The opening of the latter in 1830 heralded the railway age, and Continental Europe – particularly Belgium – soon followed suit. Twenty years later, Britain had more than sixteen thousand miles of railways.

In England the railways were developed by private enterprise, moderately regulated by the government. In France there was a long, noisy debate about the vices and virtues of public versus private development. In 1842 it resulted in a national scheme for the railways, which would be constructed mainly, but not exclusively, by private companies, and laid out on a series of vectors radiating from Paris. A single state line ran to Le Havre; the private lines were the Nord, the Est, the Ouest, the Paris–Orléans, and finally the Paris–Lyon–Mediterranée. The PLM, as it soon became known, had responsibility for the development of south-east France.

By the time the main line south was under construction, the far-reaching influence of rail was becoming apparent. As George Stephenson's biographer L. T. C. Rolt wrote,

> No other invention had such an overwhelming effect on society as this first form of mechanical transport ... we have since conquered the road and the air with newer forms of power ... but no subsequent development has equalled in significance or in sheer impact on the imagination this first mighty stride which took man from a secure and settled environment hallowed by centuries into a new, exciting yet disturbing world which at once opened up limitless possibilities. The railway train was the harbinger of this brave new world.

The PLM reached the coast at Marseille, then the second city in France, in 1855. The Rhône delta to the west of the city presented the railway engineers with numerous challenges: soft ground interspersed with water channels, mosquito-laden marshes and the *mistral*. The route to Toulon, forty-two miles east, posed fewer difficulties. There, the line could follow the coast closely; it reached France's most important port in 1859. The cliffs of the Maures massif plunge so steeply into the sea between Toulon and Fréjus that the line here was obliged to turn almost north-east, skirting the northern edge of the massif before rejoining the coast three miles beyond Fréjus, at St Raphael. From there to Cannes, a further twenty-five miles, the track skirted the base of the Esterels. It reached Brougham's resort in 1863, but not without a certain amount of difficulty.

In England, the first parliamentary bill to pave the way for the Liverpool–Manchester line was defeated by Lord Derby, who objected it would ruin his fox coverts. Others said that the noise of the locomotives would cause cows to dry, kill birds, and bring undesirable characters into the countryside. To these reasonable reservations the controversialist, painter and writer John Ruskin added his own passionate objections:

> There was a rocky valley between Buxton and Bakewell ... divine as the vale of Tempe; you might have seen the gods there morning and evening – Apollo and the Sweet Muses of the Light ... You enterprised a railroad ... you blasted its rocks away ... And now, every fool in Buxton can be in Bakewell in half an hour, and every fool in Bakewell in Buxton.

In Cannes, Brougham and his friend Woolfield were all too familiar with the pernicious side of the railway. When they discovered that the planned line crossed Woolfield's grounds, they protested vociferously to the French government. At considerable cost to the developers, its course was changed. In Nice, the prospect of the railway was generally welcomed, but no one could agree where the station should go. Nice had lost its status as a free port in 1854, and trade had suffered. Some said the railway's presence at the port would foster its renaissance, particularly when the Suez Canal was completed. Others supposed that wealthy tourists would hardly wish to arrive in the squalor of the docks, and suggested a spot more than a mile from the sea. The compromise pleased few: 'The mayor's gone mad,' they said. 'He's stuck the station in the middle of the country.' The line eventually reached the town on 18 October 1864.

Thereafter the going got tougher. The Alpes Maritimes, east of the town, fell ever more steeply into a series of heavily indented bays, on whose shores lay the gems of Villefranche and Beaulieu, separated by the magical kingdom of Cap Ferrat. It was only ten miles from Nice to Monaco, but it was necessary to tunnel almost a third of the distance. The line to the principality opened on 19 October 1868. The topography eased only slightly on the approach to

Menton, and in any case the incentive to proceed was much diminished as the border with Italy approached. In 1860 the stretch of coast from Nice to Menton was ceded to Napoleon III in recognition of his assistance to Garibaldi and Cavour in the unification of Italy: a country barely free from the throes of formation was not much concerned with railway construction. The Dean of Canterbury, writing in *The Riviera, Pen and Pencil Sketches from Cannes to Genoa*, was a sceptical observer both of the construction works and the devotion of French navvies to the Protestant work ethic:

> At several points embankment work is proceeding. The 'plant' consists of a single truck of enormous dimensions and venerable in its amount of patching. When, with the usual ejaculation of 'hee-ups' and 'hee's' this great omnibus has been brought near its destination, the horses are leisurely detached from the front, and it has to be slowly pushed forward by hand to the edge of the embankment. One side of the truck is let down, at the infinite peril of the workers, and part of the load falls out. The next step is to drive wedges under the inward side, in order to tilt the truck further. This done, the group of workmen sit down and watch it, and from time to time, with amazing demonstrations of energy, give the wedge more blows. At last the load moves off and falls over the side of the embankment, the great stones bounding away over the neighbouring field or road. The next thing is to pursue these stones and bring them back by hand ... I need hardly remind the reader that with us the embankment work is accomplished by self-tilting trucks, run out at a trot towards the *end* of the embankment ... Who is responsible for this ridiculous engineering does not appear. I can only say that at the rate it is now going on, the line to Menton will take in years as long as the Italian line will take in centuries.

The Dean was unduly pessimistic. The line to Menton at the eastern end of the Riviera was opened before his book was published in 1870, and he was obliged to introduce an erratum note to that effect. The railway had arrived.

3

Its impact was immediate. L. T. C. Rolt wrote that the railway was the first major form of mechanised transport but, equally importantly, it was the first means of mass transport. In the episode that had begun his pioneering career as a travel agent, Thomas Cook had chartered a train to transport five hundred people from Leicester to Loughborough and back again. Never in the field of human transport had so many been moved so far by so few. This was 1841, in the relative infancy of the railways. A quarter of a century later, with the western European railway system approaching completion, millions travelled daily over considerably greater distances. The teeming cities of the industrial revolution were effectively created by the railways, which transported the materials from which the cities were built, the coal by which they were powered and warmed, and the labour by which they were run. Similarly, the railways brought people – particularly the English and a few rich Russians – to the Riviera in significant numbers for the first time. In 1865, a year after the arrival of the railway in Nice, a hundred thousand people alighted there; nine years later the figure had virtually tripled. Between 1861 and 1874 the colony of foreigners also grew threefold: from 7900 to 25,000 – twice the size of the town's population when Smollett was there. As a consequence, Nice became the first major community to be dependent on the tourist trade.

The nature of the visitors changed. Hitherto, it had been principally English people who had had the time and money to travel to the Riviera. With the railway less of either was needed to visit the coast. The fact that Thomas Cook felt there was a need for a guidebook to the area is significant, given the middle-class clientele that his travel agency was beginning to attract – Cook identified them as 'clergymen, physicians, bankers, civil engineers, merchants, tradesmen, manufacturers and professional gentlemen'. It was significant, too, that his 1881 Riviera handbook talked of the need for a guide that was not only comprehensive but cheap. For good or ill, its readers would not have been rubbing shoulders with the descendants of Lord Brougham. The Cannes of the 1850s was a centre of privilege and fashion. After the arrival of the railway, the French historian Prosper Mérimée, who had known the town in its youth, found it full of 'Englishmen and unpleasant Russians. This avalanche of foreigners has spoiled this beautiful country. I need to find some other secluded place as warm as this but less over-run by civilization.' What was more, given the relative ease with which they travelled, and the pleasures that attracted them, these English were the first visitors to the Riviera who were not really travellers at all: they were tourists – who required stabling, plate, bottle and entertainment, on a hitherto unprecedented scale.

Inns had long been a feature of the coast, but the tradition on the Riviera was to rent a house or, indeed, build a villa rather than stay in a hotel: it took more than a week to reach the coast from England so stays were long. Families would arrive in the late autumn and stay until spring. When the railways reduced the journey from England to thirty hours, it become practicable to visit for shorter periods, and hotels multiplied to cater for those who wanted to stay for just a few weeks. Before the coming of the railway, Cannes had only a couple of hotels. After its arrival, according to Woolfield, 'the old hotels were enlarged, new ones built with marvellous rapidity.' By 1889 it had fifty. Between 1873 and 1891 the town's population doubled.

Menton, too, expanded: by 1871, it was scarcely recognisable as the sequestered spot that Augustus Hare and J. Henry Bennet had discovered a decade previously. It now boasted thirty hotels and *pensions*, and was on its way to becoming the principal English colony on the coast. Conversely, Hyères – once the most popular English resort – suffered: to reach it, travellers had to take a thirteen-mile branch line from Toulon. In *The Garden of Hyères*, Adolphe Smith enumerated the many virtues of this most southerly of the Mediterranean 'health stations': the mildness of the climate, the protection it offered from the *mistral*, and the energy with which hoteliers were trying to improve sanitary provision. Yet in the absence of an attraction like Brougham or publicist like Bennet, and because Hyères was 'not on the main line of communication', the town had failed 'to share in the new development enjoyed by Nice, Cannes and Monaco'. It had been 'overtaken of late by some of the newer stations in the matter of public notoriety'.

It was regrettable – and regretted – that the sudden need for accommodation promoted a rash of building that put a premium on space rather than intrinsic elegance or suitability to the setting. The style of much of the new building appeared to accord with Napoleon's aesthetic that '*Ce qui est grand est toujours beau*' (big is always beautiful), an idea later taken up by Hitler and his architect Albert Speer. As early as 1870, the former Lord Provost of Edinburgh, William Chambers, complained of Menton that 'The most genial as well as the most beautiful spot on the Riviera was architecturally spoiled. There was no attempt to construct buildings in harmony with the surrounding scenery.' Augustus Hare, who at the end of the 1850s had found Menton in particular and the coast in general in a prelapsarian state, was soon writing with an even more jaundiced eye. Of Brougham's Cannes, he railed in *South Eastern France*: 'The hills are covered with hideous villas, built chiefly by Englishmen, whose main object seems to be the effacement of all the national beauties of the place – to sow grass where it will never live, to import from the north shrubs which can never grow, and to cut down all the original woods and flowers.' Stendhal – the novelist Henri-Marie Beyle – moaned that Brougham's own villa was 'so bourgeois, so denuded of all that speaks of the imagination'. Then there was the historian and essayist A. J. A. Symons, whose tubercular condition demanded that he shuttle between the sanatoria of the Riviera and their rivals in the Alps: he complained that the hotels that had sprung up all over the coast were 'built for as many consumptive foreigners to live or to die in as can be packed into their formless parallelograms'.

And there was the railway. Ruskin was scarcely alone in seeing the endless lines of steel as desecrating the landscape. He had complained bitterly in *Sesame and Lilies* about the building of the line round the head of Lake Geneva, the one spot in Europe 'whose character and influence on the human mind is special'. He might have written much the same of the coast from Nice to Menton, the most spectacular on the whole Riviera. As it was, the job was left to the Dean of Canterbury, who deplored the changes brought about by the coming of the line:

> All this is now lost to the traveller by the opening of the railway. And certainly, however slow one may be to sympathise with the lamentations over fine country being spoilt by lines of rail, one cannot forbear in this case joining the common outcry. The one perhaps the choicest bit of route to be found in the whole of Europe ... a trail which has ever been little less than Elysian. The other a series of plunges from light and dark, only varied by the shouted names of railway stations, which were once full of associations for beauty and beauty only.

4

In 1882, within little more than a decade of the coming of the railway to the coast, Dr Henry Thomas Pickering took up his pen to promote the virtues of Monaco. He opened his book with a flourish: 'The happy harmony of nature and art, of wild alpine scenery, and of orderly government, of rural surroundings and metropolitan comforts, of a rugged sea coast and a smooth railway line to bring the full benefits of civilisation within reach – all tend to make the principality the chosen spot on the Riviera.' If it was true that the railway was already transforming much of the Riviera, it virtually created Monaco – in cahoots with the genius of François Blanc.

The principality's only natural advantage was its small but sheltered harbour. It was for this that it had been inhabited since prehistoric times. The Romans used it as a staging-post to Gaul.

According to Pickering, 'The Roman coins, the beautiful gold jewellery and the elaborate sculptured work found [at Monaco] prove the wealth and fashionable nature of Roman society which congregated there during the second and third centuries of the present era.' Like the rest of the coast, its claims to civilisation collapsed with the Roman empire. The village – it was little more – re-entered history in the early fourteenth century when Charles Grimaldi was acknowledged as its sovereign by the powers in Genoa. Grimaldi fortified the Christian settlement against the Moors, but could do little to promote the prosperity of what became Europe's smallest principality. In Smollett's time, it still had a population of less than a thousand. Its quandary was summarised by the old Monégasque saying:

> Son Monaco sopra un scoglio
> Non semino e no raccoglio
> E pur mangiar voglio
>
> I am Monaco on a rock
> By the shore, I neither sow nor reap,
> But all the same I mean to eat.

With a territory amounting to little more than five square miles, much of it precipitous and barren, there was little for the Monégasques to live on other than what they could forage directly or indirectly from the sea. Menton and Roquebrune – the latter half village, half castle on the hills above Cap Martin – were part of the principality. The Grimaldis and their people lived on taxes levied on wine, tobacco, lemons and shipping through the port. Then, in 1848 – the year of European revolutions – Roquebrune and Menton played their own small parts by declaring their independence from Monaco. The loss of the tax revenues from the outlying communities led to a crisis that was solved in a remarkable way.

By the middle of the nineteenth century institutional gambling had established itself in various German principalities, but was illegal in France and Italy. This provided Monaco's incumbent Grimaldi ruler, Prince Charles III, with an opportunity. In 1856 he sanctioned the building of gaming rooms in the principality, and a society was formed to construct and run them under the beguiling name of the Société Anonyme des Bains de Mer et du Cercle des Étrangers à Monaco. This was astute: it followed the example of the German casinos in suggesting that the first rule of running a successful casino was to pretend it was a spa. 'The bathing establishment,' wrote the Prince's lawyer and business adviser Monsieur A. Eynaud, 'should in a sense act as a façade for the gambling establishment.' The sort of bathing facilities then popular at French seaside resorts were built, together with gaming rooms, on a promontory a mile from the fortified town called Les Spélugues.

Yet the difficulty in reaching Monaco other than by sea virtually put paid to the idea. It was still a four-hour journey from Nice along Napoleon's old Corniche, and perhaps half that by sea if the wind happened to be blowing in the right direction and the water was not too rough. In March 1857, the casino had only a single visitor. The concessionaires, Albert Audet and Leon Langlois, soon abandoned their 'gold mine'. Then, in 1863, a year before the railway reached Nice, François Blanc arrived in Monaco.

Born in Avignon in 1806 to a poor tax collector, Blanc had a remarkable head for figures. First he made a fortune from the casino in the German town Bad Homburg. In 1854, anxious to found a dynasty based on his success, he married a cobbler's daughter twenty-seven years his junior. Marie Hensel was pretty, entertaining, and unspoilt by education. He sent her away to Paris to acquire the limited information necessary to cut a figure in Society. Soon there were children. Then, having heard that the Monaco concession was going begging, Blanc moved to Nice and set about researching the project. The German casinos were closed from October to April so their clientele might be attracted to a winter gambling destination. There were also the large numbers of English visitors wintering in Nice and Cannes with time and money on their hands. Blanc understood the paramount importance of communications, and was delighted to discover that when Napoleon III had acquired the territory between Menton and Nice, the French authorities had agreed to drive a new carriage road from Nice to Monaco. It would be a second Corniche. Furthermore, the PLM might be persuaded to extend its railway line further east towards the principality. Here was potential. Prince Charles III was similarly excited, even more so when Monsieur Eynaud wrote to him that 'Blanc is colossally rich; he created Homburg as it is today, and he is a past master in the art of dissimulating the green cloth of the gaming tables behind a veil of elegance and pleasure.'

A meeting was set with the Prince's agent for 31 March 1863. Despite his reputation as the genius behind Bad Homburg, Blanc cut a curious figure: a small, bespectacled man with a straggling moustache, nervous manner and heavy provincial French accent, he was obliged to stand throughout the negotiations because of a boil on his behind. 'A most troublesome disability,' he said. As a negotiator, though, he was unsurpassed. One story has it that when the pair met, Blanc opened his wallet to reveal the stupendous sum of seventeen hundred thousand francs. The Prince, Blanc informed the agent, could take or leave it that day. An agreement was reached. In exchange for the concession the Prince acquired shares in a new company to be established to run it, an annual fee, and a share of the profits. In retrospect, this looks like the deal of the century. 'Monaco,' wrote Eynaud presciently to Prince Charles, 'is about to experience an entire and brilliant transformation.'

Soon Blanc was busy following the blueprint that had made Bad Homburg such a success. He chartered a steamer to ply between Nice and Monaco, and acquired a fleet of hackney carriages to make the trip by road. Hotels were built surrounding the gaming rooms, gardens laid out, and the tiny city dignified in 1866 with a name that would flatter his patron: Monte Carlo (Charleville was also considered). Eighteen months after the opening of the railway in 1870, the principality entertained 130,000 visitors. By 1879, this had risen to 315,000. Over roughly the same period, the population doubled. A new kind of state had been created, based not on the industry of the inhabitants but on the profits accrued from allowing visitors to gamble. Lord Brougham commented admiringly, 'Blanc has astonished me by the profundity and prevision of his calculation.'

The Monégasques themselves benefited from the profusion of visitors. Leaving aside the opportunities for employment in hotels, villas and the gambling establishment, in February 1869 Prince Charles abolished all direct taxation. This made him immensely popular, a cause and effect that politicians might note.

Yet plenty of people failed to see the influx as the manifestation of civilisation that Dr Pickering claimed it to be. The Anglican clergy, mindful of the morals of their expatriate flock, were in the vanguard of those who saw gambling as immoral. They pointed out, with some justice, that the tables attracted not only gamblers but people of doubtful virtue who lived off them – moneylenders, prostitutes and the like. There were also those who committed suicide as a consequence of their losses. The Bishop of Gibraltar, piqued by the refusal of Prince Charles to let him establish an Anglican church in the principality, asked, 'Is it right for Christian men and women even to enter a place where they are sure to rub shoulders with the swindler, the harlot or the thief, whose chambers are built with the wages of iniquity, and whose riches are the price of blood?' The Dean of Canterbury was similarly outraged. 'The present attraction of Monaco is the disgraceful gaming table, and it is not too much to say that its centripetal force draws thither the scum of the world.' The Baptist revivalist Charles Spurgeon called Monaco 'the Serpent in Paradise'. In 1882 a society was established to put the casino out of business. It was indicative of the status of the Riviera at the time as a British colony that it had a branch in London. *The Times* took up the cause, and anticipated with pleasure the day 'when the last croupier shall have taken his last crown from the last Monaco gambler'. Thomas Cook's contemporary handbook on the Riviera reassured its readers that 'The respectable inhabitants of Monaco, Nice and Menton are almost entirely in favour of suppressing the Casino at Monte Carlo. They affirm that the questionable visitors who now haunt the neighbourhood would disappear, and at no distant date a prosperous and moral community would settle on this beautiful spot.'

In 1875, the principality marked its coming-of-age by welcoming the greatest attraction of the day, the heir to the English throne and his wife, the Prince and Princess of Wales. Blanc survived until July 1877, when he died with a fortune of eighty-eight million francs and – as his biographer Count Corti remarked – in Monte Carlo 'a magic realm in which the rules governing the outside world cease to be valid'. For Monsieur Eynaud, Blanc had created 'a little paradise'. The French took a different view: they called the trio of resorts that emerged from the railway Riviera – Nice, Cannes and Monte Carlo – the World, the Flesh and the Devil. Still, such was their success that by the time of Blanc's death, the Riviera had become the most popular winter destination in Europe.

4

The Indiscretions of the Prince

'What men call gallantry, and gods adultery,
Is much more common where the climate's sultry.'

Byron, *Don Juan*

1

If the railway was the harbinger of tourism and prosperity to the Riviera, it also brought the royal families of Europe. On 21 October 1864, three days after the railway opened in Nice, Tsar Alexander II of Russia arrived on a special train. He was followed a week later by Napoleon III, and on the thirtieth by the man who would become King Leopold II of Belgium. British royalty – the best sort – followed in profusion. Some years later, the British Prime Minister Lord Salisbury joked that so many dukes and princes populated the Riviera that the choice lay between royalty in the winter and mosquitoes in the summer. The French novelist Guy de Maupassant complained of Cannes, 'Princes, princes, nothing but princes. If you like them, you're in the right place.'

In the last quarter of the nineteenth century, royalty seemed to have maintained its allure despite the efforts of the French in 1796 and a number of her neighbours in 1848 – not to mention the French again – to rid themselves of the monarchist plague. In England this was surprising: in the previous century George I could scarcely speak English, lived openly with his mistress, and confined his divorced wife to prison; George II impregnated a maid of honour, was closely implicated in the South Sea Bubble scandal, and patronised Handel; George III was periodically mad, appears to have married bigamously, quadrupled the national debt and lost the American colonies; George IV was pronounced a girl at birth, developed an insatiable desire for motherly mistresses, was blind drunk at his wedding, fathered two illegitimate children, and became sufficiently deluded to believe that he had conquered Napoleon. Robert Huish, one of his earliest biographers, concluded that 'He contributed more to the demoralisation of society than any prince in the pages of recorded history.' Yet despite this patchy record, in the Victorian era the institution found a superb defender in Walter Bagehot, who wrote, 'The mystic reverence, the religious allegiance, which are essential to a true monarchy, are imaginative sentiments that no legislature can manufacture in any people.'

Too often, the feet of gods – goddesses too – prove to be as firmly rooted in clay as the Hanovers'. That was certainly the case with most of those who made their way to the Riviera. A number had undertaken the difficult journey before the coming of the railway, among them two brothers of George III. Both found the climate and the relaxed attitude to behaviour congenial. In 1776 William, Duke of Gloucester, had married not only a commoner, Maria Waldegrave, but an illegitimate one. He was banished from Court, and fled abroad until 1780 when the King relented and forgave him. William's brother, the Duke of York, was described by Lady Louisa Stuart as 'silly, frivolous and heartless, void alike of steadiness and principle'. He had visited Nice in 1764 and, like his brother, found much to enjoy. Three years later the writer Horace Walpole, son of England's first Prime Minister Sir Robert, noted:

> The poor Duke of York has ended his silly, good humoured, troublesome career in a piteous manner: scampered away as fast as he could ride for a drive all round the South of France, intending to visit a lady at Genoa that he was in love with ... grew so ill that his

gentlemen carried him to Monaco, where he arrived on the third and languished with great suffering until the seventeenth.

In some respects the two dukes set the pattern for the behaviour of British royalty on the Riviera. Much was expected of the eldest son of Queen Victoria and Prince Albert: he would succeed his mother as monarch of a country whose power and influence were beginning to exceed those of the Roman Empire. The serious-minded, dutiful – and German – Prince Albert set exacting standards in the moral, physical and intellectual education of his entire family. Yet as Lytton Strachey remarked in his biography of the Queen, Bertie, as Albert's eldest son was known, 'though he was good humoured and gentle, seemed to display a deep-seated repugnance to every form of mental exertion ... the more lessons that Bertie had to do, the less he did them; and the more carefully he was guarded against excitement and frivolities, the more desirous of amusement he seemed to become'.

At the age of nineteen he lost his virginity in Ireland to an actress called Nellie Clifden. Prince Albert was appalled: 'He *must* not, *dare* not be lost. The consequences for this country and the world would be too dreadful.' An early marriage was at once prescribed by his parents to harness his appetites to the national good. In 1863, at twenty-two, he was married to Princess Alexandra, the eldest daughter of King Christian IX of Denmark. They had five children in rapid succession, but this did little to prevent Bertie straying outside his marriage. Groomed for the throne, his official activities were restricted to those of monarch-in-waiting. Given the conviction, determination and sense of duty of his mother, this meant he had little to do. Although nineteenth-century England is rarely regarded as particularly licentious, the Queen herself complained that the upper classes and aristocracy, within whose exclusive circle the Prince was most particular to restrict himself, were 'given over to frivolity, the love of pleasure, self-indulgence and idleness'. This meant, among other things, a great deal of sex. The Prince had an insatiable sexual appetite and plenty of well-connected, well-to-do and often married women to choose from. As their husbands were usually complaisant, there was no stopping him. Alongside acknowledged liaisons with Lillie Langtry, Lady Brooke and Mrs Alice Keppel, he had dozens of casual affairs. The Queen was horrified when, in 1870, the Prince was called as witness in a society divorce case. She wrote to the editor of *The Times* asking him to 'frequently *write* articles pointing out the *immense* danger of the wretched frivolity and levity of the views and lives of the Higher Classes'. The editor desisted. Two years later, the Prince paid a visit to the South of France. He stayed at the Hôtel Gray d'Albion in Cannes. He was accompanied by his wife, a doctor, two equerries, two valets, a footman and a fox terrier called Caesar. Immediately the Prince recognised an atmosphere altogether more sympathetic to his temperament than the horrors of Buckingham Palace, Windsor or – worst of all – Balmoral. 'I go to the Riviera as I would a club,' he said later. 'It's a place with good company where everyone mingles, just like a garden party.'

Cannes had changed since the death of Lord Brougham. At the time of his passing in 1868, it was still sufficiently unspoiled to attract the poet and painter Edward Lear, who wintered there between 1867 and 1869. There he wrote the first and perhaps the best of his nonsense poems, 'The Owl and the Pussycat'. By the summer of 1870, though, Lear wrote to his friend the painter Holman Hunt that Cannes had become too busy and too noisy for him. 'Cannes grows at a rate of ten new hotels and two hundred houses yearly,' he complained. Also, Brougham, for all his idiosyncrasies, was a high-minded figure not given to self-indulgence. His successor as the town's principal patron, Grand Duke Michael, son of Tsar Alexander II of Russia, was cut from a rather different cloth. Under his patronage, Cannes became what has been called the most promiscuous society in Europe.

This suited the Prince of Wales. His first long visit had occurred in the aftermath of the Franco-Prussian war and he dutifully visited his relatives who were staying along the coast. That season they included Archduke Charles of Austria, Queen Natalie of Serbia, Queen Isabella of Spain, the Duchess of Saxe-Coburg-Gotha, and the King and Queen of Würthemberg. They were perturbed by the conflict that had brought about the unified German state and the French Third Republic. Where, they asked, would it all lead? In subsequent years the Prince did his best to avoid such obligations and political ruminations, devoting himself entirely to pleasure. He found similarly inclined company at the Cercle Nautique. The club, founded by the Duke of Vallombrosa in 1864, was the smartest on the coast, intended to compete with the likes of the Travellers' and the Reform on Pall Mall. Situated on Cannes' equivalent of the Promenade des Anglais, La Croisette, it had a splendid bar, a smoking room, a gallery with a stage for theatricals, and seventeen bedrooms. With a joining fee of a hundred guineas and subsequent annual subscriptions of twenty-five, it attracted an exclusive clientele. Its tone is suggested by an anecdote about the barman who was upbraided by the club secretary, Captain Sheldon, for serving a drink to a noble guest without wearing white gloves. Having excused himself on the grounds that the footman had been unavailable, the barman was told, 'You must always keep gloves in your pocket for emergencies like these.' Punctilio was all.

The club was largely a male enclave, and for the Prince feminine company in addition to that of his wife was a *sine qua non*. For this, Cannes proved the happiest of hunting grounds, replete as it was with well-bred, good-looking women who were perfectly happy to be bedded by the heir to the greatest of the world's thrones. The Prince's favourite time for sex was shortly after lunch or after tea at five o'clock, his preferred place the Victorian equivalent of the sofa. His mistresses did not invariably agree, but they usually complied. Needless to say, word of his behaviour reached his mother, who certainly did not let her eldest son's advancing age constrain her reproofs. In 1886, when a spring visit to Cannes had become an annual fixture in the Prince's programme and he was forty-five, he replied to one of her admonitory letters, 'You are, I think, rather hard on me when you talk of the round of gaieties I indulge in at Cannes, London, Homburg and Cowes. I like Cannes excessively, especially for its climate and scenery, just as you do Aix. To be away from England in the South for three weeks is very beneficial for me.'

The Prince's code of behaviour set something of an example for the Riviera. As Evelyn Waugh's Captain Grimes muses in *Decline and Fall*, it seemed to be based on the belief that one can never 'be unhappy for long provided one does exactly what one wants to and when one wants to'. The Riviera was recognised as a place that provided an escape from English laws, customs and mores, a refuge from gossip, an escape from Frances Power Cobbe's 'moral and physical black frosts of the the North'. In short, Paradise.

Sometimes the Prince paid for sex. 'Courtesan' means someone attached to the Court, and these women shared their affections – or their bodies – between their keepers. The normal arrangement was for a courtesan to look after either one royal, or two dukes or three millionaires, which shows a nice sense of social gradation. Obviously their stock-in-trade was sex, but unlike common prostitutes they usually offered their eminent lovers beauty, grace and considerable social standing. Some even played bridge well. In many respects the Riviera set the highest standards, and the best courtesans of the day fluttered to its lights. Most famous of all was La Belle Otero. Caroline Otero was a Spanish gypsy who married an Italian baron, honeymooned in Monte Carlo and soon progressed to a career as what the French called *une grande horizontale*. Her clients included the Prince of Wales, Alfonso XIII of Spain, Leopold II of Belgium, Tsar Nicholas II, and a German millionaire of whom Otero observed, 'Such a rich man can never be ugly.' There were also Liane de Pougy, La Leno, Gina Paleme and Cora Pearl – the latter baptised as Emma Crunch.

It was in Cannes, in 1898, at Grand Duke Michael's Villa Kasbeck that the Prince encountered Mrs Alice Keppel. The twenty-nine-year-old was so captivating that she was elevated virtually overnight to the status of mistress-in-chief. The Prince was fifty-seven.

2

For the Prince of Wales, life ashore was complemented by life at sea – or, rather, life aboard a yacht moored at Lord Brougham's jetty in Cannes.

In Smollett's time and for many years after his death, the sea played only a limited part in the lives of English pleasure-seekers on the Riviera. Although the Romans had enjoyed sea-bathing on the Bay of Naples, enthusiasm for it had lapsed until 1750, when the notion found an advocate in Dr Richard Russell. A native of Sussex and a physician at St Thomas's Hospital in London, he was interested in the use of seawater in the treatment of glandular disease. In *A dissertation on the use of seawater in the affections of the glands*, he argued the case for both bathing in and drinking seawater. Such was the book's success that he set up a practice in Brighton, and the town was established as the world's first seaside resort since the time of Emperor Augustus. Soon, Weymouth followed.

In Nice, though, no one other than Smollett thought there was much to be gained by getting wet, especially in the winter. One could, of course, go on the sea rather than in it, but boats in the eighteenth and early nineteenth centuries were simply a means of communication on the coast. No one who entrusted themselves to the Riviera waves anticipated pleasure. The English colony agreed with Dr Johnson that 'No man is a sailor who has contrivance enough to get himself into a jail; for being in a ship is being in jail, with the chance of being drowned ... A man in jail has more room, better food, and commonly better company.' There was even something not quite right, not quite English, about the Mediterranean. In *The Riviera*, one of the best *fin de siècle* guides to the coast, the Reverend Hugh Macmillan wrote:

> Unlike the other great seas of the world, it has almost no tide; and there is therefore a strange sameness in its appearance and voice. In calm its lovely blue surface looks like that of a lake, a resemblance which is still further increased by the absence of that fresh, briny odour of the veritable ocean, which makes the air of our own sea-coasts so invigorating. In storm it has little or no variety. Even when blasted by one of its furious winds into seething foam, its hollows are entirely different from the magnificent rollers of the Atlantic coming in with strong breeze and rising tide; they are monotonous in their shape and movement, and break in ceaseless crashes upon the same shingly ridges.

Still, there was, perhaps, something about the sea if one confined oneself to looking at it. In 1887 Stéphen Liégeard, a minor French poet, published a guide to the coast that captured something of its magic combination of sea and sky, not least in its title, *La Côte d'Azur.* He promised his dedicatee Xavier Marmier that, in their journey south together, 'We will forget the weakness of men, the sadness of things, the insanities of politics, the sanctities of naturalism; the cerulean waves will wash them all away.' Visitors began to look at the sea in a different light.

If they could read French, the English were further encouraged by the writings of Guy de Maupassant. In *Sur L'eau* he described a delightful nautical saunter along the coast that reinforced what the agriculturalist Arthur Young had been told a century previously: it was best viewed from the sea. It was at about this time that yachting clubs, like the Cercle Nautique at Cannes and its equivalents in Nice and Monaco, established themselves. Regattas followed, and by the time the Prince of Wales had become a regular visitor they formed an essential part of the social season.

The Prince had long been interested in yachting. As a boy of ten on board the Royal Yacht *Victoria and Albert* he had witnessed the inaugural race in 1851 of what became known as the America's Cup. In 1865 he bought his first racing yacht, the 36-ton cutter *Dagmar.* She was followed in 1876 by the 205-ton schooner

Hildegarde. Then came the cutter *Formosa*, which won the Queen's Cup at Cowes, and the schooner *Aline*. Finally, in 1892, he commissioned his own craft, the 212-ton *Britannia*. A hundred and twenty feet long, she carried more than ten thousand square feet of sail. With her long bowsprit, pencil-thin hull, billowing foresails and foam spurting from her prow, she was the embodiment of grace and power.

It became his habit – and the Prince was very much a man of habit – to despatch *Britannia* in February to the Mediterranean. There, from 1894 to 1897, she participated in the Riviera regattas. According to the British magazine *Yachting*, this was 'a time of year when we [in England] are generally experiencing a kind of weather which totally removes any idea of yachting from our minds'. *Britannia* was astonishingly successful: in her first season she was unbeaten at Marseille, Cannes and Nice; in 1895 she won six out of the ten races she entered. In 1896 she had a poor year in light winds that did not suit her, managing only two wins from ten starts. But in 1897, her last Mediterranean season, she won five of the sixteen races in which she was entered – at Marseille, Hyères, Toulon, Cannes and Nice. She was easily the best big yacht of her day, and, by some counts, of all time.

The Prince took pleasure in her victories, but was not precisely a participant. In the 1890s racing was left to the professionals. *Britannia* had a professional seaman as her captain or sailing master (Mr W. Jameson and then Mr J. Carter) and a crew of twenty-eight. During a race the Prince – like most owners – was no more likely to be seen aboard his yacht than the late Queen Mother on one of her horses in the Derby or the Cheltenham Gold Cup. Pride aside, though, the boats had their purposes, of which the first was relatively practical. A generation after the coming of the railway Nice was becoming a busy, crowded city. In *South-Eastern France*, published in 1890, Augustus Hare called it a 'great, ugly, modern town'. During the regatta season it was even worse. In his 1887 book *Shooting and Yachting in the Mediterranean*, A. C. Bagot gave a delightful account of a Mediterranean voyage in his 130-ton barque, its principal purpose being 'to try our luck on woodcock and pig in Albania'. On his return from the Ionian he put in at the port:

> Nice was in full feather, preparing for the annual regatta, and the streets presented a somewhat Margatean aspect, being full of French yachtsmen arranged in the 'latest thing' in blue serge, with the widest trousers, the yachtiest caps, and the most buttoning coats imaginable. Needless to remark, as in our own country, these very salt-water gentlemen owned no craft, and studiously avoided going outside the harbour.

Neither an hotel nor an esplanade is a private place, and it was becoming increasingly necessary to try to avoid the 'Margatean aspects' of the coast. What could be better than to withdraw with a few select guests to the canopied after-deck of one's yacht, and watch the *hoi-polloi* on the crowded shore? Only to leave them entirely by drifting down the coast to some sheltered bay where the long afternoon might be whiled away under the shade of the awning. In *King Edward VII as a Sportsman*, Captain the Hon. Seymour Fortescue wrote that *Britannia* was the Prince's home on the Riviera, 'and he made passages from port to port when it suited his convenience'. Second, the boats were extraordinarily powerful and prestigious status symbols. Even in a smart hotel or villa, and even with a dozen or so staff, a man was just a man. A man with a boat was quite a different proposition, as every yachtsman knew. After all, as a means of getting from A to B, for all man's ingenuity, few less swift and less comfortable means of transport have ever been devised. A yacht's value lay in its inutility. Erskine Childers, in his masterpiece *The Riddle of the Sands*, talked of his hero Arthur Davies's 'antitype, the Cowes Philanderer'. In any port on any coast, a boat was a social and sexual passport. The bigger the boat, the more doors she opened. At the same time, the teak-decked, brass-burnished, cotton-sailed yachts of the 1890s and the Edwardian age had a grace and elegance that has never been surpassed. A yachtsman once said with some justice that there was nothing lovelier made by man.

Given her name, her owner and her victories, *Britannia* came to symbolise both her country and Britain's world dominance in the closing years of the nineteenth century. It was agreeable enough for the Prince, but less so for those who resented Great Britain's position in the world. Kaiser Wilhelm II, the Prince's nephew, was periodically a guest on board *Britannia*. He much admired his uncle's yacht and the status she conferred. In 1896 he bought the cutter *Thistle*, which he renamed *Meteor*, and took her to Cowes where she was trumped by *Britannia*. His response was to order a yacht even larger than *Britannia*, named *Meteor II*, which, in 1897, beat *Britannia*. The Prince of Wales complained, 'The Regatta [at Cowes] used to be a pleasant recreation to me: since the Kaiser takes a hand, it is a vexation.'

Such contests reflected the growing rivalry between England and the newly unified Germany. 'Germany's a thundering great nation,' Childers had Arthur Davies say. 'I wonder if we shall ever fight her.'

3

Little though Queen Victoria approved of her son's antics, in the last quarter of the nineteenth century she became almost as regular a visitor to the Riviera as he. Her motives in being there, though, were rather different. After the death of the Prince Consort in 1861 the Queen had virtually removed herself from public life. As the years of her seclusion passed, her subjects became increasingly angry with her and with the institution of monarchy. Her retinue and, eventually, the government persuaded her doctors that travel abroad might encourage her to resume her duties at home. The summer of 1868 saw her in Lucerne, when the Alps were beginning to be developed as a holiday destination. In 1879 she was on the Italian lakes. Then, in 1882, she paid her first visit to the Mediterranean coast, staying at Menton, which was now the largest British colony on the Continent. In *The Mediterranean Passion* John Pemble recorded, 'Bath chairs monopolised the Promenade du Midi by day, and by night their premature retirement imparted a hospital hush to the atmosphere.' Here the Queen's youngest son, Prince Leopold, was treated for haemophilia. However, her visit was compromised by the mood of the retainer about whose relationship with the Queen there was so much speculation. John Brown, wrote the Queen, 'had an increasing hatred of being abroad'. In 1891, she spent some weeks in the medieval hill town of Grasse, at the Grand Hotel with the Prince of Wales, and the following year she was at the Hôtel Cost-belle in Hyères. From 1895, for five consecutive years, she spent March and April in Nice, staying in Cimiez. On her last visit she wrote, 'In this paradise of nature ... I shall mind returning to the sunless north, but I am so grateful for all I have enjoyed here.'

The Queen saw no virtue in economising on her travel arrangements to the coast, or on her retinue. Public transport was unthinkable, so she crossed the channel on the Royal Yacht *Victoria and Albert*, escorted by torpedo boats lest the Kaiser was about, then took a special train south, her private carriage filled with Louis XVI furniture. She preferred to travel leisurely, so the train chugged along at no more than 30 m.p.h. It stopped for an hour in the morning to enable the Queen to dress and the gentlemen to shave. Foreign food being unreliable, Irish stew – kept warm by cushions – sustained the party on the journey. China, glass, cutlery, table linen and furniture, such as the Queen's bed, were in the goods van. She was normally accompanied by her secretary and physician, ladies-in-waiting, a chef, a dentist, an oculist, her favourite Indian servants and her carriage horses. All in all it was quite a party, varying from year to year between sixty and a hundred. She was charged accordingly by the hotels in which she stayed. The going rate in the 1890s was 80,000 francs – the hotel's gardener earned four francs a day. Still, this was not quite a holiday. Government papers and other correspondence were couriered out daily to the Queen, and she set aside much of the morning to deal with them.

Since Lord Brougham had long ago set the seal of political approval on the coast, the prime minister of the day was often conveniently at hand to discuss with her any pressing matters of state. W. E. Gladstone had discovered the Riviera in 1883, when he was already seventy-three. Later he wrote, 'I am stunned at this wonderful place, and so vast a change at a moment's notice in the conditions of life.' His last meeting with his monarch, in March 1897, took place in Cannes. The Queen described her long-serving prime minister and his wife as 'both looking much aged'. Gladstone was eighty-seven, the monarch seventy-eight.

Lord Salisbury was prime minister during much of the 1890s, and was an admirable representative of a more leisurely, civilised age. He famously said that in his foreign policy he preferred 'to drift lazily downstream using a boathook to occasionally avoid collision'. In *My Early Life*, Winston Churchill – soon to become a Riviera regular – recalled that Salisbury would never have dreamt of calling a cabinet meeting when there was racing at Newmarket. Salisbury had developed the habit of holidaying in France during the 1880s. After returning to office in 1885, uniquely combining the posts of foreign secretary and prime minister, he and his wife spent a month in Monte Carlo at the Hôtel de Paris. There, Salisbury was refused entry to the casino because he was not carrying his passport, although he explained: 'You see, I'm the man who issues them'. The couple disliked hotel life and decided to buy a plot of land in Beaulieu. This was no more than a fishing village, so sheltered as to justify its description as La Petite Afrique. 'Above it,' wrote the Reverend Hugh Macmillan in *The Riviera*, 'rise gigantic cliffs quite perpendicular, with picturesque sky-lines fringed with pine-trees, and the ruddy limestone interstratified with patches of red sandstone, producing quite a feast of glowing colours.' There Salisbury built the red-shuttered villa La Bastide, and created the garden to which he devoted his leisure hours. The Queen's maid-of-honour

Marie Mallet described it as 'a glorious garden, where tulips, anenomes, irises and forget-me-nots grow wild in great masses'.

When Salisbury was at Beaulieu he placed himself at the Queen's disposal, at hand to comment on the crises that erupted as the century and the Queen's life drew to a close. First there was the Jameson Raid in South Africa, which in January 1896 drew an intemperate response from the Kaiser, who implied that the Germans would intercept on the Boers' behalf. Then came the Fashoda incident, a squabble between France and England that nearly caused the Queen to cancel her visit in 1898. However, the British ambassador in Paris wrote to Salisbury that her holidays had 'come to be regarded in France as an outward and visible sign of the friendly sentiments entertained by her Majesty for the French people', and she went ahead as usual. When the Boer War broke out in 1899, though, indignation on the Continent at the British attack on Transvaal and the Orange Free State meant that her trip was cancelled. By then, though, the Queen had already made an immense contribution to the coast's fame. In her last years she reigned over an empire of 320 million people that covered a quarter of the world's surface. Many of her subjects could not have located Europe, let alone France, on a map but knew that she holidayed on the Riviera. The Côte d'Azur had become not only the world's first major tourist destination but the centre of the fashionable world. It wasn't England, but it had become as much part of the English social calendar as Ascot, Goodwood, the Derby and Cowes.

In 1901 the Queen died and was succeeded by the Prince of Wales as Edward VII. According to the poet, diplomat and traveller Wilfred Scawen Blunt, the King sent a note to all his former mistresses saying that although he had been called to serious duties, he hoped still to see them from time to time. But he never again visited the Riviera.

5

Lost Caviare Days

> 'I have already made up my mind I do not like Nice; it is garish and very dusty and most unattractive, nothing picturesque about it, even the villa gardens are tiny and covered in dust, and houses everywhere, no escape from them unless you drive for miles. Coming abroad only to see huge hotels and hordes of smart people depresses me more than I can say.'
>
> Marie Mallet, *Life with Queen Victoria*

1

While various species of royalty were doing their best to vulgarise Cannes and ruin Nice, a group at the lower end of the social spectrum was turning its attention to the western end of the Riviera. Some at least were not English.

Although sufferers from tuberculosis and other diseases continued to patronise resorts like Menton and Hyères, by the 1890s the pretence that one went to the Côte d'Azur for other than hedonistic purposes had been dropped. Medical opinion now favoured the cold, clean air of the Alps rather than the Riviera for the treatment of tuberculosis and, besides, the coast now offered other attractions. Even in 1870, Dr William Chambers had declared in *Wintering at Mentone*, 'Fashion, ennui, and the love of gaiety seems to send quite as many abroad as absolutely ill health.' J. Henry Bennet thought similarly of visitors to Nice, seeing them as 'cured invalids of former days'. But not everyone was like the Prince of

Wales in his pursuit of frivolity and Mrs Keppel: some came searching for the rather more elusive qualities of the coast's light and colour. In *The Riviera* the Reverend Hugh Macmillan had written:

> What strikes the visitor most when passing eastward beyond the smoke of Marseilles and Toulon is the peculiar quality of the light that shines on sea and shore. Fresh from cloudy northern skies that limit the horizon and bring the heavens like a roof close to the earth, imparting to the landscape a grey gentleness of tint and a mysterious depth of shadow, he is suddenly transported to a land where the brilliant sunshine and the translucent atmosphere give the feeling of vast aerial space, and naked reality surrounding him near and far. The light has a sparkling crystalline lustre, as if each particle of air through which it passes were the facet of a gem. The dull red brick under its magic touch becomes almost transparent, the grey rock breaks into opaline lustres, and the blue waters near the shore gleam like the flickering hues upon the neck of a dove. Pictures done in this light seem in our country gross exaggerations of colour, but the artist knows how impossible it is to transfer to his canvas the transparencies of light and the radiances of burning hues, which are at once his joy and his despair.

Despite the difficulties posed by the southern shades, though, in the last two decades of the nineteenth century and into the twentieth, a series of painters began to interpret the coast, ultimately with dazzling results.

In 1883 Claude Monet paid his first visit to the Mediterranean coast, with Pierre Renoir. They went to Marseille, Hyères, Monaco, Menton, and the Italian Riviera to the east. As a native of Le Havre, Monet was bowled over by the luminescence of the southern coast, and wrote to his mistress Alice Hoschede, 'I should like to paint orange and lemon trees standing against the blue sea ... as to the blue of the sea and sky, it is impossible.' In 1884 he met Guy de Maupassant, whose narrative of the coastal voyage, *Sur l'eau*, had been well received in artistic circles, and who introduced him to Antibes. Unlike Cannes, its neighbour, Antibes was still a village with a population of less than 7000 and, as Murray's *Handbook* recorded, 'a situation hardly to be surpassed for beauty'. There, in the first months of 1888, Monet set to work. To the sculptor Auguste Rodin he wrote: 'I fence and tussle with the sun ... one should paint here with gold and gemstones.' He sold ten of the thirty paintings he produced to Vincent van Gogh's brother, Theo, a dealer working at Boussod & Valadon, formerly Goupil's. Theo van Gogh wrote to him: 'You have really won over the public, mulish as it is. The people one sees at Goupil's are full of admiration.' The poet Stéphane Mallarmé declared: 'This is your finest hour.' The following year Renoir was wintering near Grasse at Magagnosc, a village set in a classical landscape of olive groves and fig orchards: 'It doesn't seem as if misfortune could ever reach you in this wonderful region,' he remarked at the time.

At much the same time in St Tropez, thirty miles west, an artist's colony was being established. Situated on the southern side of the Golfe de St Tropez, the town was unique among the Riviera resorts in facing north. This largely disqualified it as a 'winter health station' on the grounds that it was open to the *mistral* that swept down from the Esterels. However, a golden evening light shot across the bay between it and St Maxime on the opposite shore, and for those in search of light, it was irresistible. Then as now, St Tropez was difficult to reach: the main Paris–Lyon–Mediterranée railway line ran some miles north of the town on the far side of the Massif des Maures and although a light railway had been constructed along the coast from Hyères to St Raphael via St Tropez, it was not a great success. As late as 1928, the novelist Douglas Goldring recorded in his guide to the Riviera that

> To set out from Hyères with the intention of arriving at St Raphael, is to embark on an adventure. The fifty-mile journey takes anything from four to six hours, or longer. It all depends on what the engine is feeling like that morning, and whether the stoker happens to be in an energetic mood. The passenger gazes on scenery of enchanting loveliness, endures eternities of boredom and delay, alternating

> with periods of panic, terror, and whether he will arrive at his destination at all, and, if so, at what hour, are matters beyond his capacity to determine.

Yet as one of Goldring's fellow passengers observed, 'We don't really want it any different. But for the wretchedness of this railway the whole coast would be ruined.' A quarter of a century earlier, St Tropez had been a sequestered spot, as easily approachable by sea as land.

Torpes, from whom St Tropez takes its name, was a servant of the Emperor Nero. In AD 66 he was tortured and beheaded for his adherence to Christianity. By tradition his body was set adrift with a dog and cockerel, and washed up at the settlement then known as Heraclea Caccabaria. Given that the animals had left the corpse untouched, the episode was declared a miracle and the village's Christian inhabitants renamed it St Torpes.

During the Dark Ages and the medieval period, like the rest of the settlements on the coast, St Tropez had been besieged, destroyed and rebuilt. From the sixteenth century it was occupied by the Genoese, who built the ramparts and the citadel. The Reverend Samuel Baring-Gould wrote, 'The women of St Tropez are noted for their good looks due to the infusion of Italian blood.' In 1887 when de Maupassant sailed to St Tropez in *Bel Ami*, sardine scales glistened 'like pearls on the cobblestones', and the town was a 'charming, simple, daughter of the sea'. The painter Paul Signac was similarly taken by it when he sailed into the port in 1892. He rented then subsequently bought a house there, dividing his time until 1914 between St Tropez and Paris. Signac formed the nucleus of a group that the critic Louis Vauxcelles described as a 'flock of migratory birds ... a valiant little colony of artists painting and conversing in this enchanted land'. Here, Signac produced his masterpiece *Au Temps de Harmonie* in which his figures lounge, labour, paint, teach and love against an idealised background of sea and shore. In 1904 Matisse visited him in St Tropez, and was inspired to paint *Luxe, Calme et Volupté*, a pessimistic reinterpretation of Signac's picture. At first glance it is an idyllic scene, with an ancient sailing boat and a group of bathers, but there is also a modern tourist in contemporary clothes, striking a discordant note. Tourism, as well as death, was in Arcadia.

A little later Augustus John spent a summer at Martigues on the Rhône delta, just west of Marseille. At the time he was regarded as the equal of Matisse. Six feet tall, bearded, with long flowing hair and strikingly handsome, John had married a fellow Slade student, Ida Nettleship, then established a *ménage à trois* with Dorelia MacNeill. His life was punctuated by tragedy, not least Ida's death after the birth of their fifth child in 1907. Three years later, during a difficult period in his relationship with Dorelia, he decided to explore Provence, whose reputation for beauty and licentiousness had long fascinated him. He left London in early January 1910, and on the seventeenth wrote to Dorelia that 'The sun of Provence is curing me of all my humours.' He explored the Roman town of Arles, then went on to Marseille. Of the great port, he said, 'In some respects it beats Liverpool even.'

In the spring he was joined by Dorelia and three of his children. They settled for the summer at the Villa St Anne at Martigues on the Étang de Berre, on the western fringes of Marseille. 'An enchanting spot this,' he wrote to the Bloomsbury socialite Ottoline Morrell, 'at the mouth of an island sea where it joins the Mediterranean. The population are handsomer than the country folk. I have seen so many powerful women whose essential nudity no clothing can disguise.' To his American patron John Quinn he wrote, 'I am installed in this little house with a batch of family and hard at work. The weather has been glorious and we have been out of doors for weeks.'

One of the attractions of the place was the villa's owner, Albert Bazin. Undeterred by the success of the Wright brothers in 1903, Bazin was devoting himself to the development of aeroplanes that flapped their wings like birds. Each failure simply spurred him on to his next attempt. John was delighted by him, and was soon pressing his claims on Quinn.

Despite the distraction of Bazin, the prostitutes in Marseille, and a trip to Nice – 'a paradise invaded by bugs (human ones)' – John's painting prospered. When he returned to London in September 1910, he had accumulated sufficient material for a one-man show, *Provençal Studies and Other Works* – thirty-five drawings and etchings, fifty studies in oil. Most critics saw a new power in these works, inspired by the Provençal sun, and compared John with Gauguin, van Gogh and Matisse. His greatest advocate, the critic Laurence Binyon, wrote,

> These small studies ... make an extraordinary impression and haunt one's memory. A tall woman leaning on a staff; a little boy in scarlet on a cliff-edge against blue sea, a woman carrying bundles of lavender: the description of these says nothing, but they themselves seem creatures of the infancy of the world, aboriginals of the earth, with an animal dignity and strangeness, swift of gesture, beautifully poised. That is the secret of Mr John's power. He is limited ... but in it there is a jet of elemental energy, something powerful and uncontrollable, like life itself.

The impressionists and post-impressionists – John is less easily categorised – were the pioneers in visualising the Riviera, and the huge number of their works helped transform it from a place into a myth. They captured some of its beauty and, often, the coruscating change it was undergoing.

2

Of the various agents of that change, among the most pernicious was the motor-car, introduced to the coast at just about this time.

Steam-driven road carriages dated back to 1800 and the inventor of the steam engine, Richard Trevethick, but never caught on. In 1887, though, Gottlieb Daimler used the petrol-driven internal combustion engine in his 'four-wheeled, wooden-built, light waggonnette'. That year two Frenchmen were granted patents for similar carriages, and in 1894 a French newspaper sponsored a procession of motor-cars from Paris to Rouen. Six years later Lord Salisbury's nephew Arthur Balfour, himself a future prime minister, told the House of Commons that the world in future might see 'great highways for rapid motor traffic'. With the French establishing themselves alongside the Germans and Italians as leaders in the new industry, the Riviera was soon embracing the attractions of the car. An 1898 poster for the Paris–Lyon–Mediterranée railway used a picture of a car in its promotion of the Nice Carnival, and in 1902 the first motor race took place in Nice, for the Henri de Rothschild Cup. Three years later a new world speed record was set during the race: a remarkable 100 k.p.h. In 1905 Paul Signac was picking up his new Peugeot in Marseille, and by 1911 C. N. Williamson had published *Motoring on the Riviera.* The motor-car, he told his readers, 'added tenfold to the variety and charm of holidaying on the Riviera. It [provides] independence from the inconvenient timetables of the PLM, so that social engagements can be kept anywhere along the coast without having to catch the train at unreasonable hours, or waste time if one arrives early at one's destination. It enables every man to cultivate his individual tastes, whatever they may be.'

Like the railway, though, the car was by no means universally welcomed. Early models were slow, unreliable and uncomfortable, and the locals in the South of France – as elsewhere – were ill-adapted to them. In Nice, on 23 March 1899, Queen Victoria's maid-of-honour Marie Mallet wrote in her journal: 'This afternoon such a pleasant drive with the Queen. We went up the valley of the Paillon right into the country and enjoyed the peace and absence of automobiles more than I can say. They make driving here a hideous nightmare and kill at least three people a week.'

Leaving aside the threat to human life, one of the other problems was the dust that cars threw up from the unmetalled roads, spraying verges, animals and pedestrians alike. This was particularly irritating in Monaco, where in 1898 spectators at the newly inaugurated Concours d'Elégance found themselves coated in it. (Prizes were awarded for the elegance of the cars and their female passengers.) Camille Blanc, one of François' two sons, was now managing director of the Société des Bains de Mer and asked the Italian Dr Guglielminetti to develop a road surface that would eliminate dust. Monte Carlo was the first place to lay a tarred road. Anxious to exploit the fashionability of motor-cars among those who could afford them, the Principality hosted the first of the Monte Carlo rallies in January 1911. Cars converged on the resort from Paris, Boulogne, Brussels, Berlin, Vienna and Geneva, and the twenty-three starters were required to average 10 k.p.h. The winner, Henri Rougier, started from Paris and covered the 570 miles to Monaco in just over twenty-eight hours. The rally – supposedly the first of its kind – was a success in so far as cars proliferated on the coast. From England there were Rolls-Royces, Argylls, Napiers and Wolseleys, and from the United States, Wintons, Packards and Loziers. In 1913, Robert de Souza, a columnist in one of Nice's newspapers, complained that the Lower Corniche from Nice to Villefranche was no longer suited to idlers and promenaders: it had become 'a "great" artery of circulation'.

3

Artists have always enjoyed a mixed press, and certainly the presence of Renoir, Signac and Augustus John on the Riviera was by no means universally welcomed as the coast approached its apogee in the *belle époque*. Robert Standish, the biographer of the prolific Riviera novelist E. Phillips Oppenheim – the Jeffrey Archer of his day – referred scathingly to 'the artistic colony ... few of whom appear to have done anything other but talk, drink and let their hair grow'. By the early years of the twentieth century it was becoming all too apparent that the coast, alongside the artists, was attracting undesirables of another sort too.

As far back as 1870 the Dean of Canterbury had written that Monte Carlo drew the 'scum of the world'. This may be too harsh a judgement for modern taste on gamblers and their parasites, yet in the years that followed, there was a growing sense that the Riviera was attracting considerably fewer upper-class English Christian gentlemen, who were married and temperate in their habits. Those who came found themselves magnets for the less fortunate. Prostitutes, confidence tricksters and beggars flocked to where there was a high concentration of their natural prey. The riches of Nice, the superficially splendid buildings, the wide boulevards, the promenading dukes and countesses belied its tens of thousands of poor. In a community of more than 100,000, four out of ten lived in dwellings unfit for human habitation. In the season, beggars flocked there like locusts. On 4 March 1899 Marie Mallet drove over to the ancient port of Villefranche with the monarch. 'Beggars were the chief excitement. The Queen clasped a sky-blue purse which she opened hurriedly from time to time to appease the awful deformities posted at regular intervals along the road.'

At the same time, the Riviera seemed increasingly a haven for those whose inclinations made living in their home countries either unpleasant or untenable. Oscar Wilde, the most gifted dramatist of his generation, master of the epigram, dandy and man-about-town, was sent to prison in 1895 to do two years' hard labour for homosexual practices. The sentence, the most severe that could be handed down, was described by Mr Justice Wills as totally inadequate for the worst case he had ever tried. When Wilde was released in May 1897 he was a broken man, dying of syphilis. He fled to Dieppe. Urged – for obvious reasons – to acquire a taste for the female sex, he resorted to a local prostitute. 'The first these ten years,' he commented, 'and it shall be the last. It was like chewing cold mutton.'

He trailed around Paris, Naples and various other Continental watering-places until his death in November 1900. It was to the generosity of the raconteur and socialite Frank Harris that he owed three months on the Riviera between December 1898 and March 1899. He stayed at the Hôtel des Bains at La Napoule, five miles west of Cannes, occasionally venturing east down the coast. 'Yes: even in La Napoule there is romance,' he wrote to a friend, Leonard Smithers. 'It takes the form of fisher-lads, who draw great nets, and are bare-limbed: they are strangely perfect. I was at Nice lately: romance there is a profession plied beneath the moon.' More conventionally, he also saw Sarah Bernhardt in *Tosca*. When he encountered the Prince of Wales in Cannes he raised his hat but the Prince failed to recognise him and asked his companion who the man was. On being told that it was Wilde, whose plays he admired, he ordered his carriage turned round. When he caught up with Wilde, he reciprocated the gesture.

Kenneth Mackenzie Clark was another figure who typified the *belle-époque* coast. 'My parents,' wrote Clark's son, the art historian Kenneth Clark, 'belonged to a section of society known as "the idle rich", and although, in that golden age, many people were richer, there can have been few who were idler. They took no part in public affairs, did not read the newspapers, and were almost entirely without the old upper-class feeling of responsibility for their tenants. My father gave so little time to his business interests that in the end he lost nearly half his fortune.' Like many other idle and rich Englishmen, Clark *père* made it his habit in the years before the First World War to spend two or three winter months on the Riviera. At first the family stayed in Monte Carlo, normally on their yacht *Katoomba*. There, the gaming tables proved an irresistible attraction. Later the family sailed to Menton, where the social life was less exacting. When the existing yacht began to seem too small, a new and larger craft was ordered, the third of its line. When it had been completed on the Clyde, it was sailed to Menton. There *Katoomba III* was much admired.

The Blue Train service from Calais to the Côte d'Azur came to epitomise the Riviera. Introduced on 8 December 1922, it heralded a return to normality after the horrors of the First World War. The standards of luxury it introduced attracted a clientele so exclusive it was nicknamed the millionaires' train.

Above: The earliest English visitors came in winter and found the remains of the Roman civilisation as appealing as the climate. The great tower of the Emperor Augustus symbolised his conquest of the tribes in the maritime Alps, and the real beginnings of the French Riviera.

Left: As popular in his day as Dickens, the Scottish novelist Tobias Smollett was crabbed, cantankerous and tubercular. Even he found something to praise in pre-Revolutionary Nice, and his celebration of the town's climate and vegetation attracted more English visitors to the coast.

The journey from Calais took a fortnight by coach, the horrors of French food were to be endured, and the prevalence of infectious disease often led the local authorities to take drastic, usually ineffective, precautions to prevent its spread. Here, Victorian travellers from Marseille are fumigated against cholera.

Before the deluge of visitors brought by the coming of the railway, the coast was as unspoilt by civilisation as by sanitation. This print shows Marseille at the western end of the coast.

Above: Ever since the arrival of the railway, the prosperous English families insisted on travelling south in the greatest degree of comfort possible. In the 1880s, trains with compartments had four seats, three of which converted into bunks; the fourth concealed a lavatory.

Left: Queen Victoria's stays in Nice over five consecutive years set the seal on the coast's popularity. By the time of her death in 1901, it had become the world's first major tourist destination.

From its earliest days, the casino at Monte Carlo attracted critics as well as gamblers. 'Is it right for Christian men and women,' thundered the Bishop of Gibraltar, 'even to enter a place where they are sure to rub shoulders with the swindler, the harlot or the thief, whose chambers are built with the wages of iniquity, and whose riches are the price of blood?'

Self-effacing Americans like the financier J. P. Morgan had introduced themselves to the coast during the *belle époque*.

In the years up until the outbreak of the First World War, the notorious arms-dealer Sir Basil Zaharoff characterised the essence of the coast.

Sir J. Rolls asking directions from an Automobile Association scout. The presence of the AA was indicative of the extent to which the Riviera remained a predominantly English colony.

The railway arrived in Marseille in 1855, progressing in a leisurely fashion over the next fifteen years to the eastern end of the Riviera at Menton. The art of the railway poster developed at the turn of the century, and contributed much to the iconography of the coast.

The Prince of Wales found the Riviera as irresistible as had his grandfather, King Edward VII. It was the setting of much of his romance with the American divorcee Wallis Simpson, and the couple's subsequent life as the Duke and Duchess of Windsor.

> On the third day [wrote Clark] my parents gave a luncheon party for some local residents. Amongst them was Madame Herriot, proprietress of a store named the Louvre, then the most prosperous in Paris. 'It is delightful,' she said to my father. 'I would give *anything* for a yacht like this.' 'Anything?' 'Yes, anything.' My father named an enormous sum. 'But it must include everything.' 'Yes, everything.' 'Even the notepaper.' 'Yes, the notepaper.' 'And I must have it *tomorrow*.' 'Yes, tomorrow.' Accommodation was found in the neighbourhood, we all packed hastily, and Madame Herriot came on board next morning with her cheque.

The episode demonstrates the attitude then prevalent on the Riviera towards money and possessions. Recalling the excesses of the epoch in *Tender is the Night*, F. Scott Fitzgerald wrote of 'the resplendent names of Cannes, Nice, Monte Carlo ... whispering of old Kings come here to dine or die, of rajahs tossing Buddhas' eyes to English ballerinas, of Russian princes turning the weeks into Baltic twilights in lost caviare days.'

At much the same time as Clark and Wilde were raising the tone of the Riviera, someone altogether more sinister was disfiguring its boulevards. This was the legendary arms dealer Basil Zaharoff, described by the MP and professional Irishman T. P. O'Connor as 'a most impressive figure, with his steely-blue eyes and excessively dark eyebrows, almost melodramatic eyebrows – a citizen of the world, as at home in the Unter den Linden and the Champs-Élysées as in the Kartnerstrass in Vienna or Broadway in New York.' Zacharias Basilius Zachorot was born in Anatolia in 1849, son of a commodity dealer. It was as a businessman that he first appeared in London. There he married the daughter of a British builder, having courted her in the guise of a Russian prince. Arraigned at the Old Bailey on a charge of embezzlement, he was only released after providing compensation of a hundred pounds. Abandoning his wife, he fled to Cyprus. There he lived under the assumed name of Z. Z. Williamson. Later, he surfaced in New York where he married bigamously, was exposed, changed his name to

Basil Zaharoff, and began his spectacular career as an arms dealer. First, he acted as an agent for Thorsten Nordenfelt, the Swedish inventor of a machine gun and a submarine. Then he contrived the merger of Nordenfelt's company with that of rival manufacturer Hiram Maxim, creator of the definitive machine gun. This could fire six hundred rounds a minute, and was described by the explorer and journalist H. M. Stanley as 'invaluable for subduing the heathen'. Zaharoff became the company's main agent for the guns, a submarine, one of the earliest effective torpedoes, and a series of naval surface ships.

From 1895 onwards he took to wintering on the Côte d'Azur. First he stayed at the Hôtel de Paris in Monte Carlo, then in his own villa at Beaulieu. When, in 1897, Maxim Nordenfelt was acquired by the English firm Vickers, Zaharoff became the principal agent of the largest arms manufacturer in the world – just a year before Germany enacted laws to transform her fleet from a collection of ramshackle gunboats to one that was capable of challenging the supreme naval power of the day, Great Britain. This led to the huge increase in British naval estimates, and the naval race that culminated in the First World War. Vickers was one of a number of firms that did well by selling guns to both sides in the Boer War. Such were Zaharoff's efforts on the company's behalf that in 1902, the year the war ended, he earned £34,000. By 1904, the year of the Anglo-French entente, this had risen to £40,000. The following year, with a Franco-German crisis, he pocketed £86,000. At the time, a top lawyer would earn around £10,000.

Where better for such a man to live than the Riviera? 'All the deranged and crazed souls of the world, all the misfits and hysterics tend to rendezvous here, all in dead earnest,' wrote the novelist Jean Lorrain in *Le Crime des riches*. 'O Riviera! Riviera, the blue paradise to confidence men and tricksters.'

4

It was when Pierre Renoir was painting in Magagnosc that he heard about an old olive grove overlooking Cagnes, the medieval hill town between Antibes and Nice. The property boom that had followed the coming of the railway had continued for a generation, and the towns, villages and hillsides of the coast were now littered with villas. Cagnes was no exception, and the grove at Les Collettes was threatened with development. Renoir bought it to use as an outdoor studio, but as his rheumatism worsened, he decided to settle in the south and build a house on his plot. 'The architect,' wrote his biographer Francis Fosca in *Renoir*, 'wanted to erect one of those pretentious villas so common on the Côte d'Azur – a bizarre mixture of something between a Genoese palace and the Petit Trianon. Needless to say, Renoir disagreed and demanded a simple house that would fit into the surroundings, without a suburban garden with neat lawns and flowerbeds full of begonias.'

If the style of villas was bad, the hotels were worse. In the 1860s after the arrival of the railway they had been enlarged and new ones built, at first on a relatively modest scale. They proved such a success, though, that more ambitious plans were hatched for a series of residences – the *hotels-palais* – which were intended to be fit for a king. They were imposing, which, in the architectural language of the day, meant they were large. The Carlton in Cannes had nearly three hundred rooms, the Grand in Nice six hundred. The interiors were similarly monumental: there were huge sweeping staircases to showcase Parisian gowns, vast ballrooms and dining rooms that would not have disgraced the courts of Nebuchadnezzar. The Riviera Palace in Nice opened in 1884, then the Excelsior Regina in 1897. It had 400 rooms, 233 bathrooms, and took 4000 workers eighteen months to build. Queen Victoria stayed there during its inaugural year, 1898–9. The Alhambra and the Winter Palace followed, with the Ruhl et des Anglais, named after Henri Ruhl, the architect of nearly thirty of these monstrosities. In Monte Carlo there was the Hôtel de Paris and the Hermitage, at Beaulieu La Réserve and the Metropole, at Antibes the Hôtel du Cap, at Cannes the Majestic and, of course, the fabulous Carlton.

The largest, grandest and most absurd of them all was the Negresco in Nice. Henri Negresco was a Romanian who had been a violinist in a gypsy orchestra. He was a moustached Lothario who saw that his talents might be even better expressed as a maître d'hôtel. Negresco commissioned Edouard Niermans, architect of the Moulin Rouge and Folies Bergères in Paris, to create his fantasy. The result was a rectangular edifice, occupying a whole block of the Promenade des Anglais, distinguished by two cupolas at the eastern and western corners. These were said to have been inspired by the courtesan La Belle Otero, or more precisely by '*les boîtes à lait de la Belle Otero*'. Each of its four hundred rooms was provided with a private bath. There were also novelties like lifts, electric lights and even telephones. The hotel's centrepiece was the gigantic oval ballroom, crowned with a glass dome. Someone came up with an imaginative idea for the launch: that Louis Blériot, hero of the first cross-Channel flight in 1909, should land his aeroplane on its roof. He refused. Less spectacularly, the hotel persuaded eight kings to attend its opening in November 1912. During its first year the hotel recouped almost an eighth of the total investment.

In September 1913, Basil Zaharoff pulled off one of his best deals: Vickers was awarded what amounted to a monopoly to supply guns to the Russian army. On 28 June 1914, the heir-apparent of the Austro-Hungarian empire, Archduke Franz Ferdinand, was assassinated in Sarajevo. On 28 July Austria declared war on Serbia, and on 3 August Germany against France. Twenty-four hours later Britain joined in and the world was at war. From his fastness on the Côte d'Azur, Zaharoff commented, 'These fool politicians think that when war comes, it will be short and sharp. How wrong they are and how little they understand the situation. It will be a long and hard war, and only because of this the Central powers will be defeated.

They cannot hope to last in a long war. So logic decrees a long war it must be.' It would be some time before the British public discovered that the Turkish guns that decimated the expeditionary force at the Dardanelles in 1915 were of British manufacture, delivered by Zaharoff himself.

5

In the century since the Napoleonic wars, and in particular the fifty years since the coming of the railway, the Riviera had been transformed. Once it had enjoyed geographical, social, cultural and economic isolation, and its few inhabitants had lived lives – according to early English visitors – of Arcadian innocence. Decades of progress had brought a profusion of visitors, a huge growth in the local population, the construction of sewers, the transformation of Nice from small town into large city, and the development of a series of satellite resorts: Brougham's Cannes, J. Henry Bennet's Menton, François Blanc's Monte Carlo, and Queen Victoria's Cimiez. It had also seen the inception of the world's first tourist economy, occasional triumphs and repeated architectural disasters, a remodelled but by no means refined landscape, and the arrival of the motor-car.

All this did not meet with everyone's approval. The publisher John Murray IV wrote of his father's achievement in publishing the famous handbooks to the Continent: 'He built up a series which held the field against all competitors till the time when cheap travel introduced the vast horde of travellers who cared little for intellectual information and required a different *vade mecum* – travellers to whom where to feed was a more important question than what to see.' The alpinist and traveller Frederic Harrison observed sadly, 'We go abroad, but we travel no longer.' The French journalist Robert de Souza fulminated in the main Nice daily newspaper, *l'Éclaireur*: 'Go on foot from Nice to Menton to see trolley poles, factory chimneys, shapeless and grotesque caravanserai. All this done to one of the most beautiful places in the world. It's a pudding of local greed, stupid foreigners, shameless innkeepers and tasteless architects.' In 1913, de Souza fired his broadside against the new Nice, and indeed the coast as a whole: his book *Capitale d'hiver* was a tirade against a century of development that had left cities like Paris and Rome 'spoiled, trampled, massacred'. With some justice he singled out Nice as 'the most lamentable and significant example'. At the end of his five hundred carefully argued pages, he declared, 'If the town of Nice – and by the town I mean the whole of the coast, from the Var to the Italian frontier – if this town doesn't take the opportunity to reflect, to work methodically and hard, and to make durable progress as a result of these reflections, it is lost.'

PART TWO

6

America to the Rescue

'I shall lie on a beach
On a shore where the rippling waves just sigh
And listen and dream and sleep and lie.'
Max Plowman, *When it's Over*

1

With the outbreak of war in August 1914, the leisurely, self-indulgent and escapist tempo of the *belle époque* was lost, and the Côte d'Azur entered the modern world – the world of Gallipoli, Ypres, the Somme, Passchendaele and Verdun. In *My Early Life*, Winston Churchill contrasted the battle of Omdurman in 1898 with the conflict that was to follow:

> It was not like the Great War. Nobody expected to be killed. Here and there in every regiment or battalion, half a dozen, a score, at worst thirty or forty, would pay the forfeit; but to the mass of those who took part in the days of the little wars of Britain in those vanished days, this was only the sporting element in a splendid game. Most of us were fated to see a war where the hazards were reversed, where death was the general expectation and severe wounds were counted as lucky escapes, where whole brigades were shorn away under the steel flail of artillery and machine guns, where the survivors of one tornado knew that they would certainly be consumed in the next or the next after that.

Although the Riviera was six hundred miles from the killing fields of the western front, its distance from the fighting, the excellent rail links and the numbers of existing sanatoria meant that it had to revert to its traditional role as a 'health station'. In Nice, the French authorities immediately requisitioned several hotels for use as hospitals; the first wounded arrived in late August in the aftermath of the battle of Mons. By the end of September, the city was hosting 4500 injured; by the end of the year, eighteen further hotels had been requisitioned, and the Casino de la Jetée Promenade had became a depot for the wounded.

Hotels at Hyères, Menton and Cannes also became hospitals. According to the *Menton and Monte Carlo News* of April 1915:

> The most perfect hospital at Menton is without question the one now installed in the Hôtel Imperial and called the Hospital of the Entente Cordiale. It is very doubtful if any other town on the Riviera has a hospital that can rival or even equal this one in comfort, with its vast airy wards and comfortable beds, in luxury with its hundreds of baths and beautiful surroundings, in the perfection of its appointments, in the equipment of its theatre, in the number of skilled doctors and trained nurses, and in the excellence of the general management.

In Monaco, Prince Albert declared the principality's neutrality, but allowed the establishment of hospitals and convalescent homes for Allied wounded. The gaming rooms remained open. When the Italian front opened in 1915 on the Austro-Italian border within a hundred miles of Monaco, the principality was overrun.

At the same time the Niçois, pragmatic in ways that were to be repeated in 1940, did their best to sustain Nice as the tourist city it had become. 'Nice must live,' declared one of its two major dailies, *Le Petit Niçois*. 'Faithful to its traditions, Nice must receive its guests with a smile of welcome. Nice must attract, and keep, all its old friends and clients. Nice must summon up all its customary seductiveness and charm.' For obvious reasons, Germans and Austrians took their holidays elsewhere, while most of the British and

Russians were otherwise occupied. Nevertheless, in the winter season of 1914–15 Nice still attracted more than half the normal number of tourists. Some of the hotels – the Negresco and the Winter Palace – sloughed off the wounded in favour of more lucrative trade. The cinemas and theatres soon reopened. To an Englishman, Herbert Gibbons, this seemed incongruous. At the height of the Verdun offensive in 1916, when it seemed that Paris itself might fall, he found in Nice 'no mass instinct of national danger, no sickening anxiety'.

Then there were the Americans, arriving on the coast for the first time in force. For a time the United States had taken an isolationist stance on the war, claiming that the troubles of Europe were not its concern. Public opinion, though, was disturbed by the sinking of the British liner *Lusitania* in April 1915, not least because 118 American citizens drowned. Then, in January 1917, came the German announcement of unrestricted U-boat warfare, which threatened American merchantmen. That same month saw the publication of the Zimmermann telegram, which seemed to suggest that Germany supported Mexico in its claims to recapture from the United States the 'lost territories' of Texas, New Mexico and Arizona. Allied statesmen – Poincaré, Asquith and Lloyd George – appealed to their American counterparts to join the battle for freedom. In March 1917, under President Woodrow Wilson, the USA finally entered the war. 'We shall fight,' he said, 'for the things which we have always carried nearest to our hearts – for democracy, for the right of those who submit to authority to have a voice in their own government, for the rights and liberties of small nations.'

The conviction of the new alliance was soon tested by the repeated offensives on the western front and the huge success of the U-boat offensive. Then, in the autumn of 1917, the Tsarist regime in Russia collapsed. On 3 March 1918 the treaty of Brest-Litovsk ended the German-Russian conflict. This coincided with General Ludendorff's spring offensive, which aimed to throw the British back to the Channel ports, the French to Paris. By the summer, though, its force was spent. The British and French, under the supreme command of General Ferdinand Foch, began a counter-offensive, supported by nine divisions of American forces under General John Pershing. In July, American detachments were sent via Nice to the Italian front. By early November the Germans and their allies were facing a rout. The French were closing on Lorraine, the Americans on Sedan. On 9 November Kaiser Wilhelm II abdicated, and two days later the Armistice was signed. A Virginian Red Cross nurse, Ella Fife, witnessed the scenes in Paris: 'Nobody will ever know the sensations I had when those first guns went off announcing "peace" to a war-sick old world ... I lay there and wept for one solid hour.'

With the Riviera designated as one of the principal leave centres for the Americans – nicknamed 'Sammies' – shoals of natives of New York, Chicago, Boston and Pittsburgh came to visit the world's most famous galaxy of resorts, the fabled Côte d'Azur. In the Riviera season that followed the end of the war, more than seven thousand Americans sampled the pleasures of the coast; before the troops' departure from Europe the following spring, 65,000 had visited. They were enchanted by it. Ella Fife wrote to her mother: 'I wish you could see this lovely place, and see the sea for miles, so blue and beautiful, dotted with little white sail boats ... like the beautiful stories and pictures I've read and seen about such places, but never dreamed I'd go to one of them.'

On the Côte d'Azur, the new world had arrived, called in, it was said – by those who remembered George Canning – to redress the balance of the old.

2

As a story, though, this had begun years earlier. The sheer size, the variety of scenery and climate, and the geographical isolation of the USA meant that in the early nineteenth century Americans had few incentives to venture beyond their own shores. Given that so many were of European origin, though, some longed to visit the Old World. In the days of the great sailing ships, however, this meant an expensive, time-consuming, often hazardous voyage. In 1805 the American chemist Benjamin Silliman crossed the Atlantic on his first trip to Europe in the *Ontario*. She was lost with all hands on the return voyage – fortunately *sans* Silliman.

With the coming of steam transatlantic travel, pioneered by Brunel's *Great Western* and *Great Britain*, America moved closer to Europe because the voyage was cheaper and quicker. By the 1860s the services had expanded sufficiently to be dubbed the 'Atlantic ferry', and in the aftermath of the Civil War, large numbers of Americans began to visit a continent they knew only by reputation. Many were understandably bemused by the experience, wondering why their forefathers had left Europe in the first place. As the essayist Ralph Waldo Emerson remarked, 'It is for want of self-culture that the superstition of travelers, whose idols are Italy, England and Egypt, retains its fascination for all educated Americans.' Then, in 1867, Mark Twain set out on the journey to France, Italy and Palestine that he would chronicle two years later in *Innocents Abroad*. It made his name as a humorous writer, largely at the expense of his credulous fellow Americans. 'Travel is fatal to prejudice, bigotry and narrow-mindedness,' he wrote, 'and many of our people need it sorely on these accounts.'

Twain felt no call to visit Nice – dismissed by a contemporary American guidebook to Europe as 'a town of no great note' – but a few years later, in 1870, Americans constituted more than one in seven *hivernants* in Nice. By then a far more subtle observer of Americans abroad was at work. Starting with *Roderick Hudson* in 1875, the novelist Henry James made the interaction of European and American values his principal theme. Christopher Newman in *The Americans*, Isabella in *The Portrait of a Lady*, the eponymous heroine of *Daisy Miller*, and Chad Newsome in *The Ambassadors* are all innocents drawn into the wiles of the cultured and corrupt Old

World. Part of *The Ambassadors* is set on the Riviera. Here James Strether, yet another innocent American, learns the subtleties of the coast's *fin de siècle* social code: '"Decent men don't go to Cannes with the – well with the kind of ladies you mean." "Don't they?" Strether asked with an interest in decent men that amused her. "No, elsewhere, but not to Cannes. Cannes is different."' Henry James himself was an occasional visitor to the coast. Staying with his friend and fellow writer Paul Bourget in Costabelle near Hyères in April 1899, he commented, 'Such a wealth of comfort could sap creative juices.'

Yet despite the likes of Strether – and James himself – it was less with their innocence than their austerity, modesty and self-effacement that Americans first made a mark on the coast during the *belle époque*.

John Pierpont Morgan was one of a group of magnates who pioneered the industrial revolution in the USA and turned her into the country that, in the early twentieth century, rivalled Britain as an economic power. The son of a highly successful banker, Morgan built his father's concern into the most successful private bank in the USA, developed the country's rail system and, in 1901, founded the US Steel Corporation. This was the world's first billion-dollar concern and the largest company in the world. A lumbering giant of a man with a menacing stare, his nose perpetually disfigured by acne, Morgan could never have been considered good-looking. But this did not prevent him keeping as many as seven mistresses at a time and – it was said – generously funding the New York Lying-in Hospital to accommodate those he impregnated. Arguably the greatest art collector of the age, he was among the American millionaires who ransacked Europe for its treasures during the *belle époque*. His collection included works by Rubens, Rembrandt, Velázquez, Gainsborough, Constable and Turner. He once paid $21,000 for a small Louis XVI gold box, ten times that for a Cellini cup, and $484,000 – then a king's ransom – for a Raphael altarpiece.

Such a man was naturally attracted by the Riviera. There he disgraced himself in the eyes of the French by acquiring a series of Jean Honoré Fragonard's pre-revolutionary masterpieces and moving them from Grasse to the New York Metropolitan Museum, of which he was one of the founders. An enthusiastic gambler, he once stormed out of the casino at Monte Carlo having been refused permission to double his bets to $20,000. He owned in succession three yachts, all named *Corsair*, of which each was larger than its predecessor. *Corsair III* was a rather bulky black steamer, often seen mooching in and out of Cannes. At 302 feet she was the size of a destroyer, one of the largest pleasure-craft ever built, the perfect symbol of Morgan's wealth and power – and of his status as an *arriviste*.

Morgan's colleague Charles M. Schwab was born in 1862 in Williamsburg, Philadelphia. He started life as a stake driver at the magnate Andrew Carnegie's Carnegie Steel. By 1897 he had risen to become its president. In 1901 he was appointed the first head of US Steel after it merged with Carnegie's firm. He was rumoured to have been paid $1 million. As a monument to endeavour, Schwab spent four years building Riverside, a mansion in New York modelled on a Loire château. It occupied an entire block, had a power plant that consumed ten tons of coal a day, and a refrigerator that could hold twenty tons of meat.

Schwab's mentor, Carnegie himself, was an austere emigrant Scot whose first job in America had been as a bobbin boy in a textile factory. He believed that wine, gambling and women compromised the efficiency of his employees. Schwab took pains to conceal from him that he had played roulette at Monte Carlo every year since his first visit to Europe in 1886.

Running US Steel was hardly a full-time job so Schwab spent as much time as J. P. Morgan on the Riviera, sometimes an entire winter season. He knew how to spend his money: although he travelled alone, in January 1901 on his voyage out to the Mediterranean he took eight suites on a luxury French liner. When he arrived in Paris, he bought a car and drove to Nice, his luggage and retinue trailing in his wake. He retained the legendary tenor Enrico Caruso to entertain his guests at dinner for a fee of $10,000. He was known for his aphorisms and once remarked that 'The person who does not work for the love of work but only for money is not likely to make much money nor find much fun in life.'

James Gordon Bennett, born in 1841, was the son and heir of the millionare founder of the *New York Herald*, one of the first modern newspapers. He was best known for despatching the journalist H. M. Stanley to locate the explorer David Livingstone in Africa with the simple words, 'Find Livingstone.' In 1877, having tired of the United States, he settled in Europe and established homes in Paris and Beaulieu, the exquisitely sheltered spot between the ancient port of Villefranche and Monaco. He used Villefranche as his market town, regularly exhausting its supplies of meat, bread, vegetables and wine. He insisted that a red carpet was laid out across the quay when he was there so that his shoes were not soiled. If he thought service in a restaurant was slow, he would pretend to chew the carpet or bellow like a cow. In 1887 he founded a Paris edition of the *Herald*, supposedly with a view to promoting international understanding, then as ever in short supply. In reality the paper, which ran at a considerable loss, was intended to confer social distinction on its proprietor. As others have since discovered, it worked – after a fashion.

As often as not Bennett ran the *Herald* from his villa in Beaulieu. From its inception the paper praised the coast to the skies. It promised 'southern sunshine, opening of the season at all the famous resorts, and monarchs galore'. Bennett thought nothing of throwing his money about. In Monte Carlo he patronised a particular restaurant that cooked chops just as he liked them. One day he arrived with a few other millionaires to find all the best tables taken. He at once bought the restaurant, ejected the other diners, ordered and ate his chops, then gave the restaurant to his favourite waiter by way of a tip – with the proviso that his table should be reserved for him in perpetuity. His yacht *Lysistrata* cost $635,000: she had three decks, a Turkish bath, a crew of a hundred and – for the provision of fresh milk – an Alderney cow. There he hosted splendid parties. During the course of one, he ordered, without warning, the yacht to sea. Then as now, few visitors to the Riviera appreciate that boats can move. With a tactful sense of social distinction, he compensated three outraged female guests by presenting the titled pair with a diamond tiara apiece, the commoner with a pearl necklace.

These men were out to put the Old World in its place. They showed that, contrary to accepted European wisdom, business success mattered more than ancestry, social class or academic prowess. The *belle époque* Riviera was the ideal setting and backdrop for their antics, especially since, with their presence, the Prince of Wales and Queen Victoria had made it the most exclusive, glamorous and fashionable destination in the world – a staging-post to heaven.

3

The British had originally come to the Riviera to get away from their climate. Steel magnates and servicemen aside, the Americans who came after the First World War were also escaping. In their case, though, it was less from the winter weather than the cultural climate.

Leaving aside objections to Prohibition, it was the materialism of President Coolidge's post-war America that musicians, artists, writers and intellectuals found stultifying and claustrophobic. The philistinism of the age was brilliantly captured in Sinclair Lewis's novels *Babbit* and *Dodsworth*. In the latter a character deplores the idea of visiting the Old World. 'Europe? Rats! Dead as a door-nail. Place for women and long-haired artists … only American loans that keep them from burying the corpse! All this art! More art in a good shining spark plug than in all the fat Venus de Milos they ever turned out.' The American poet and critic Malcolm Cowley took a similar line in explaining the exodus of the cultural élite: 'Feeling like aliens in the commercial world,' he wrote, they 'sailed for Europe as soon as they had enough money to pay for the steamer tickets'. The strength of the dollar against the franc meant that it was cheap for Americans to live in France. By 1921 there were six thousand in Paris. Many were then drawn south by the Riviera's fabulous reputation, among them two great artists, Edith Wharton and Isadora Duncan.

Wharton contrasted sharply with the Americans who had hitherto somewhat ostentatiously represented the Land of the Free on the paradisal coast. She had been born in 1863 into a venerable American family that traced its descent to the early Virginian settlers. This wealthy and traditional east-coast society saw itself threatened by the burgeoning power of industry and commerce, well represented by the likes of J. P. Morgan. Educated by tutors and governesses, the young Edith had learned French, German and Italian during the family's extensive travels in pre-war Europe. In 1885 she married Edward Wharton, a wealthy Bostonian, and in 1907 they settled in Paris, which was then approaching its apogee as the capital of the world's imagination, the city of Picasso, Diaghilev and Gertrude Stein, of Joyce, Gide and Valéry. There, Wharton published the short stories, verses and novels that established her as a major writer. Her theme was the failure of her own wealthy and traditional society to adapt itself to the challenges of the industrial age: her world, she observed in *House of Mirth*, had a 'blind dread of innovation, an instinctive shrinking from responsibility'. In *Ethan Frome* she examined her fractured marriage, which ended in divorce in 1913. Wharton was a woman of rare intellect, learning and sensitivity whose novels bear comparison with those of the fellow American who became her confidant, mentor and friend, Henry James.

According to her first biographer, Percy Lubbock, it was the rich history of the Riviera that had drawn Wharton there during the *belle époque*. It also predicated her return after the end of hostilities in 1918. 'As soon as ever the war-shadow lifted, she had sloped off to the south for a winter of content – to the blessed light of the olive land, the classic shore, the Roman Province.' Soon she had bought an old grey house flanked by two small towers that stood above Hyères. 'I am thrilled to the spine,' she wrote.'*Il y va de mon avenir*, and I feel as if I were going to get married – to the right man at last!' There, according to Lubbock, 'If you looked back to a century of polite behaviour, from the rocky hillside of Provence, it was an age that opened, through a vista of old rough history, broadening away to the great bowl of the midland sea, brimmed with light – to Rome, to Carthage, to the Grecian Isles, to Tyre.'

It was at the villa that Wharton wrote the novel for which she is now best remembered, the Pulitzer Prize-winning *The Age of Innocence*. In it she remarks that 'New York was divided into the two great fundamental groups of the Mingotts and the Mansons and all their clan, who cared about eating and clothes and money, and the Archer-Newland-van-der-Leyden tribe, who were devoted to travel, horticulture and the latest fiction, and looked down on grosser forms of pleasure.' For New York, read the Côte d'Azur. During the *belle époque* it had become something of a hostage to the Mingotts and the Mansons. Despite its charms, in the 1920s Wharton watched it turn into their enclave.

Isadora Duncan was born in 1878 in San Francisco, and brought up in a household dominated by the arts: poetry, classical music and, above all, dance. 'I spent days and nights,' Duncan wrote later, 'seeking that dance which might be the divine expression of the human spirit through the medium of the body's movement.'

As a teenager she performed in vaudeville shows and contemporary productions like Shaw's *Pygmalion*, but when she ventured to Edwardian Europe her genius was recognised in the salons of London, Paris and Berlin. Inspired by what she viewed as the free, natural movements of classical Greek folk dances, of dance as an ultimately sacred art, she re-created the medium as a major art form. Soon she had established schools in Berlin, Salzburg, Vienna and Moscow. As radical in her personal life as in her art, Duncan refused to be bound by what she regarded as the chains of marriage. She had two children, Deirdre and Patrick – by her lovers Paris Singer and Gordon Craig – but in 1913 they drowned when the car in which they were being driven fell into the Seine. She never recovered from the tragedy. For a time she stopped dancing, and for the remainder of her life was an alcoholic. It was in the years after the war, until her grisly death in 1927 when her scarf caught in the wheel of her car, that she became one of the leading figures on the Côte d'Azur. 'Art meant Isadora,' remarked the novelist John Dos Passos. 'Art was whatever Isadora did.'

Like many others in the brave new post-war world, Duncan found that fame alone paid few bills. On returning at the age of forty-three to the coast she had known in its *belle époque*, she had to throw herself on the hospitality of her brother Raymond, who had a business in Nice selling sandals. She slept in his office on a sheepskin-covered bench. Eventually she took a room at the coast's most expensive hotel, the Negresco, at a *prix d'artiste*. Then she found an old wooden barn on the Promenade des Anglais, that would double as a studio. It was her centre of gravity during the final years of her life, when – like Edith Wharton – she divided her time between the coast and Paris. In the capital she stayed alternately in the most fashionable hotels and in moth-eaten *pensions*, according to the generosity of her friends. 'She lived,' wrote Dos Passos, 'in the chatter of scandalised tongues, among the kidding faces of reporters, the threatening of bailiffs, the expostulations of hotel managers bringing overdue bills.'

In his memoirs the Hollywood director Jean Negulesco recalled driving with Duncan, the writer and artist Jean Cocteau, and the pianist Walter Shaw to Marseille for a midnight *bouillabaisse*:

> The port was full of sailors, and so was the restaurant – young sailors. Cocteau and Walter were in heaven. We didn't finish ordering before Walter brought to the table a handsome, blushing young sailor. An animated quarrel started between Isadora and Jean

> Cocteau as to who would get this tempting morsel. Jean was ahead in the argument when Isadora started to moan like a child. 'Sweetest Cocteau, you had the one last night, let me have this one.' And turning to us, 'Make him realise how unfair he is.' In happy chorus we gave him our pacifying verdict. 'She is right. It's her turn.' To which he sulkily agreed. 'She can have him. But this is the last time.'

The *matelot* himself was not consulted. Towards the end of her life, Duncan observed, 'There are only two things left, drink and a boy.'

4

In 1920 the Riviera woke up to discover that the tide had retreated. The Americans who had flocked to the coast after the war had gone home, and many who had haunted the Riviera during the *belle époque* had also disappeared. 'After World War I,' commented Charles Graves, one of the coast's historians, 'the social atmosphere of the South of France altered completely. No more grand dukes, no more Baltic barons, no more German princelings, no more Austrian archdukes. The Russian Revolution and the inflation of the mark put them out of business.'

Despite the likes of Isadora Duncan, the clientele that Henri Negresco saw as the cream of society had largely disappeared. He sold his gargantuan edifice on the Promenade des Anglais, and went north to die in Paris. Monte Carlo, which attracted a comparable clientele, faced similar problems. In 1918 Prince Louis had refused Camille Blanc's proposal that economic circumstances dictated he should take a reduction in his annual income from the tables. Although the end of hostilities saw a rise in the number of visitors to the principality, there were certainly far fewer then there had been up to 1914 and the Salle des Bains de Mer was in crisis. Prince Louis turned to his neighbour Basil Zaharoff.

Like most arms dealers, during the years between 1914 and 1918

Zaharoff had never had it so good. He had even turned himself into something of a statesman by inducing the British government in 1915 to use him as an agent to persuade neutral Greece to join the Allies. Then Prime Minister Lloyd George asked him to detach Turkey from her alliance with Germany. His success in both ventures was rewarded with the GBE in March 1918, and the GCB the following January. Also, in recognition of his philanthropy in establishing the chair of Aviation at the University of Paris and of French Literature at Oxford, he received the Grande Croix and the Légion d'Honneur from France, and an honorary DCL from Oxford. In 1918, he drew up Monaco's first written constitution with his friend the French Prime Minister Georges Clemenceau.

For Zaharoff the affairs of the Société des Bains de Mer were intriguing. He had long held shares in it, and he harboured the modest ambition to put himself and his Spanish mistress, the Duchess of Madeira, on the Monaco throne. He made himself invaluable by placing £1 million at Prince Louis's disposal, dispensed with Camille Blanc, and introduced his own nominees to run the tables under the directorship of René Léon. Soon, all was in order once again. H. G. Wells, although well past his best as a novelist, had achieved huge popularity in 1920 with *The Outline of History* – the story of the world according to Wells. His affair with Odette Keun, a member of the artistic community at Magagnosc, brought him to the coast, where he made a pronouncement on the controversial Zaharoff that demonstrated the moral flexibility and intellectual suppleness the Riviera expected of its adherents:

> The picture of an Anatolian Greek overwhelmed by his riches, adorned by the highest honours France and Britain could bestow, amusing himself by running a gambling place in his declining years, displayed against a background of innumerable millions of men maimed, tortured, scalded, mutilated and killed, may be an effective indictment of our political traditions, but in no sense is it a personal condemnation. Millions would have played the same game had they thought of it and known how.

In September 1924 Zaharoff married his mistress, thereby creating a vacancy for the position. When she died two years later his aspirations for the throne were dashed, but his riches remained. He died in his bath at the Hôtel de Paris in Monte Carlo.

7
Summer Turns to High

> 'The word paradise, with its sense of a limited enclosure outside time, became the word – *quel paradis!* – to describe the Côte d'Azur.'
>
> Charles Graves, *Royal Riviera*

1

It was in the summer of 1924 that the American novelist Scott Fitzgerald and his wife Zelda first visited the Riviera. As a couple, they were for their generation the epitome of grace, glamour and success just as John F. and Jacqueline Kennedy, Richard Burton and Elizabeth Taylor, Laurence Olivier and Vivien Leigh were to be.

Francis Scott Fitzgerald, born in Minnesota and educated at Princeton, had enlisted in October 1917. The war ended before he had the opportunity to join his compatriots in France, so he returned to the literary career he had begun at university. An autobiographical novel of his life there, *This Side of Paradise*, appeared in 1920, soon to be followed by *The Beautiful and the Damned*. He then tried his hand as a short-story writer, with considerable financial success. By 1924 he was earning $25,000 a year. He had also become the acknowledged chronicler of the uncertainties of the post-war generation, coining the phrase 'the Jazz Age' in homage to the new music of the era, and catching much of the insouciance and inconsequence of the *années folles*. 'America,' wrote Fitzgerald, 'was going on the greatest, gaudiest spree in history and there was going to be plenty to tell about it. The whole golden boom was in the air – its splendid generosities, its outrageous corruptions in the tortuous death struggles of the old America in Prohibition.'

In the spring of 1924 Fitzgerald and his wife set sail on the *Aquitania*, following the beaten track of American artists and intellectuals in escaping to the Elysian fields of Paris. 'We were going to the Old World,' he wrote, 'to find a new rhythm for our lives, with a true conviction that we had left our old selves behind forever.' There the Fitzgeralds met Gerald and Sara Murphy, Americans of a slightly older generation. The Murphys had settled on the Bohemian Left Bank Quai des Grands Augustins where Gerald had established himself as a notable painter – Fernand Léger thought him the only painter of significance among the Americans in Paris. Soon the Murphys were urging their new friends to visit the summer Riviera: the deserted hotels were cheap, the weather wonderful. With some misgivings, the Fitzgeralds, with their daughter Scottie, took the train south in late May. In Zelda's autobiographical novel, *Save Me the Waltz*, she wrote:

> The tea-party told them nobody stayed on the Riviera in summer – that the baby would take cholera if they carried her to the heat. Their friends expected they'd be bitten to death by French mosquitoes and find nothing to eat except goat. They told them that they'd find no sewage in the Mediterranean in high summer and remembered of the impossibility of ice in high-balls; there was some suggestion of packing a trunk with canned goods.

It was certainly true that for the traditional English colonists, summer on the Riviera was anathema. This was partly for social reasons. The brown – male – bodies Oscar Wilde had admired were those of soldiers, seamen, and peasants obliged to labour in the vineyards during the heat of the day. Middle and upper-class Victorians had preferred alabaster skin as a token of racial and social purity, but there were practical reasons, too, for avoiding the sun.

In *Tuscan Studies*, Lucy Baxter, daughter of the Victorian poet William Barnes, deplored the Italian habit of sea-bathing in July and August: 'To our English minds this seems inconceivable. During those two months the scorching rays of "Sol Leone" render the sands a burning desert, the sea is as warm as the hot air above it, and the close lodgings are too stifling to endure. Of what use is a month at the seaside to us if our children cannot dig in the sands, and our boys and girls take long walks, seaweed and sea-anemone hunting?' To the heat was added the usual British phobia about sanitation, hinted at in 'close lodgings'. In Nice in 1883 the Paillon river was finally channelled underground. Until then it had been little more than an open sewer. Unpleasant enough in winter and spring when the water from the Alps flowed freely, in summer it became what the local newspaper called 'a receptacle of putrefaction, an oven of pestilence'. Also, in the infancy of organised refuse collection, most of the Riviera resorts simply bundled up their rubbish and dumped it a couple of miles out to sea. If the breeze was onshore, it returned. Finally, bathers were thought vulnerable to the exotic sea life that inhabited the Mediterranean, not least the man-eating octopus.

In any case, for those who found the English summer as unpalatable as the winter, there were French Channel resorts like Deauville and Trouville, the Italian lakes and the Swiss Alps, all of which had been developed as summer destinations during the second half of the nineteenth century. No Englishman dreamed of staying on the Riviera after Easter. 'Before about 1922,' the art historian Kenneth Clark remarked in his memoirs, 'it was considered suicide to stay on the Riviera after the end of April ... I asked our Scottish gardener what the natives did during the months between May and December. He said it was terrible, and that he made it a condition that he could return to Pitlochry during at least these months.'

Americans like the Fitzgeralds, though, came to the South of France relatively free of British prejudices. America was scarcely a class-free society, but its notions of class were different and arguably less rigid. They didn't object to a suntan and had different ideas about heat: Nice in summer was no hotter than Washington or Atlanta. Young Americans visiting the summer Côte d'Azur for the first time found in it something of the paradisal quality that the English had discovered there in winter more than a century previously. Ella Fife, the young Virginian nurse on her first visit to Cannes in 1919, 'couldn't think of anything more ideal than spending a summer here'. The gun-toting Ernest Hemingway entitled the novel he set on the 1920s Riviera *The Garden of Eden*. Fitzgerald himself wrote lyrically of the coast's summer air, 'vivid with dresses just down from Paris and giving off a sweet pungent odour of flowers and chartreuse and fresh black coffee and cigarettes mingled with another scent, the mysterious thrilling scent of love. Hands touched jewelled hands over the white tables; the vivid gowns and shirt-fronts swayed together and matches were held, trembling a little, for slow-lighting cigarettes.'

The Fitzgeralds tried Hyères, Cannes and Monte Carlo. Eventually they found a suitable villa in Valescure, just outside what was then the tiny resort of St Raphael. Exposed to the *mistral*, it was then a fishing village that had attracted few summer or winter visitors; it boasted a golf course and a small English colony. The Fitzgeralds were enchanted. 'It is twilight as I write this,' noted Fitzgerald in a letter, 'and out of my window darkening banks of trees, set one clump behind another in many greens, slope down to the evening sea. The flaming sun has collapsed behind the peaks of the Esterels, and the moon already hovers over the Roman aqueducts of Fréjus, five miles away.' It was there that he wrote much of his masterpiece, *The Great Gatsby*. There, too, he began what became the best novel of the coast, *Tender is the Night*. For Fitzgerald – at least at first – the Côte d'Azur was the place where he wanted 'to live and die'.

2

The Divers, the central couple in *Tender is the Night*, were based on the Fitzgeralds and the Murphys. The latter had first visited the coast at the invitation of the composer Cole Porter. A contemporary of Gerald Murphy at Harvard, Porter had rented the Château de la Garoupe on Cap d'Antibes, the tree-covered cape that divides Juan-les-Pins from Antibes. The Murphys and their three children found that in summer Antibes was deserted. Even the telephone service shut down in the lunch-hour, the cabbies dozed in the shadow of their traps, and the shops were shuttered. At the end of the Cap d'Antibes there was a tiny beach, La Garoupe. 'It was only forty yards long,' wrote Gerald, 'and covered with a bed of seaweed that must have been four feet thick. We dug out a corner of the beach and bathed there and sat in the sun, and we decided that this was where we wanted to be.' They found a suitable property on the cape, overlooking La Garoupe lighthouse. It was in need of restoration, but was admirably situated in seven acres of its own grounds, overrun with exotic plants trailing down towards the sea. They called it Villa America.

In the summer of 1924 the Murphy family stayed at the Hôtel du Cap while they supervised the work on their new home. It was in the fashionable art-deco style: beige walls set off striped awnings and bright yellow shutters, which opened on to a flagged terrace shaded by a linden tree. The interior walls were white, the floors black, the furniture covered in black satin, the austerity offset by linen and china of vibrant blue, yellow and apple green. The villa was completed by 1925, and over the next two summers the Fitzgeralds were often to be found there. Fitzgerald's list of his fellow guests at the Murphys' is a name-check of the contemporary cultural élite. He wrote facetiously that 'There was no one at Antibes this summer except me, Zelda, the Valentinos, the Murphys, Mistinguet [Maurice Chevalier's lover], Rex Ingram, Dos Passos, Alice Terry, the MacLeishes, Charlie Brackett, Maude Kahn, Esther Murphy, Marguerite Namara, E. Phillips Oppenheim, Mannes the violinist, Floyd Dell, Max and Crystal Eastman, ex-Premier Orlando, Étienne de Beaumont – just a real place to rough it, an escape from all the world.'

To the Fitzgeralds, during those golden summers, the Murphys seemed to have solved the problem of how to lead fulfilling lives. Murphy's father ran a smart New York leather-goods firm called Mark Cross, the Louis Vuitton of its day. This had made Gerald financially independent. He was something of a dandy, affecting the latest fashions and a cane – which the diminutive Fitzgerald could never carry off. He had married his childhood sweetheart, who happened to be a beautiful heiress – she and her sisters had been presented at Court in London in the dazzling Season of 1914. Murphy had been a great social success at Harvard and again when he was introduced to artistic circles in Paris. He counted Picasso, Gertrude Stein, Diaghilev, Stravinsky, Cocteau and Braque among his friends. Perfectly dressed, perfectly poised, perfectly married and – particularly from Fitzgerald's point of view as a professional writer – perfectly creative and perfectly rich, the Murphys had life cracked. A coterie of the famous gathered around them, like moths to a flame. In *Tender is the Night* Fitzgerald based Gausse's Hôtel des Étrangers, with its 'prayer rug of a beach', on the Hôtel du Cap, and the summer lifestyle of the Divers on that of the Murphys. Here, family, company, conversation, creativity and sun combined to form a Utopia unobtainable in the USA. For a time it seemed to the Murphys and the Fitzgeralds that it could only occur on the Riviera. 'One could get away with more on the Summer Riviera,' wrote Fitzgerald in *The Crack-Up*. 'And whatever happened seemed to have something to do with art.'

Yet for the Fitzgeralds, the proximity of all this perfection was unsettling. While Fitzgerald was completing *The Great Gatsby*, his wife embarked on the sort of affair that was *comme il faut* on the Riviera. Edouard Jozan was a young officer from the naval air station at Hyères. In *Save Me the Waltz*, Zelda's heroine Alabama asks of the character based on Jozan, 'Do you think he actually *is* a god? He looks like you – except that his face is full of the sun.' Fitzgerald's discovery of the affair doomed the marriage. He had finished *The Great Gatsby* and found himself, as so many of his predecessors had on the Riviera, with too much time on his hands. He had a weakness for drink and was now overcome by it. 'I cannot consider one pint of wine at the day's end,' he wrote, 'as anything but one of the rights of man.'

It was at the Colombe d'Or *auberge* in St Paul de Vence, a *village perché* in the hills behind Cagnes, that the Fitzgeralds and the Murphys ran into Isadora Duncan, now established in her studio on the Promenade des Anglais. Zelda overheard her giving Fitzgerald the name of her hotel, and threw herself over the parapet of the terrace on which they were sitting to the walled garden below. 'I was sure,' recalled Gerald Murphy, 'she was dead.' Fortunately the drop was less than it looked – only a few feet – and dinner resumed. At the end of the evening the couples left in two cars. The Fitzgeralds followed the Murphys for a few miles until they came to a level crossing. Fitzgerald turned on to the track, bumped along for a few yards, stalled and fell asleep. A farmer found them the following morning and pulled the car clear just before the first train arrived.

It was the shape of things to come. Fitzgerald descended further into alcohol, while Zelda, who preferred a more direct form of self-destruction, dived from considerable heights into the rocky Riviera seas. It was not long before she was consigned to an asylum.

3

In *Tender is the Night*, Fitzgerald observed that in 1925 Gausse's Hôtel des Étrangers 'was almost deserted after its English clientele went north in April ... now it has become a summer resort of notable and fashionable people.' The Murphys and their entourage were notable and fashionable people, and the less notable followed in their footsteps, much as they had in Lord Brougham's a century previously, or in Queen Victoria's during the *belle époque*. Of course, they were not alone as summer trailblazers. Among other pioneers were Frank Jay Gould, Coco Chanel and Jean Cocteau.

Gould was another American millionaire, one of the six children of the railroad king John Gould. He was a former watchmaker who had the unenviable reputation of being the most unpleasant among a group of people virtually defined by their gracelessness, a class described by Fitzgerald in *The Great Gatsby* as the 'pioneer debauchees, men who during one phase of American life brought back to the Eastern seaboard the savage violence of the frontier brothel and saloon'. Gould's son Frank was little better, and a confirmed drunk. Like James Gordon Bennett before him, he identified the Riviera as the best place to while away his days and in 1913 established himself there, in permanent exile. As a property speculator, he proved himself an astute businessman, and it was for the creation of modern Juan-les-Pins that the French government made him a Commander of the Légion d'Honneur.

A more fitting tribute might have been the guillotine. As its name suggests, the village of Juan-les-Pins had pine trees and little else except a beach. When 'the season' was winter, this meant nothing. However, it was the only beach of any size in the area, and it faced south-west so it got most of the day's sun. When 'the season' became summer, its fortunes were transformed. A Niçois restaurateur, Edouard Baudoin, spotted the opportunity and in 1924 he opened a shabby casino there. It was an immediate success. A couple of years later Gould bought the casino, then built a 200-room hotel, the Provençal, and developed the town by laying out a series of building plots on a grid system, divided by avenues. If he had not incorporated some parkland, it would have had all the charm of contemporary Chicago. By 1928 the novelist Douglas Goldring, in his guide to the coast, described the place as 'the most fashionable and frequented bathing resort on the Eastern Riviera'.

A year later Arnold Bennett described it in similar terms, noting in an introduction to a French guide that 'If Juan-les-Pins "rises" any further, the beach, like New York, will have to rise upwards and be arranged somehow in two storeys.'

Gabrielle 'Coco' Chanel was born in 1883 in the poorhouse in Saumur on the Loire. She opened a couture house in the fashionable Channel resort of Deauville before the First World War, then another in Paris in rue du Cambon. 'For four or five years I made only black', she wrote. 'My dresses sold like mad . . . .' In *The Decade of Illusion*, Maurice Sachs, the French chronicler of the *années folles*, wrote, 'Chanel created a feminine character such as Paris had never before known. Her influence went beyond the reach of her work. Her name was etched on minds in the same way as the names eminent in politics or letters. She represented, in sum, a new being, all-powerful in spite of the legendary weakness of women and, it seemed, essential to the city's life.' Her liaisons were a subject of considerable international interest, and the Duke of Westminster, the richest man in England, was besotted with her. Noël Coward remarked that he was 'a floridly handsome man who, had he lived in an earlier age, would undoubtedly have glittered with rhinestones from head to foot'. For three years Chanel was his acknowledged mistress, and the couple spent much of their time together on his four-masted schooner *Flying Cloud*. But Chanel refused his marriage proposal. As she said, 'There have been many duchesses of Westminster but only one Coco Chanel.'

An acute observer of fashion, Chanel devoted the summer of 1923 to acquiring a suntan. When she strolled down the yacht's gangplank one day in Cannes it was said that she was as brown as a cabin-boy. Her return to Paris was a sensation and, as the female icon of the day, where Chanel went, others followed. 'I think she may have invented sunbathing. At that time she invented everything,' said Prince Jean-Louis de Faucinge-Lucinge, later director of Monaco's Société des Bains de Mer. The following summer he and his young bride followed suit on their honeymoon in an otherwise deserted Cannes. 'It was delicious. We immediately started sunbathing, which was something new at the time. A lot of sunbathing, exaggerated sunbathing. It was a study, it took time, hours and hours of sunbathing.'

4

A few miles to the west of Monaco, a rather different pioneer of the summer scene was at work in the Hôtel Welcome, Villefranche-sur-Mer.

Villefranche, the Portus Olivulae of the Romans, was refounded in the fourteenth century by Charles II of Anjou. Protected from the easterlies by Cap Ferrat and from the northerlies by the mountains of Le Vinaigrier, Pacanaglia and Soleillat, it had, with nearby Beaulieu and Menton, the most benign climate on the coast. Its sixteenth-century citadel was indicative of its martial history, the deep water of the harbour providing a haven for warships. Later it became the favourite destination of the Mediterranean squadrons of any navy that could find an excuse to visit it; the town's cafés, restaurants, brothels and hotels catered for the amusement of sailors on runs ashore. These *matelots* were the principal attraction for the artistic colony that established itself in the port in the mid-1920s: 'From all over the world,' wrote Jean Cocteau, 'men who have lost their hearts to masculine beauty come to marvel at the sailors lounging around the town alone or in groups, answering stares with smiles and never refusing propositions.'

Cocteau was the leader of the artistic community in Villefranche. Born in 1889 in a suburb of Paris, he became one of France's most prolific and eclectic artists. He was novelist, script-writer, dramatist, poet, essayist, sculptor, painter and critic all rolled into one; W. H. Auden once remarked that his complete works could be contained less in a library than a warehouse. By the early 1920s he was a national celebrity, one of a group of brilliant homosexual artists in the vanguard of the modernist movement. In *Brideshead Revisited*, Evelyn Waugh characterises Anthony Blanche as dining with Proust and Gide, and being on 'closer terms' with Diaghilev and Cocteau. Once, when Cocteau was short of money, the Duke of Westminster – whom he had met through Coco Chanel – suggested he should write a history of the ducal dogs.

Homosexuality had been legalised in France under the Code Napoleon of 1804. This was, of course, no guarantee of its social acceptability. Still, at least Cocteau could not find himself in the same position as Oscar Wilde. The most profound of his many affairs was with Raymond Radiguet, whom he met when Radiguet was fourteen. Cocteau compared him to Rimbaud: before he died of typhoid at the age of twenty, the precocious and unstable Radiguet had produced two novels of astonishing maturity: *Le Diable du corps* and *Le Bal du Compte d'Orgel.* (Zelda Fitzgerald attempted to learn French by reading the latter.) Cocteau was devastated by his lover's death, and retreated into opium. In the summer of 1924, following a period of detoxification, he settled in Villefranche. He set himself up in the small quayside Hôtel Welcome, and soon attracted a retinue. He described it in his memoir *Professional Secrets*:

> The Hôtel Welcome, in Villefranche-sur-Mer, is a source of myths, a site which the young enthusiasts of lyricism should transform into an altar and cover with flowers. Poets of all kinds, speaking every language, lived there and by a simple contact of fluids transformed the extraordinary little town, whose steep chaos ends at the water's edge, into a veritable Lourdes, a centre of legends and inventions.

The Hôtel Welcome attracted an inspiring and competitive group. The visitors' book read like a check-list of the 1920s avant-garde, and included Monroe Wheeler, Bébé Bernard, Francis Rose, Glenway Westcott, Evelyn Waugh and his brother Alec. There, Cocteau discovered his 'personal mythology or artistic philosophy'. Around this time he said 'I am the lie that always speaks the truth', an insight into the relationship between the world observed and its representation in art. At the hotel he wrote much of the novel for which he is best remembered: *Les Enfants Terribles* is a prescient, dystopian vision of adolescence in which young men fail to mature into adulthood and idle their way meaninglessly towards violent death. Meanwhile, the visiting fleets of the world's navies provided Cocteau with an inexhaustible supply of men, including, in late 1926, the aspiring writer Jean Desbordes.

In due course Cocteau moved on to Toulon. In 1931 this was still the great naval port that Napoleon would have recognised: a virtually landlocked harbour dominated by the two limestone precipices of Mount Coudon and Mount Faron. It had a profusion of cheap hotels and was swarming with sailors. Desbordes, whom Cocteau had helped with his novel *J'Adore*, accompanied him, but the relationship was petering out. By his own account, Cocteau spent that summer principally in the company of opium, a monkey, and an Annamese boy.

The Fitzgeralds left Europe in the autumn of 1931. Like many visiting American artists and intellectuals, they were impoverished by the collapse of the dollar that followed the Wall Street crash of 1929, and disillusioned by their experiences in the Old World. Fitzgerald died in 1940, the genius of the *The Great Gatsby* largely unrecognised.

The Murphys lost their son Baoth to meningitis in 1935, his younger brother Patrick to tuberculosis in 1937. Gerald wrote to Fitzgerald: 'Only the invented part of our life – the unreal part – has had any scheme of beauty. Life has stepped in now and blundered, scarred and destroyed. In my heart I dreaded the moment when our youth and invention would be attacked in our only vulnerable spot – the children, their growth, their health, their future. How ugly and blasting it can be, and how idly ruthless.'

The idyll offered by the summer Riviera had been an illusion, as Fitzgerald eventually realised. *Tender is the Night* records his awakening. In 1934 he advised his editor not to mention the Riviera in publicity material for the novel: 'Its very mention invokes a feeling of unreality and insubstantiality.' As for the book itself, he wrote of it that 'The novel should show a man who is a natural idealist ... giving in for various causes to the ideas of the haute bourgeoisie, and in his rise to the top of the social world losing his idealism, his talent and turning to dissipation. Background is one in which the leisure class is at their most brilliant and glamorous.' The novel lacks the genius of *The Great Gatsby*, but captures the greater commonplaces of life: betrayal, disappointment, infidelity and failure. It was set largely on the Riviera, which always seemed to promise so much more.

8

From a View to a Death

> '1930 was the last of the great years. After that the Riviera became too crowded ... I have not been back since 1937 and I have no desire to do so. I prefer to remember it the way it was.'
>
> Tom Finnery, proprietor of the Hôtel du Cap

In February 1929, when Evelyn Waugh arrived in Monaco, he witnessed the casino staff clearing away some unseasonal snow:

> The triumph of industry and order over the elements seems to me typical of Monte Carlo. Nothing could be more supremely artificial, except possibly the India rubber bathing beach which they had just decided to install ... the immense wealth of the Casino, derived wholly and directly from man's refusal to accept the conclusion of mathematical proof; the newness and neatness of the buildings, the absolute denial of poverty and suffering in this place, where sickness is represented by fashionable invalids and industry by hotel servants, and the peasants in traditional costume come into town to witness in free seats the theatre ballets of *le pas d'acier* and *Mercure*, all these things make up a Principality about as real as a pavilion of an International Exhibition.

He had travelled to the Riviera with his wife, who was developing pneumonia. When they arrived she was seriously ill, and on their subsequent voyage around the Mediterranean she nearly died. This experience doubtless coloured Waugh's view of the Riviera, which he also took to task for the prevalence of tourists and the plague of cars. 'The word "tourist" seems naturally to suggest haste and compulsion,' he wrote. As for the cars, 'There are very few roads in Europe now where one can walk without a furtive circumspection: one may sing away for a mile or so, then there is a roar at one's heels and one is forced to leap for the gutter in a cloud of dust.'

Two other artists visited the coast at this time and recorded for posterity what they felt and saw. One was the film-maker Jean Vigo, who moved to Nice in 1929 to recuperate from tuberculosis. In October of that year the world was overtaken by the Wall Street crash, and the beginnings of the depression. In Britain, a coalition government was formed to deal with the national emergency. Struck by the contrasts in the city between the wealthy pleasure-seekers and the misery of many of its indigenous inhabitants, Vigo set out in 1930 to make a documentary of its condition, hiding his camera in a cardboard box to make an early essay in *cinéma vérité*. In this way, he captured a series of marvellously spontaneous and candid shots, both of the bourgeois visitors on the Promenade des Anglais, and the city's *vélos*, street cleaners and beggars, dramatising the political struggle that was erupting over the demand by the working classes for paid holidays. This was the battle that would eventually lead to the introduction in 1936 of *congés payés*, the paid holidays that were one of the turning-points in the emancipation of labour in France.

Vigo did not see Nice as a paradise. Rather, he talked of filming 'the last gasps of a society so lost in its escapism it sickens you'. He made his masterpiece *L'Atalante*, then died of leukaemia aged twenty-nine.

The other artist was D. H. Lawrence. In 1912 he eloped with Frieda Weekley, a cousin of the German fighter ace Baron Manfred von Richthofen. Soon afterwards he published *Sons and Lovers*, the book that made his name, then *The Rainbow* in 1915, and was prosecuted for obscenity. In 1919 he contracted tuberculosis and left England. He spent the next three years in Italy, writing *Women in Love*, then went to Mexico. Eventually his health drove him back to

Europe, and it was in December 1927 that the Lawrences arrived in Bandol, between Marseille and Toulon. Here the country was still unspoiled and tourists were few. According to a contemporary guide, the little resorts were patronised by 'French people from the North who prefer to avoid the company of the foreign invaders of their shores, and by a handful of English people, mostly French speakers, who like to live quietly in a French atmosphere and in the French manner'. The Lawrences stayed at the Hôtel Beau Rivage for three months, some of which Lawrence devoted to writing *Lady Chatterley's Lover*. To Aldous Huxley's wife Maria, he described the village as 'swimming with milky gold light at sunset, and white boats half-melted on the twilight sea, and palm trees frizzing their tops in the rosy west, and their thick dark columns down in the dark where we are, with shadowy boys running and calling, and tiny orange lamps under the foliage'.

The following autumn, the Lawrences stayed first at the Beau Rivage, then moved to a villa, the six-roomed Beau Soleil. In the course of that winter, Lawrence wrote the series of poems he called *Pansies*, in a jocular reference to Pascal's *Pensées*. They seem only minimally inspired by the coast, and fall far below the standard of Lawrence's best verse. The poems published after his death as *Last Poems* are of a different order, clearly written while he was under the spell of the coast and the sea, of which he wrote, 'I still love the Mediterranean, it still seems as young as Odysseus, in the morning.' In 'The Greeks Are Coming' he sees

> Little islands out at sea, on the horizon
> Keep suddenly showing a whiteness, a flash – and a furl, a sail...

'Middle of the World' begins:

> This sea will never die, neither will it ever grow old
> Nor cease to be blue, nor the dawn
> Cease to lift up its hills
> And let that slim black ship of Dionysus come sailing in
> With grape-vines up the mast, and dolphins leaping.

'Bavarian Gentians', which he had begun to compose in southern Germany the previous autumn, is about death:

> Reach me a gentian, give me a torch!
> Let me guide myself with the blue forked torch of this flower
> Down the darker and darker stairs, where blue is darkened on blueness
> Even where Persephone goes, just now, from the frosted September
> To the sightless realm where darkness is awake upon the dark
> And Persephone herself is but a voice...

By now Lawrence was dying. He left Bandol on 6 February 1930 for a sanatorium at Vence, the Roman town of Ventium. One of the eight main cities of the Alpes Maritimes, it stood on a rock promontory protected by its medieval ramparts, bordered by ravines and sheltered from the *mistral* by mountains to the north. Aldous Huxley had said that for the previous two years Lawrence had been like a flame that miraculously burned without fuel to feed it. When he and his wife arrived in Vence, he saw that 'The miracle was at an end and the flame was guttering to extinction.' Lawrence lingered for a few weeks, then died on 2 March 1930. He was buried two days later. The postscript to his penultimate letter, written to Maria Huxley, was bleak: 'This place no good.'

The Australian literary and television critic Clive James observed that 'Lawrence was in search of, was enraged over the loss of, a significance this world does not supply and has never supplied.' Despite the illusion to the contrary, this was as true of the Riviera as it was of anywhere else. It was a century since Lord Brougham had founded modern Cannes, seventy years since the coming of the railway. Now the coast – both in winter and summer – had been sufficiently developed for it to seem that paradise was at bay. The unacknowledged legislators of the world – the Renoirs and Johns, Fitzgeralds and the Waughs, the Vigos and the Lawrences – were beginning to notice.

9
Wallis in Wonderland

> 'It is fitting that the Riviera of the Twenties and Thirties should have been a favourite refuge of the Prince of Wales – a place where one could strip off not just one's clothes but everything that locked one into a public role … a repudiation of one's workaday identity.'
>
> Ian Littlewood, *Sultry Climates*

1

On 9 October 1934 the rowdy streets of Marseille echoed to the sound of an assassin's bullet. Hitler had come to power eighteen months previously as Germany's chancellor. If this had alarmed France, Germany's subsequent withdrawal from the League of Nations caused consternation. Early in 1934, French foreign policy was placed in the hands of Louis Barthou. He was a cultured and able man with a healthy dislike of Fascism, and aimed to encircle Germany with French allies, principally the Soviets, but also Poland, Czechoslovakia, Romania and Yugoslavia, which was then ruled as a royal dictatorship by King Alexander I. Invited to pay an official visit to Paris, the King had landed at Marseille where he was met by Barthou. The great seaport was *en fête*, the narrow streets thronged with welcoming citizens, flowers, the *tricouleur* and the Yugoslavian flag. A motorcade made its way up from the port towards the St Charles railway station, high above the harbour.

Winston Churchill, who had spent three weeks that August at the Château de l'Horizon at Cannes, takes up the story:

> Once again from the dark recess of the Serbian and Croat underworld a hideous murder-plot sprang upon the European stage and, as at Sarajevo in 1914, a band of assassins, ready to lose their lives, were at hand. The French police arrangements were loose and casual. A figure darted from the cheering crowds, mounted the running board of the car, and discharged his automatic pistol into the King and all the other occupants, all of whom were stricken.

Within hours Barthou was dead, as was, Churchill noted, the coherence and force of the French foreign policy that aimed to contain Hitler.

This cast a pall over the autumn of 1934, and on a Riviera already deep in the throes of the depression. At first France, as one of the less industrialised of the western nations, had been affected only moderately by the Wall Street crash of 1929, but the Riviera hardly represented France. In 1929, Americans like the Fitzgeralds and the Murphys had spent three times more money there than other tourists, and they were the first to go. American visitors to France fell from 265,000 in 1929 to 135,000 five years later. In 1931 they were followed by the British, when the devaluation of sterling made travel abroad prohibitively expensive. From 1927 to 1932 the number of visitors to Nice dropped from two million to fewer than 700,000, and unemployment in the city tripled. Hotels slashed their rates and started issuing false guest lists in an effort to attract custom. Many closed, including the Polonia, the London Palace, the Savoy, the Grand Hôtel de Cimiez, and the Majestic. In his novel *The Razor's Edge* Somerset Maugham wrote:

> An estate agent told me that on the stretch of the coast that reaches from Toulon to the Italian border there were forty-eight thousand properties, large and small, to be sold. The shares at the Casino slumped. The great hotels put down their prices in a vain attempt to attract. The only foreigners to be seen were those who had always

been so poor they couldn't be poorer, and they spent no money because they had no money to spend.

Worst of all, sleeping cars were added to the Blue Train for passengers in second and even third class.

In the mid-1930s, the economies in Britain, the USA and Germany began to pick up. France, though, was still in the depths of recession. In 1936 there were still more than half a million officially unemployed, there was a sharp fall in agricultural prices, and a new French government. The Popular Front had been formed as a combination of left-wing moderate forces to combat Fascism, and Léon Blum swept to power as the country's first socialist prime minister. France was behind the times in much of her social legislation, and a series of initiatives was set up to improve the lot of the working classes, among them the right to the fortnight's paid holiday that was already enjoyed in Great Britain and Nazi Germany. At the same time the minister of leisure and sports, Léo Lagrange, brought in the cheap railway ticket that enabled working-class families to take full advantage of their holidays. On 31 July 1936 every factory in France closed for a fortnight. More than half a million cheap tickets were sold and, with the Riviera's summer season now firmly established, many workers from the industrial north visited the fabled Côte d'Azur. A reporter for *Le Figaro* on the train for Nice observed patronisingly:

> Red ties, scarlet handkerchiefs, wild roses lost in masses of well brushed suits, cardigan sweaters buttoned right up to their celluloid collars. The women, too, had made commendable, often pleasing attempts at elegance. There were berets, and flowered hats, and feathered hats ... But also a sportier look – of knickers, and bulky wool jumpers embroidered with their wearers' initials.

When the first train carrying the cheap-ticket holders arrived at Nice, it was welcomed by a brass band and representatives of the tourist board, the *syndicat d'initiative*. The following year almost a quarter of a million workers visited the Riviera. 'Thanks to *congés payés*,' a left-wing newspaper noted, 'the French worker has had a chance to know the paradise long perceived as inaccessible to the common people: the Côte d'Azur.' However, the proprietors of some shops thought that such visitors lowered the tone of the coast and put up signs that read: '*Interdit aux congés payés*.' Some hotel staff were surprised to discover that their new visitors could use a knife and fork. The right-wing *Action Française* commented, 'In opening the way to the red trains, we close it to the famous Blue Train.' A contemporary cartoon showed an elderly lady peering through a lorgnette at the new arrivals: 'You don't think, do you, that I'm going to go into the same water as these Bolsheviks?'

2

None of this was thought worth mentioning by Charles Graves in his popular history of the coast, *Royal Riviera*. 'The major event of the winter season of 1936,' he wrote, 'was the arrival of Mrs Wallis Simpson, shortly before Edward VIII's abdication.' Today the liaison between the Prince of Wales and the American divorcée would have entertained tabloid readers for months. At the time, though, the British press maintained a seemly reticence about the private lives of the royal family virtually until Mrs Simpson's dramatic arrival in Cannes on 4 December 1936.

Edward VIII was the eldest son of George V. He was burdened with the usual difficulties of the heir to the throne of having too much time and money on his hands, and the more common one of a poor relationship with his father. 'The King is in very good form,' the King's confrere Lord Hardinge of Penshurst once wrote to his wife, 'which I hope will survive the arrival of his sons.' As Prince of Wales, Edward VIII had perhaps more in common with his grandfather, the unswervingly promiscuous Edward VII. Certainly the life he led as king-in-waiting between his coming-of-age in 1915 and the death of his father early in 1936 bore similarities to that of the earlier Prince of Wales. Both men were popular, self-indulgent, devoid of intellectual or creative interests, and obsessed by women or – arguably – sex. In the case of the elder Prince of Wales it was Lillie Langtry, Lady Brooke and Mrs Keppel; with the younger, it was Mrs Freda Dudley Ward. Her husband was a Liberal whip, whose duties largely confined him to the House of Commons, which allowed the lovers full rein. On 12 March 1918, Lady Cynthia Asquith noted in her diary: 'Saw the Prince of Wales dancing round with Mrs Dudley Ward, a pretty little fluff with whom he is said to be rather in love. He is a dapper little fellow – too small – but really a pretty face. He looked as pleased as Punch and chatted away the whole time … He obviously means to have fun.' The couple was still having fun twelve years later when the Prince, then thirty-six, met Wallis Simpson.

Bessie Wallis Warfield was born in Pennsylvania in 1896. Her parents traced their descent proudly to English colonial settlers, and their daughter's relatives on both sides were bankers, businessmen and public servants. Despite Wallis's intention to marry money, she settled in 1916 for Earl Winfield Spencer, an officer in the Air Arm of the US Navy. 'Win' transpired to be a neurotic alcoholic. A trip with her aunt brought her to Europe, and when she met American-born Englishman Ernest Simpson the marriage was doomed. Later, she described him in her autobiography *The Heart Has Its Reasons*: 'Reserved in manner, yet with a gift of quiet wit, always well dressed, and a good dancer, fond of theatre, and obviously well-read, he impressed me as an unusually well-balanced man.' Others thought him fat and stupid. In December 1927 her petition for a divorce from Spencer was granted, and she married Simpson in London in July 1928. Simpson's sister, Mrs Kerr-Smiley, was something of a society hostess – it was in her house in Belgrave Square that the Prince of Wales had first met Mrs Dudley Ward. It was through her, too, that the Simpsons met Lady Furness, who was also having an affair with the Prince of Wales. In the autumn of 1930 Lady Furness introduced them to the Prince.

He was at once attracted to Wallis. She was then thirty-four to the Prince's thirty-six, and she herself wrote, 'Nobody ever called me beautiful or ever pretty ... No-one has accused me of being intellectual' but she was petite, smart, danced well, and was rumoured to be good in bed. She was fascinated by the Prince, or perhaps by what he represented: 'His slightest wish seemed always to be translated instantly into the most impressive forms of reality. Trains were held; yachts materialised; the best suites in the finest hotels were flung open; aeroplanes stood waiting ... It seemed unbelievable that I, Wallis Warfield of Baltimore, Maryland, could be part of this enchanted world ... All I can say is that it was like being Wallis in Wonderland.' Much of their courtship was played out on the summer Côte d'Azur.

With Wallis installed as the Prince's new companion, the couple spent the summer of 1934 cruising the Riviera on Lord Moyne's yacht *Rosaura.* During the trip, according to Wallis in her memoirs, the couple crossed the grey line between friendship and love, and the Prince decided, on reaching Cannes where the trip was supposed to end, to go on to Genoa. Lord Moyne agreed. The following summer the couple made the village of Golfe-Juan their base, renting the Villa le Roc. When the mood took them they cruised with friends, and the Duke of Westminster put his yacht *Cutty Sark* at their disposal. Another companion was Daisy Fellowes, a rich Franco-American who scandalised the *bourgeoisie* with her taste for black men, and who once gave a Diaghilev ballerina cocaine for a headache.

Press photographs of the happy couple disporting themselves on the playground of the rich played badly at the time of the Jarrow March. The Prince of Wales' father, King George V, was inexpressibly pained by his eldest son's friendship with Wallis. To the Prime Minister Stanley Baldwin, he remarked, 'After I am dead the boy will ruin himself in twelve months.' In January 1936 he died and the Prince of Wales became Edward VIII. A crisis developed in which the Riviera played a fitting part.

3

At the time of his father's death, no one had supposed that the new King wished to marry his mistress: no one married his mistress. Also, as King, Edward could not marry a divorcée. However, as the summer of 1936 approached it became clear that the King indeed intended to marry Wallis Simpson. He was advised to avoid holidaying on the Riviera because of continued social unrest in France that the Popular Front was still attempting to address (it was even suggested that 'The Red Flag' had been sung within earshot of the villa he had intended to rent in Cannes), so he and Wallis cruised instead along the Dalmatian coast in the yacht *Nahlin*. The Prince's enjoyment of the Côte d'Azur had been widely reported in the American press, which delighted in his romance with Wallis – it was emblematic of the American dream of success. When he and Wallis returned to London in October the *New York Woman* pointed out that if Ernest Simpson wanted a divorce, the King could not be sued in England for adultery. On 26 October the *New York Journal* announced KING WILL WED WALLY because, it went on, Edward believed that 'the most important thing for the peace and welfare of the world is an intimate understanding and relationship between England and America'. Two days later it announced that Mrs Simpson had been granted a divorce in Ipswich on the grounds of her husband's adultery with a girl called Buttercup Kennedy at the Café de Paris in Bray. The best headline ran: QUEEN'S MOLL RENO'D IN WOLSEY'S HOME TOWN.

A fortnight later it was apparent that the British press was about to break its silence on the 'King's friendship', and the constitutional implications. The King's private secretary Alexander Hardinge told him that the government might be obliged to resign over its handling of the matter. A general election would have to be called, the chief issue of which would be his affair with Wallis. The House of Commons talked openly of abdication, and the socialite Chips

Channon recorded in his diary, 'We are faced with an impasse. The country, or much of it, would not accept Queen Wallis, with two live husbands scattered about.' Lurid rumours circulated about Wallis: that she was illegitimate, that she was a lesbian *and* a nymphomaniac, a spy for the Nazis and probably the KGB, that she was Nazi foreign minister Ribbentrop's mistress, had a child by Count Ciano, his Italian counterpart, and that she had learned sexual techniques in the brothels of Hong Kong. Most seem unlikely. But as papers released by the Public Records Office in 2003 disclosed, while she was sleeping with Simpson and the Prince of Wales, she was apparently also having an affair with a second-hand-car dealer from York called Guy Marcus Trundle. According to Special Branch reports, he was a 'charming adventurer, very good-looking, well-bred and an excellent dancer'.

On 15 November the King told Prime Minister Stanley Baldwin that he intended to abdicate and marry Mrs Simpson, which precipitated a first-class constitutional crisis. In early December the British press finally broke the news. Although in both America and France the matter had been treated as the love story of the century and Wallis Simpson as a latter-day Cinderella, British opinion reflected in the papers was less indulgent. 'The monarchy,' wrote the Archbishop of Canterbury, Cosmo Lang, 'was being vulgarised and degraded ... mud was being thrown on sacred things.' On 3 December, Wallis left for the South of France, trailed by a posse of more than twenty newsreel cameramen, reporters and photographers. She broke the journey overnight at Blois in the Loire valley, with the press encamped in her hotel lobby. The next morning her car was blocked in to prevent her leaving without them. When she reached Cannes, she went to the Villa Lou Vieie, owned by her friends Herman and Katherine Rogers. The local press were lying in wait so she was driven through the gates sitting in the car's footwell with a rug over her head.

The King was in a quandary so Baldwin summarised the options open to him: he could give up the idea of marriage to Wallis; he could marry against the advice of ministers; he could marry and abdicate.

But Edward wanted to keep the Crown *and* marry his mistress. In the hours that followed Mrs Simpson's departure for Cannes, he turned to Winston Churchill. The pair had been friends for twenty-five years, and Churchill understood the strength of the King's feelings for Wallis. On 4 December he attempted to persuade him to take time to consider the matter fully before he carried out his threat to abdicate. In a letter to Baldwin, Churchill explained, 'I told the King that if he appealed to you to allow him time to recover himself and to consider now that things have reached this climax, the grave issues, constitutional and personal with which you have found it your duty to confront him, I was sure you would not fail in kindness and consideration. It would be a most cruel and wrong thing to extort a decision from him in his present state.'

On the Riviera Mrs Simpson was still besieged by several hundred reporters and photographers. From the Villa Lou Vieie she spoke to Edward once, sometimes twice daily on the telephone. The line was poor, 'hardly more than an acknowledgement of the possibility of long-distance communication', as she put it in her memoirs. She maintained to the King that he was within his rights as monarch to marry whom he chose, and that he would carry public opinion with him.

As it turned out, Churchill and Wallis were disappointed. On Sunday 6 December, Baldwin told his ministers that the matter had to be resolved before Christmas. The chancellor, Neville Chamberlain – soon to replace Baldwin as prime minister – pointed out that the uncertainty was ruining the Christmas shopping. On 11 December 1936 the King announced his abdication over the radio: he found it impossible to reign, he said, 'without the help and support of the woman I love'. Wallis heard the broadcast at the Villa Lou Vieie; Churchill was in tears at his country home, Chartwell; in New York, public interest was such that in the course of the broadcast not one single telephone call was made. It was the first abdication in British history since Richard II's in 1399.

The couple were married the following June. Wallis wanted the ceremony to take place at the Villa La Croe in Antibes, a large, green-shuttered neo-classical house, built in 1933 by the English newspaper magnate Sir Pomeroy Burton. Winston Churchill later described it as a 'lovely little palace'. This venue was rejected by the new king, George VI, because the Riviera was associated with playboys. The medieval Château de Cande near Tours was regarded as a more dignified environment for the wedding.

Afterwards the couple toured Germany as the Duke and Duchess of Windsor. They were introduced to Goering and visited Hitler. 'She would have made a good Queen,' the Führer pronounced. It was at this time that the former prime minister David Lloyd George, who was celebrating his golden wedding anniversary in Antibes, remarked, 'I have never doubted the fundamental greatness of Hitler as a man. I only wish we had a man of his supreme quality at the head of affairs in our country today. Mussolini is temperamentally an aggressor. I have never thought that Herr Hitler was, and I do not believe it now.'

In the spring of 1938 the Windsors took a ten-year lease on Villa La Croe. It was the best possible setting for a life without purpose.

4

The Duke and Duchess soon set about establishing their court on the Côte d'Azur. As King George VI had observed, the Riviera was hardly a byword for rectitude, but when Wallis had arrived in Cannes in December 1936 she had been widely ignored. 'I hear that in Monte Carlo, all the English and French leave as soon as she walks in,' wrote Queen Maud of Norway. 'I wish something harsh would happen to her.' There was competition, too. Royalty was one thing, ex-royalty quite another. The coast had always attracted monarchs who, for one reason or another, had fallen from grace: the ex-king of Spain, the ex-king of Portugal, the ex-king of Yugoslavia, the ex-king of Egypt and the ex-emperor of Vietnam, Bao Dai. There was even a group in Monaco known as the Society of Royal Bastards, who lived on claims of descent from – among others – the Duke's grandfather. Far from being leader of the field as King of Great Britain, the Duke of Windsor was now an also-ran.

Still, the Windsors retained a certain glamour, had a pleasant villa and kept a good table. The Duke insisted his wife was addressed as Her Royal Highness, although the style had been denied her by George VI. They might have chosen to make friends with Thomas Mann, Aldous Huxley and Lion Feuchtwanger, or the French existentialists Simone de Beauvoir and Jean-Paul Sartre, but instead they hobnobbed with Duff Cooper, then secretary of state for war, and his glamorous wife, Lady Diana, the playwright Noël Coward, the newspaper magnate Lord Beaverbrook, and the singer Maurice Chevalier. There was also the man who, like the Duke himself, had left England because, as he put it, 'To me England has been a country where I had obligations I did not wish to fulfil'. This was Somerset Maugham, who had fled England to avoid sleeping with women, and to pursue another Anglo-American romance.

The novelist and dramatist was by then at the height of his fame. Before the First World War four of his plays were running simultaneously in the West End. In 1915, his autobiographical novel *Of Human Bondage* gave him an international reputation, and he vied with Agatha Christie as the best-selling author of his time. He served as a secret agent in Switzerland and Petrograd, experiences that inspired the novel *Ashenden*. Having survived tuberculosis, he travelled to the South Seas and visited Tahiti; the result was *The Moon and Sixpence*, about an Englishman who abandons the pleasures of marriage and stockbroking to die in a leper's hut. Maugham's own attempt at marriage having failed, he formed an attachment to Gerald Haxton, usually referred to as his 'secretary'.

An American some eighteen years Maugham's junior, Haxton was as boisterous and outgoing as Maugham was reserved and shy. He had been deported from England as an undesirable alien following his arrest in 1915 for gross indecency, and also had weaknesses for gambling and drink. Another of Maugham's *protégés*, Beverley Nichols, wrote, 'He had an aura about him of corruption.' Given the mores of the time and Maugham's wealth, the South of France was the obvious place for the pair to go.

In 1926 Maugham purchased the Villa Mauresque. It was on the tip of Cap Ferrat, the peninsula that divides Villefranche from Beaulieu. The area had been developed as his own private paradise in the *belle époque* by King Leopold II of Belgium, and the Villa Mauresque was built by the Archbishop of Nice at the beginning of the century in the Moorish style. Even by the standards of local architecture it was ugly, so Maugham stripped away the Moorish extravagances and installed a square indoor patio open to the sky. He also added a workroom whose windows faced away from the temptations of the sea. There he set up his own court in the years that led up to the Second World War. Despite Haxton's efforts to gamble away his income at Monte Carlo, Maugham lived in style: he had thirteen servants, a collection of modern art including Laurencin, Toulouse-Lautrec, Matisse, Monet, Rouault, Pissarro, Utrillo and Renoir, and an eclectic guest-list.

Maugham, though, was far from uncritical of Riviera society, and it was he who coined the phrase that it will never live down, 'a sunny place for shady people'. He was sharp, too, about the absence of the work ethic that had been recognised by Smollett more than a hundred and fifty years previously. 'It is easy to be idle on the Riviera,' he wrote in the memoir *Strictly Personal*. 'Especially in summer, what with bathing, conversation, tennis and bridge, and parties, the days were full enough without work.' Maugham had Haxton's gambling stakes and his own lifestyle to support so he continued to write, producing *Cakes and Ale*, a satirical portrait of the novelist Horace Walpole that is often regarded as his masterpiece, *The Razor's Edge* and the short story *The Three Fat Women of Antibes*.

Maugham was not the Riviera's presiding artistic genius, and neither was his creativity particularly associated with the region. Between the wars, though, he was regarded as representative of the coast: rich, louche and perverted. In *Prater Violet*, Christopher Isherwood depicted the Riviera as the natural setting for an implicitly homosexual romance – like Maugham's. 'Love had been J. for the last month – ever since we met at that party. Next week we should go away together. To the South of France perhaps. And it would be wonderful. We would swim. We would lie in the sun. We would take photographs. We would sit in the cafe. We would hold hands, at night, looking out over the sea from the balcony of our room.' For Isherwood, the coast was still a vision of felicity, outside the normal bounds of human behaviour.

5

Leaving aside the matter of the Duchess's styling as a royal highness, other aspects of protocol in the Windsors' life on the Riviera were somewhat ambiguous. The couple had done little to help themselves with their interest in the Fascist regimes, and the American ambassador to Great Britain was aware of this. He was Joseph Kennedy, lover of Hollywood's Gloria Swanson, father of the future President John F. Kennedy, and frequenter of the coast. Playing golf behind the Duke's party one day at Antibes, he made obvious his desire to avoid an encounter. The Duke took public umbrage. His friend and adviser Walter Monckton induced Winston Churchill, among others, to pour oil on the waters.

Churchill was then in the process of relaunching his career as a statesman by rallying those opposed to the British government's appeasement of Hitler. In 1935, while staying at the Château de l'Horizon in Cannes, he had delivered a characteristically trenchant riposte to a Frenchwoman who questioned resisting Italy's invasion of Ethiopia. 'Who is to say what will come of it in a year, or two or three? With Germans arming at breakneck speed, England lost in a pacifist dream, France corrupt and torn by dissension, America remote and indifferent – Madame, my dear lady, do you not tremble for your children?' With the outbreak of civil war in Spain and Hitler's reoccupation of the Rhineland, his words proved prescient. At the end of March 1937 he was staying on Cap Martin, the spit that divides Monaco from Menton. From there he wrote to the Duke of Windsor: 'I paint all day, and as far as my means go, gamble after dark.' As war became a certainty, Churchill both corresponded with and visited the Windsors. He was conciliatory over the ambassador's tactlessness but in January 1938, at the Villa La Croe, he and the Duke had something of a showdown. Vincent Sheean, a fellow guest of Churchill, recorded the scene:

> After a long and stately meal in the white-and-gold dining-room, the Duke of Windsor and Mr Churchill settled down for a prolonged argument, with the rest of the party listening in silence. The Duke had read Mr Churchill's recent articles on Spain, and his recent one in which he appealed for an alliance with Soviet Russia. We sat by the fireplace, Mr Churchill frowning with intentness at the floor in front of him, mincing no words, reminding HRH of the British constitution on occasion – 'When our kings are in conflict with our constitution, we change our Kings,' he said – and declaring flatly that the nation stood in the gravest danger in its long history. The kilted Duke in his Stuart tartan sat on the edge of the sofa, eagerly interrupting when he could, but receiving – in terms of utmost politeness as far as the actual words went – an object lesson in political wisdom and public spirit. The rest of us sat fixed in silence; there was something dreadfully final, irrevocable about the dispute.

On the Riviera, there was trepidation as 1938 slipped into 1939. France was threatened by Germany as she had been in 1914, and the Riviera itself was in immediate proximity to Mussolini's Italy.

On 22 May 1939, Mussolini and Hitler made a formal military alliance, the 'Pact of Steel', and the head of the Luftwaffe, the portly Field Marshal Hermann Goering, was seen observing the annual military parade in Nice – in his voluminous sky-blue uniform, he was difficult to miss. The summer season that year was the hoteliers' best yet, albeit with an underlying mood of hysteria. There were stories of spies being put ashore at Cap Martin and Cap Ferrat, of German military intelligence officers at the Monte Carlo casino. At Cap d'Antibes the writer and critic Cyril Connolly saw placards on trees reading, 'Mort aux Juifs'.

Then, on 23 August 1939, the Molotov–Ribbentrop agreement concluded a non-aggression pact between the Soviet Union and Nazi Germany. That day there was chaos on the coast, and the occupants of hotels and villas in Monaco virtually fled. On 1 September Hitler ordered his armoured divisions into Poland, and Prime Minister Neville Chamberlain realised that appeasement had failed. On 3 September, first Britain then France declared war on Germany.

Major Edward ('Fruity') Metcalfe was in charge of the Windsors' domestic arrangements at La Croe. That day he wrote to his wife in England about the scenes at the villa. It had been proposed that an aircraft should be sent to return the Windsors and their staff to England. Major Metcalfe, having despatched eight of the domestic servants and a secretary from Cannes station, returned to find that the Duke and Duchess had taken offence, as Frances Donaldson recorded in *Edward VIII*.

> Well, anyhow they came in to me after about half an hour and said, 'We are *not* going – the plane is coming for *you* and Miss Arnold tomorrow.' I looked at them as if they really *were* mad – Then they started off. 'I refuse to go *unless* we are invited to stay at Windsor Castle and the invitation and plane are sent personally by my brother etc' – I just sat still, held my head for about 20 minutes and then I started. I said *I'm* going to talk now ... after what I've said you can ask me to leave if you like but you're going to listen now. You *only*

> think of yourselves. You don't realise that there is at this moment a war going on, that women and children are being killed while you talk of your PRIDE. You talk of one of HM Government planes being sent out for Miss Arnold and me!! You are just nuts ... it's too absurd even to discuss. I said a lot more in that strain. They never uttered. After this I said now if this plane *is* sent out to fetch you, which I doubt very much then get in it and be b—y grateful. I went to bed then.

Metcalfe was right. The aircraft did not materialise and the Windsors were obliged to drive to Cherbourg. There, at Churchill's instruction, they were met by the Duke's cousin, Lord Louis Mountbatten, who brought them home on the destroyer he then commanded, HMS *Kelly*.

Those who were obliged to remain saw the coast fall into the hands of the Vichy regime, then the Italians, then the Germans. On 10 September 1943, SS Hauptsturmführer Alois Brunner arrived in Nice. He had been most successful in rounding up Jews in Austria and Greece. Now he established himself at the Hôtel Excelsior, charged with doing the same job on the Riviera. The world had turned upside down, and Paradise had been turned into Hell.

10

The Dark Years

'I will corrupt the countries I occupy.'
Adolf Hitler

1

Although the dogs of war had been unleashed in September 1939, for the next seven months they stayed in their kennel. Britain had an army that amounted to no more than six divisions and, under Neville Chamberlain, little will to fight. The French had a vast conscript force ten times the size of the British, but under Prime Minister Paul Reynaud and his minister of war Edouard Daladier, a similar disinclination for hostilities. Reynaud was notoriously in thrall to his mistress, who disliked the idea of war. Many French servicemen manned the Maginot Line, the great concrete and steel fortification on the border between France and Germany designed to avoid repeating the impasse of the encounters of the western front, and over the winter, the remainder worked with the British Expeditionary Force under Lord Gort to fortify positions on the Franco-Belgian border where the Maginot Line ended. Hitler, who had been as surprised by the speed of his blitzkrieg success in Poland as the declaration of war by France and Britain, contemplated his next move at his leisure. He thought little of the Maginot Line, and supposed that Britain would come to terms. The British called this period the Phoney War, the Germans the *Sitzkrieg*, the sitting war.

Despite the urgency of their departure from the South of France, the Windsors were soon contemplating a return. The Duke took the view that he had been accorded insufficient respect on his arrival in England, and that his brother George VI had been actively hostile to him. At the King's instigation, however, the Duke had been offered a position on the Military Mission to France, in a liaison role between Lord Gort and General Gustave Gamelin, in command of the French forces. This might have been construed as a generous offer to someone who, although enjoying the rank of field marshal by virtue of birth, had had the minimum of military training. Acceptance, though, involved demotion to major general, which the Duke told the war minister Leslie Hore-Belisha, on 16 September 1939, he would prefer to avoid. The minister implied that he could take it or leave it. He took it.

By early October, he and the Duchess were back in France, staying at the Ritz Hotel in Paris, and soon the Duke was inspecting the Maginot Line with Major Metcalfe as his equerry. 'The Duke of Windsor,' Metcalfe summarised, 'has some nebulous job at Gamelin's H.Q.'

Then, on 9 April 1940, German forces rolled into Denmark. The Danes offered no resistance. A month later, on 10 May, Hitler launched an assault in the west, attacking the Low Countries simultaneously with France, surprising the latter by penetrating the supposedly impenetrable Ardennes. That day, Winston Churchill replaced Chamberlain as prime minister. On 16 May the Windsors left for Biarritz, on France's Atlantic coast. Having accompanied the Duchess to her hotel, the Duke returned to the Military Mission in Paris. Heinz Guderian's XIX Panzer division crossed the river Meuse at Sedan, and by the twentieth his forces had reached the Channel. The Duke, accompanied by Metcalfe, continued to visit various sections of the front, as the débâcle became increasingly apparent. Daladier had replaced Gamelin with Weygrand, but the new commander-in-chief fared no better than his predecessor: his counterattack at Arras on 21–23 May failed. With the German Panzer divisions heading for

Paris and the Belgian army capitulating, the Duke left on 28 May for Biarritz. The following day, he and his wife drove to Villa La Croe.

They found the Riviera in a curious limbo. During the First World War, it had been six hundred miles from the trenches of northern France, and some semblance of normality – or what, on the Riviera, passed for normality – had been maintained. Since October 1936, though, the South of France had fallen under the shadow of the Axis established between Rome and Berlin. Although Mussolini had hovered uncertainly on the sidelines of conflict in September 1939, the threat to the Riviera remained: the Italian border at Ventimiglia was scarcely fifteen miles from Nice. In the face of the danger in the north, Gamelin requisitioned the railway rolling stock that might have brought winter tourists to the coast to take troops to the front. The Riviera hotels lost half of their business, the shops selling luxury goods were deserted, the holiday villas shuttered, pleasure boats hauled ashore, foreign visitors largely gone. A blackout was imposed, German civilians were interned, and some modest efforts were made to fortify the coast.

Those, like the Windsors, who could escape when war had been declared did so. There were others for whom such an exodus was difficult or impossible. As the Windsors' friend and dining companion Somerset Maugham pointed out in his memoir of the period, *Strictly Personal*,

> The Riviera isn't only a sunny place for shady people. The people whose pictures you see in the illustrated papers and whose doings the gossip writers tell you of hadn't come this year ... there were invalids ... numbers of elderly persons, retired soldiers, Indian civilians and their wives, who after many years spent in the service of their country had made their home on the Riviera because the climate was mild and the living was cheap. There were a lot of people who had been in commerce or trade ... there were old governesses, teachers of English, chauffeurs, butlers.

This was the rump of the old English colony, which amounted to thirty or forty thousand people at least until the summer of 1939.

Some had no lives or homes to return to in England and remained on the coast during the winter of the Phoney War. The French newspapers were not to be relied upon. As May turned to June they listened to the news broadcast by the BBC in London with increasing trepidation. On 10 June 1940 the Windsors were sitting on the terrace at La Croe, entertaining the singer Maurice Chevalier to lunch. They had hoped, the Duchess wrote, 'that he might be inspired to supply a last flash of lightheartedness in that dismal atmosphere'. As it was, they were toying with the *salade Niçoise* when news was broadcast that Italy had declared war on France and England. The game was up. Chevalier left without finishing his lunch. The Windsors telephoned the British consul in Nice, Major Dodds, for advice. He suggested they join his own party to drive to the Spanish border the following morning. This they did. As they passed through Cannes, the Duchess wrote later, 'I saw in the roadstead two rusty, nondescript cargo ships that had been diverted to pick up the rearguard of the British Riviera colony.' The Windsors crossed into Spain that day, soon to be on their way to the Caribbean. They spent the rest of the war in the Bahamas, where the Duke had been appointed governor.

His former subjects on two cargo vessels, the colliers *Ashcrest* and *Saltersgate*, had a less comfortable time. There were some thirteen hundred of them and the ships were not properly adapted to transport refugees. Somerset Maugham, obliged through force of circumstance rather than penury to take passage on *Saltersgate*, wrote in his memoir of the period:

> The conditions were so strange to most of us that it took a day or two to find our bearings. One lady, when she came aboard, told an officer she wanted to go first class, and another called the steward (there was only one) and asked him to show her where the games deck was. 'It's all over the ship, madam,' he replied. A third, when she discovered that our drinking water came from the ship's pump, remarked with horror that she'd never drunk tap water in her life.

The voyage to England, via Marseille, the Algerian port of Oran, and Gibraltar, took almost three weeks, during which four people lost their minds – 'one,' said Maugham, 'owing to a sudden and enforced deprivation of alcohol'. It was a pathetic end – and end it was – for the English colony on the Côte d'Azur.

2

By the time the refugees had reached England, the French prime minister had resigned. He was replaced on 16 June by a Riviera farmer and vine grower, the First World War hero Marshal Philippe Pétain. At Verdun in 1916 he had famously proclaimed, '*Ils ne passeront pas.*' Now an octogenarian, he entertained no hope of victory, and was soon suing for peace. The armistice with Germany was signed on 22 June 1940 in the same railway carriage in which Germany had been humiliated in November 1918.

The extent of the German advance in the north meant that France was divided into two along a line drawn between Tours and Dijon. The Atlantic coast to the industrial north came under direct Nazi rule. The southern zone, which included the Rhône valley and the Mediterranean coastline, fell under Pétain's puppet government, established on 29 June in the spa town of Vichy. Pétain also retained control of the French fleet, at the time the fourth largest in the world. On 10 July the Third Republic formally gave way to the État Français. Three months later Pétain arranged to meet Hitler at Montoire, and set out his policy for the new France. He made clear that he intended to co-operate with the Nazi regime. In a broadcast to the French people, he declared, 'I enter into the way of collaboration.'

Given the stringencies of Nazi rule, in particular the regime's monstrous attitude towards minorities like Communists, homosexuals, gypsies and Jews, thousands fled south during the summer of 1940 to the Vichy zone. It became known as the Great Exodus and the Riviera was one of its principal beneficiaries. Throughout the autumn, the exiles from the north were welcomed by the proprietors of *pensions*, hotels, theatres, cabarets and cinemas. The winter season at Nice racetrack broke all records. The following spring the casinos reopened. In summer a regional tourism committee was formed to welcome the new visitors. Soon, as well as the northern French, there were almost fifty thousand Jews on the coast. From the Hôtel Roosevelt in Nice, centre of Orthodox Jewry, 'One could see rabbis in their traditional apparel walking through the streets, listen to Talmudic discussions and hear the old tunes of Hebrew prayer and Talmudic study.' A Parisian newspaper described it as '*le ghetto parfumé*'.

The opinions of Paris were echoed in Vichy. Anti-Semitism was an intrinsic part of French life. Well before the Statut des Juifs of June 1941, it had been government policy to persecute Jews. The artist Marc Chagall, who had been granted French citizenship in 1937, was blasé about the threat, despite his Russian-Jewish blood. Varian Frey was head of an organisation called the American Emergency Rescue Committee, established to provide escape routes for prominent Jews. When she arrived in Chagall's hideaway of Gordes, forty miles north of Marseille in the winter of 1940–41, the artist felt her concern for him was excessive. She had brought with her an invitation for him to go to the United States, which was also extended to Picasso, Raoul Dufy, Max Ernst and André Masson. How could he go to America, Chagall asked, a country with which he was relatively unfamiliar? Were there trees or cows there? He changed his mind when he, his wife and daughter were stripped of French citizenship. In April 1941 he moved his family to Marseille in preparation for flight. While they were waiting for their visas, he and his wife were arrested in a round-up at the Hôtel Moderne, and were saved only by Frey's intervention. On 7 May Chagall and his family crossed the border into Spain, thence to Madrid and Lisbon. He and his family set sail for New York on 11 May.

Others were less fortunate. In August 1942 France joined Bulgaria as the only country not under direct German rule to hand over Jews for deportation. Those who had fled south began to fear for their lives in their own land. On 26 August 1942 the French police rounded up six hundred in Nice. They 'surrounded hotels, villas, whole blocks of houses and dragged out of their beds terrified Jews ... the shouts, the wailing and groaning broke the stillness of the morning.' They were sent to Drancy, the notorious transit camp outside Paris, and from there to Auschwitz. In all, close to five thousand Jews were despatched from Nice, few of whom survived.

Three months later, on 8 November 1942, came Operation Torch, the Allied landings in North Africa. Opposition to the invading forces should have come from 120,000 Vichy French troops in Algeria under Admiral Jean Darlan, Pétain's second in command. Darlan, though, was a pragmatist who thought caution the better part of valour: his troops offered only token opposition. 'After the treachery in North Africa,' declared Hitler, 'the reliability of French troops can no longer be guaranteed.' Something had to be done. Operation Anton followed: the Axis occupation of the French southern zone. The port of Toulon was of strategic importance, and more than a hundred battleships, cruisers, destroyers, minesweepers and submarines were based there. On 10 November German forces seized all of southern France with the exception of the eight *départements* east of the Rhône, which fell to four divisions of the Italian 4th Army under General Vercellino. Toulon, though, was left to the 7th Panzer Division, which was ordered to forestall the French fleet's escape or sabotage. Before dawn on 27 November the Panzers moved into the city. Every effort had been made to cut communication links. Nevertheless one duty officer, Lieutenant Commander Paul le Natec, had warned the fleet. As the first German units arrived the ships were already being scuttled. A German battle group commander rushed up to the pier where the cruiser *Algérie* was moored. There in the half light he found her admiral and flag captain.

'We have come to take over your ship,' he said.

'You are a little late,' announced the French admiral. 'It is already sinking.'

'Will it blow up?'

'No.'

'In that case, we will go on board.'

'In *that* case,' replied the Admiral, 'it will blow up.'

The port was in German hands by 8.30 a.m., but by then only twelve vessels were still afloat.

Axis efforts at the eastern end of the coast were similarly muted. General Vercellino's forces went so far as to rename Nice's Avenue de la Victoire Avenue Mussolini, and to ignore the claims of Prince Louis on the neutrality of Monaco. But their views on the Jewish question were less sound: many soldiers were rooted in the coast's community and had relatives there so they were unlikely to impose on them a draconian regime. Angelo Donati, an Italian of Jewish extraction, was actually installed in the Prefecture of Nice. The *carabinieri* protected the city's Jewish monuments and broke up a march of French anti-Semites on a Nice synagogue. The deportations ceased and Italians were even to be seen fraternising with Jews. Donati developed a plan to remove the entire Jewish community to Italy. By February 1943, things had become so bad from the German point of view that Foreign Minister Joachim von Ribbentrop complained personally to Mussolini who, mindful that the Wehrmacht was heavily engaged at Stalingrad, was increasingly sensitive to Allied opinion. Nothing was done.

By now, though, Mussolini's hold on power was fast weakening. Two weeks after the Allied landings in Sicily on 10 July 1943, King Victor Emmanuel dismissed him. The new royalist Italian government, led by Marshal Badoglio, was in secret negotiations with the Allies to change sides. Hitler harboured suspicions about what was going on, and began to make arrangements to supplant the Italians in the south-east of France with the Wehrmacht. He was not the only one thinking ahead. Donati put into action his plans for the evacuation of the Jewish colony. It would take time to transport thirty thousand refugees, and all depended on when the Italian armistice was announced. All too soon, on 8 September 1943, General Eisenhower made the announcement, and a day later the Germans were crossing the Var. On 10 September they arrived in Nice. The German commander installed himself in the Hôtel Atlantic, the navy in the Hôtel Suisse, the Gestapo in the Hermitage. The French Gestapo – the Milice – took the Concordia. SS Hauptsturmführer Alois Brunner installed himself in the Hôtel Excelsior. His victims were trapped.

Working in conjunction with the Milice, Brunner's men set to work and within a few days had picked up more than 150 Jews as they tried to escape. They systematically raided the city's hotels, ten or a dozen each night: anyone suspected of being a Jew, based on their appearance, official papers or even circumcision, was seized. No mercy was shown to the elderly, the infirm, pregnant women or even the blind. They were brought to the Excelsior, relieved of their money and possessions and, in some cases, tortured to reveal the whereabouts of other members of their family. A few days later they were despatched to Drancy. According to one account, 'The road between the sinister hotel-prison Excelsior and the station became a Calvary for the Jewish population of Nice. Two or three times a week the same heart-rending procession takes place, before a silent, tearful crowd held back by a large police contingent.' Brunner knew his job. By the end of the month, a German report noted enthusiastically that 'The city of Nice has lost its ghetto appearance. The Jews no longer circulate. The synagogues are closed. And the Promenade des Anglais offers to Aryan walkers numerous chairs which, up to now, were occupied by Jews.' Up and down the coast, in Hyères, Fréjus, St Raphael, Cannes, Antibes, Nice and Menton, public buildings were hung with the swastika.

Now it was the turn of the Wehrmacht, the Gestapo, the SS and the Milice to enjoy the Riviera's bars, brothels, cinemas and cabarets. Some foreigners living in Nice at the time thought it was all the same to the Niçois. Elizabeth Foster, an elderly American, who lived in the city throughout the war, noted in her journal, 'If one lives on the Riviera it is very hard to believe in the Resurrection of France. I try not to forget that the Riviera is, as someone said of Palm Beach, an atmosphere which "melts the moral marrow".'

In Monaco the situation was much the same. Its Italian community was Fascist, Prince Louis a sympathiser of Pétain. With the coming of the Italians and subsequently the Germans, the principality became a rest and recreation centre for the Axis forces, including the SS and the Gestapo. The latter were accommodated in the Hôtel de Paris, where the management had had the wisdom to wall up a cellar full of its best wines. They indulged themselves at the casino, strutted around the remains of Augustus's monument at La Turbie, and patronised the principality's brothels. Monégasque lawyers and bankers busied themselves providing services for companies profiting from the war. The US State Department took the view that 'Monaco is, to all intents and purposes, belligerent.'

3

Despite the lack of moral fibre that Elizabeth Foster observed on the Côte d'Azur, a resistance movement of some substance existed.

In France resistance was inspired by Charles de Gaulle. The General, appointed under-secretary of state for war to Reynaud during the battle of France, flew to London just before the armistice was signed. There, on 18 June, he broadcast an appeal to those among his compatriots who wanted to continue the fight. The following month, he was officially recognised by the British as leader of the Free French. Vain, arrogant and notably dismissive of the efforts of his hosts in Britain, de Gaulle was nevertheless a moral force to counterbalance the iniquities of the Vichy regime.

It was Napoleon Bonaparte who wrote, 'To live with defeat is to die a little each day.' Such was the bitter experience in France after the fall, and it took time for even the most robust among the French to answer de Gaulle's call. The movement began incidentally and spontaneously, with groups of people at local level jostling the occupying forces in the streets, evading minor regulations and printing clandestine papers. Churchill, schooled in the value of guerrilla resistance by his own experiences in the Boer War, understood the value of these activities. In 1940, the Special Operations Executive (SOE) was formed at his instigation. Intended to 'set Europe ablaze', it sent agents all over occupied Europe to finance, arm and reinforce local resistance.

A Cambridge graduate named Peter Churchill was the first SOE agent sent into the Côte d'Azur, selected because of his fluency in French and his considerable local knowledge – he had holidayed on the Riviera before the war. He knew that a set of steps in a hotel grounds coming up from the beach in the Golfe de la Napoule, west of Cannes, was invisible from the coast road. Early in January 1942 he was ferried out by submarine to within three miles of the spot, canoed ashore and landed safely. He set himself up in a flat in Cannes, made himself popular by patronising one of the local restaurants, Chez Robert, and pursued his calling in a gentlemanly fashion. A rendezvous with one of his contacts, a Madame Rondet, involved 'an excellent loup de mer ... with a dry white wine' in the characteristic setting of 'the vast expanse of the blue Mediterranean, calm and untouched below a cloudless sky'. Later he met an agent called Lise, and married her. It was spying as Ian Fleming imagined it.

Peter Churchill's cavalier style conceals the value of the work that he, his fellow agents, and the local resistance were accomplishing. After the Allied invasion of North Africa, it was expected that Italian troops would replace the Vichy forces on the Côte d'Azur, and the agents developed plans in the summer of 1942 to blow up bridges, roads and tunnels. They were countermanded by London: the absorption of Axis forces into garrisons subduing the local population was thought preferable to their presence on the battlefront. Churchill had to stand by as General Vercellino's forces drove into

Menton in November 1942: 'Below the feathers of the Bersaglieri hats,' he wrote, 'their faces seemed ready enough to break into an answering smile.'

When the Allies landed in Sicily on 10 July 1943, the Côte d'Azur became of strategic significance. The landings showed that the Allies could mount successful amphibian operations, and Hitler anticipated that other attacks would follow. The Channel and Mediterranean coasts of France both offered relatively easy access to Germany. Also, of course, the coast was the corridor to Italy: the railway from Marseille to Menton became one of several routes vital for maintaining supplies to Axis forces that were attempting to contain the Allies as they worked their way up through Italy. The coast became an obvious target for observation, disruption and sabotage.

The Allied offensive was clearly encouraging to the local resistance movement. In many respects the efforts of the Nazis to conscript local labour were even more so. By the middle of 1943 the Wehrmacht was sustaining heavy losses. Although more French bore arms for the Axis than for the Allies during the war, neither France nor Italy was regarded as a suitable source for large numbers of front-line troops. In March 1943 Hitler appointed Fritz Sauckel chief of labour allocation. His strategy was to use the workforce of Nazi-occupied and satellite countries for agricultural and industrial purposes, freeing native Germans for military service. Faced with the stark choice of deportation to Germany – *service du travail obligatoire* – or joining the resistance, many Frenchmen who had hitherto been deaf to General de Gaulle's call to arms were galvanised into action. Tens of thousands took to the open country and the hills to form guerrilla bands or *maquis*. (The term was apparently derived from the name for the scrub on the Mediterranean island of Corsica, long notorious for its bandits.) On the Côte d'Azur, whose mountainous interior was suited to the congregation of *maquis*, companies of about a hundred strong were formed at Cannes, Cagnes, Beaulieu, Cap Martin and in the Esterels.

These groups busied themselves with watching the Germans at

work. The Nazis had established Organisation Todt to construct fortifications, defences and harbours. As the Allied threat grew, it was tasked with constructing the 'Atlantic Wall' from Norway to the Spanish frontier, and the 'Ligurian Wall' between Toulon and Spezia – half-way between Genoa and Pisa. The summer of 1943 was tropical and all along the coast Polish workers, stripped to the waist, laboured over bulldozers and concrete mixers to fortify the beaches and esplanades where once the rich had strolled. Soon everywhere was littered with gun emplacements, tank traps, earth embankments, slit trenches and minefields. The resistance described, mapped and radioed the intelligence to London.

Once the coast had been dressed for invasion, conditions for the local populace were dire. Fresh vegetables had long since disappeared. So, too, had household essentials like string, cooking utensils and shoe polish. Cosmetics were unobtainable. Cigarettes were rationed, and – in an egalitarian gesture – women were allowed none at all. Even wine was rationed, and Marshal Pétain had declared that on three days a week no alcohol should be served in the nation's bars, restaurants and cafés. The essentials of carbohydrate, protein and vitamins were so reduced that nutritional experts stated they were sufficient to sustain human life only if the recipient stayed in bed all day. Some did just that. Fingernails grew brittle and fell off; teeth dropped out of diseased gums. The national loaf, augmented by sawdust and rats' faeces, caused outbreaks of diarrhoea and boils. There was one last refuge of civilisation: the Carlton Hotel on La Croisette in Cannes put up the few remaining rich refugees from the Vichy regime and black marketeers. The latter were known as BOFs because of the goods in which they traded: *beurre*, *oeufs*, *fromage*. By tradition, the hotel offered a special dish at black-market prices. In the winter of 1943–4, this was a portion of plain white beans.

Hitherto, the resistance on the coast had been of an essentially passive nature. By early 1944 the *maquis* in Cannes, led by a charismatic and courageous schoolteacher called Ange-Marie Miniconi, had grown to two hundred. At the end of January it conducted its first successful sabotage operation, damaging the track of the railway at Antéore, fifteen miles west of Cannes. This was the beginning of a concerted operation intended to culminate in the liberation of the coast.

Quite what form liberation would take was not apparent. The original intention of Allied military planners in 1943 was to conduct a simultaneous invasion of France on both the Channel and Mediterranean coasts. 'Hammer', the Channel operation, was intended to crush the occupying Wehrmacht forces in France against its southern counterpart, 'Anvil'. This raised practical problems, the most important being that it would draw troops from the Italian campaign where the American Seventh and British Eighth armies had yet to reach Rome. There were also insufficient landing craft for both operations. In early 1944, the dual operation was abandoned. The Channel strategy was renamed 'Overlord' and set for the early summer. Anvil was postponed by two months, and rechristened 'Dragoon'. The local resistance was to be signalled that the invasion was imminent by one of the personal messages that followed the BBC news bulletin beamed into France – 'Gaby is sleeping on the grass', and 'Nancy has a stiff neck'.

The coast was defended by the German Eleventh Army under the command of General Friedrich Wiese. He had at his disposal in the South of France almost a quarter of a million troops, but a tiny complement of seventy-five ships and 180 aircraft. In early May 1944, his preparations, fortifications and plans had been inspected by Field Marshal Erwin Rommel, Montgomery's antagonist at El Alamein, who expressed himself dissatisfied, and the labours of Organisation Todt were redoubled. The number of permanent fortifications was tripled to 340, more than sixty thousand land and sea mines were laid, and a low-lying area close to the mouth of the Rhône, thought suitable for an Allied airborne landing, was flooded. Areas vulnerable to sea landings were implanted with 'Rommel's asparagus', underwater posts tipped with explosive charges that would detonate on contact. The D-Day landings in Normandy eventually took place on 6 June 1944. By that time the aerial bombardment of the southern coast in preparation for Dragoon had already begun, and by early August appeared to be reaching a climax. With raids on the third, fourth, sixth, seventh and eighth, General Wiese assumed that invasion was imminent. As with the Channel landings for the forces defending the north coast of France, his problem was to guess or discover where it would come.

The Allied invasion force comprised 60,000 troops of the American Seventh Army and the French First Army. The Seventh was led by General Alexander Patch, who had won the first American land victory of the war at Guadalcanal. The Free French had General Jean de Lattre de Tassigny, chief of staff of the Fifth Army during the battle of France. An invasion fleet of 880 vessels from Naples, Oran, Palermo, Sorrento and Malta assembled off Corsica in the first few days of August, and set off for the coast on the eleventh. Spotted by reconnaissance aircraft of the Luftwaffe, its manoeuvres on the thirteenth led Wiese to believe that a two-pronged assault on Genoa and Marseille was planned. On the night of the fourteenth, under cover of darkness, the fleet changed course. That same evening the coded messages were broadcast: 'Gaby is sleeping on the grass'; 'Nancy has a stiff neck'. On the morning of 15 August, an airborne division was dropped eight miles north-west of Fréjus near Le Muy, and the two armies made their way ashore on the forty-five-mile stretch of coast between Cavalaire and Agay – five miles east of St Raphael. That night, the inhabitants of St Tropez were woken by the German occupying forces and evacuated from the port. Then mines laid around the harbours and its buildings were exploded, rendering the port useless to the Allies.

With their overwhelming numbers and detailed intelligence of the defending forces of the Nineteenth Army, the French and Americans experienced relatively little resistance. Winston Churchill observed the landings on the Pampelonne beach near St

Tropez from the American destroyer *Kimberley*: 'As far as I could see,' he wrote, 'not a shot was fired at the approaching flotillas or on the beaches.' Nor was it. By then the opposition had been silenced. The Americans found resistance stiffer on the neighbouring beaches of Agay and Dramont. A unit of French commandos who landed on the Pont de l'Esquillon six miles west of Cannes fared worst. Resistance intelligence suggested the area was free of mines. Hours before their arrival German sappers had laid a new field. Out of a unit of almost seventy, eleven were killed and seventeen badly wounded. The next day, 16 August, General Patch had nevertheless established Seventh Army headquarters in a hotel west of St Tropez. Two days later it was apparent that the Germans had decided to withdraw rather than stage a major resistance or counterattack. By the twentieth the Allies had landed 115,000 personnel at the relatively modest cost of 1966 wounded or killed.

A plan by the Germans to blow up Cannes was thwarted by the resistance. The schoolmaster Ange-Marie Miniconi had been tipped off that the Nineteenth Army under the local commander Colonel Schneider was intending to blow up all the public buildings and the hotels: the *mairie*, the Hôtel de Ville, the Palais de Justice, the records office, the post office and all the great hotels on La Croisette. In the precarious few days between the invasion and the Wehrmacht's withdrawal, Miniconi tracked down the colonel in a bar and – at enormous personal risk – tried to persuade him that such an action would be a pointless and reckless act of destruction. The colonel, swilling his wine in the crowded, smoky little room, listened to him in silence. Early the following morning Miniconi was escorted by German agents to the cellar of the Hôtel Splendide, a drab hotel-cum-brothel close to La Croisette. There in the cellar he found the master detonator for an explosion that would have destroyed much of the old town. Within minutes, he had disarmed it. Cannes was saved.

Hyères was taken by a French battalion on the twenty-first, after relatively heavy fighting. Marseille and Toulon had been fully prepared for defence in response to an order from Hitler dating from March 1944. In Toulon the Wehrmacht's 242nd division held out for a few days, surrendering on 24 August. The 244th division was already besieged in Marseille. There was some savage house-to-house fighting until, on the twenty-seventh, General Schaefer's forces had been pushed back to the dock area. The general realised the situation was hopeless, and the following day he surrendered. To the east, Nice fell with scarcely a struggle. By the end of the month, as the main thrust of Dragoon forced its way up the Route Napoleon towards Grenoble, small bodies of troops, no more than a company, started infiltrating the coast east of Nice. On 3 September 1944, two bemused American marines appeared on the Place d'Armes in Monaco, asking where the hell they were.

For the coast the war was over. It was five years – almost to the day – since Hitler's invasion of Poland and France's declaration of war on Nazi Germany.

PART THREE

11

Après le Déluge

'"Is there any other point to which you would wish to draw my attention?"
"To the curious incident of the dog in the night-time."
"The dog did nothing in the night-time."
"That was the curious incident," remarked Holmes.'

Arthur Conan Doyle, *Silver Blaze*

1

Of the many curious incidents that took place on the Riviera between its foundation by Lord Brougham and its liberation by Allied forces in August 1944, perhaps the oddest was the almost complete absence of the French from the story of their own southern coast. It was after the end of the Second World War that they returned to claim it.

Few natives discover the wonders of their own lands. The Romans discovered Britain and the Spanish – or, if you prefer, the Chinese – the New World; the British saw the potential of the Alps while an Austrian stumbled on Tibet. The familiar can never be wondrous, and it is scarcely surprising that the Provençal peasants of the late eighteenth and early nineteenth centuries were slow to promote the attractions of their home. Although some dewy-eyed early visitors like J. Bunnell Davis, author of *The Ancient and Modern History of Nice*, attributed an Arcadian innocence to the local peasants, Smollett had found them dissolute, idle, superstitious and unclean. By the time Brougham had built the Château Eleonor and established a steady stream of titled guests to Cannes, the locals had been firmly put in their place. When the publisher John Murray issued his definitive *Handbook* to the coast in 1892, he could pronounce that 'The character of the people appears influenced by the fiery sun and soil, which looks as though it never cooled. Their fervid temperament knows no control or moderation; hasty and headstrong in disposition, they are led by very slight religious or political excitement, or sudden impulses, to the committal of acts of violence unknown in the North.'

At the time the British excluded the French from much to do with their own coast. The qualifications for membership of the Riviera club were either blue blood, money, or preferably both. The French were insufficiently rich and, since the revolution, largely shorn of an aristocracy, so did not qualify. The second tier of Riviera immigrants comprised those entrepreneurs who developed the facilities for the British visitors and *hivernants* and were either British or another species of foreigner. Lord Woolfield and his gardener, John Taylor, developed an estate-agency business that operated until the early 1970s. Many of the principal hoteliers were Swiss or Italian. Even the third tier of maids, butlers, postillions and, later, chauffeurs was often British – experience suggested that local domestics helped themselves to the wine and became unduly familiar with their superiors. The running of the golf and tennis clubs was, naturally enough, a British preserve, given French ignorance of either game. The Richmond tea-rooms in Menton were run by a Yorkshirewoman who provided roast beef and Yorkshire pudding for the homesick.

The French, of course, could not be entirely excluded. Someone had to sit in the Préfecture, clean the lavatories, where they existed, and drive the trains. The locals complained, '*Lu estrangie mastegon, lu Nissart panon lu plat.*' (The foreigner chews, the Niçois wipes the dish.) Such nonentities, though, could be roundly treated with the nice degree of patronage and condescension shown by the *Menton and Monte Carlo News* when it talked of 'our Gallic friends', a commonplace phrase among the English colonists. Even a Francophile, like the British secret agent Peter Churchill, found the pretensions of the locals risible: 'The French are, to an objective observer,' he wrote, after the Second World War, 'a vain race. Their innate courtesy to strangers influences them to conceal as much as possible their conviction that French art, industry, literature, language, scenery, cities and villages – and womenfolk – are the finest on earth.' So extreme was the exclusion of the French that some have even concluded that they were subjected in the coast's heyday to a form of tacit apartheid: the French should know their place, which might be in Paris or Lyon but certainly not on the Côte d'Azur. The art historian Lord Clark recalled in his memoirs a French visitor who installed himself in one of the *belle-époque* hotels in Menton dedicated to an English clientele. He was regarded as an eccentric and referred to slightingly as 'the Frenchman'.

French artists and Bohemians had started to resist this sort of thinking at the turn of the century with the establishment of the artists' colony at St Tropez that revolved around Paul Signac, then Cocteau's homosexual circle at Villefranche in the 1920s. In the 1930s the writer Colette, creator of the socialite Chéri, came to St Tropez. It took the war, though, to flatten the social structures of the coast that had emasculated the French, and to present the French with the opportunity to develop their own backyard. They were led by men like Prince Rainier of Monaco, Jean Médecin ('le Roi Jean'), the mayor of Nice, and his son Jacques, who succeeded him as mayor. There were women, too, of course, most spectacularly Brigitte.

The liberation that followed the Allied landings of August 1944 did not see the re-creation of the south of France as a land of milk and honey overnight. First, there was the '*épuration*', or purge, when the French avenged themselves on their tormentors. As so many of the oppressors had been their own fellow-citizens, they had ample scope. *L'épuration* was six months of national blood-letting that –

according to apologists for the Vichy regime – saw more than 100,000 people killed. Most were executed without trial, some forced to dig their own graves. Minor offenders lost their jobs. Women who were supposed to have consorted with the Germans – 'horizontal collaborators' – had their heads shaved, and their faces daubed with swastikas.

Then attention turned to the economy. After the years of Nazi occupation, it was in ruins: factories, blast furnaces, farms and commerce had been ravaged. Across France, half a million homes had been destroyed, two million damaged. The transport infrastructure, particularly the railway system, had virtually collapsed. In its absence neither home nor factory could be fuelled. As late as March 1945 France's minister of production declared, 'We are still in the stage of emergency repairs.' In the Alpes Maritimes, which had suffered the consequences of the Allied invasion, 14,000 buildings had been damaged or completely destroyed, 130 bridges were down. 'In a year,' wrote one journalist of the Promenade des Anglais in a local newspaper, 'the German barbarians have managed to transform this magnificent vista into a twisted scrap heap of iron and stone.'

Several hundred Germans had been captured during the invasion and had yet to be repatriated. They were set to work rebuilding Nice, removing the 43,000 mines they had planted, and clearing military emplacements up and down the coast. St Tropez faced similar problems: much of the port and the picturesque seventeenth- and eighteenth-century harbour buildings had been destroyed by German mines on the night of the Allied invasion. The novelist Colette assembled a committee to ensure that the port was rebuilt in the traditional style. The coast's reputation was such that it had been designated a rest-and-recreation zone for Allied troops. Now, Nice was allotted to enlisted men, Juan-les-Pins to the Red Cross, women and nurses, Cannes to officers. The Riviera command was given the *belle-époque* Hôtel Negresco on the Promenade des Anglais. The Colombe d'Or *auberge* in St Paul de Vence – where Scott Fitzgerald

At the height of the Abdication Crisis in December 1936, Mrs Simpson fled to Cannes to avoid the attentions of the press. She failed.

Left: The strength of the dollar against the franc and the philistinism of post-war America drew American bohemians and intellectuals to the coast in the roaring twenties. F. Scott Fitzgerald, pictured with his wife, Zelda, wrote one of the best novels about the coast, *Tender is the Night*.

Below: By the early thirties the summer season had firmly established itself on the coast, observers noting various advantages in taking most of one's clothes off in public.

Above: The Monaco Grand Prix, inaugurated to associate the principality with glamour, ensured that it received a major annual dose of publicity.

Right: Leader of the homosexual artistic circle in Villefranche, Jean Cocteau sought inspiration, summer sun and *matelots* on the coast in the years before the war. Here he appears at the London premiere of his ballet set on the Riviera, *Le Train Bleu*.

During the Second World War the Riviera fell successively to Vichy, Italian and German control, was largely stripped of its Jewish population and was invaded by the Allies on 15 August 1944. Here the Wehrmacht enjoys the Promenade des Anglais.

During the occupation of the coast, some of the local women became horizontal collaborators, while others joined the Resistance. These are members of the Marseille *Maquis*.

The Wehrmacht withdrew from the coast after the Allied invasion without putting up much of a fight. Although wreckage still littered Nice waterfront in November 1944, the cathedral stands untouched.

After the war, the Riveria's aficionados soon returned to the coast. With Picasso, Matisse and Chagall all settling there, it was called the new Montparnasse. The Spanish genius accepted his celebrity status without reluctance; so too Jean Cocteau.

Right: Brigitte Bardot made her name at the new Cannes Film Festival by taking off (most of) her clothes, then starred in her husband Roger Vadim's *Et Dieu Créa la Femme.* Set in St Tropez, it made the small port at the unfashionable western end of the Riviera one of the most famous villages on earth.

Below: On 13 May 1971 the world's most fashionable couple, Mick and Bianca Jagger, were married in St Tropez. Bride and groom were locked out of the church, and Keith Richards, in Nazi regalia, drank himself into a stupor.

On 14 September 1982, the death of Princess Grace, following a car crash in the Monaco principality, seemed to signal the end of the story of the earthly paradise that early visitors had seen on the Riviera. At the funeral Prince Rainier is supported by his children Princess Caroline and Prince Albert.

had encountered Isadora Duncan – was reserved for generals. Monaco, regarded by the Allies as a former belligerent, was allocated 12,000 enlisted men. Prince Louis made himself unpopular by saying that it would accept only 1200 officers, but the Americans refused to compromise, and put the principality out of bounds. Bomb-disposal experts eventually removed more than six hundred mines that had been laid on the approaches to the harbour.

Many of the troops visiting the coast were from the United States. The American GIs were issued with *A Pocket Guide to the Cities of Southern France*. 'So far as your military duties permit, see as much as you can. You've got a great chance to do now, major expenses paid, what would cost you a lot of your own money after the war. Take advantage of it.' They did. Prostitutes from Marseille, Toulouse and even from Paris flocked to the area. 'The streets of Nice are not safe at night,' complained the *Aurore* in May 1945. One GI was told by an innkeeper that Germans who had fled his café during a resistance attack returned the following day to settle the bill. 'The Yanks ... would have grabbed a few bottles and tried to screw the barmaid on the way out.'

Gradually, the coast seemed to be getting back to normal. As early as November 1944 the *syndicat d'initiative* in Cannes was able to assure potential visitors that 'All equipment which made Cannes the chief port of call on the Riviera is now entirely in as good an order as the pre-war period.' Soon the English-language *Menton and Monte Carlo News* had resumed publication. The removal of emplacements and munitions continued, and some of the Riviera's visitors returned. Somerset Maugham, with a new 'secretary', repaired the Villa Mauresque, halved the size of the garden and his staff, and started writing again.

The Windsors returned to the Villa La Croe in the spring of 1946. Italian troops had been quartered in the garage, some paintings had been looted, the garden and its coastal frontage had been laid with mines; otherwise it was much as they had left it. The Blue Train made a welcome return, a powerful symbol of the resumption of normality. 'The Blue Train is waiting,' wrote Charles Graves in *The Riviera Revisited*, 'with a six-course dinner of clear soup, red mullet, pâté with truffles, *chouxfleur aux gratin*, cheese, fruit and coffee.'

2

The coast also welcomed back one of its favourite sons: Pablo Picasso. The Spanish artist had first visited the coast in the summer of 1920, when he was thirty-nine. When he was still in Paris, he had been inspired to paint an imaginary scene of a perfect coastal setting: rocks, pine trees, a beach, pure blue sea, and a brilliant sun. When he arrived in Juan-les-Pins with his mistress, the Russian ballerina Olga Koklova, he was astonished to walk into his own painting. 'I'm not trying to make anyone believe I have second sight,' he remarked of the experience, 'but everything was there, just as it had been in the picture I painted in Paris. I was absolutely amazed. And it was then that I grasped that this landscape was my own.' In the 1920s and 1930s Picasso spent several summers on the coast, mainly in Juan-les-Pins and Golfe-Juan. Inspired both by the extraordinary light and his proximity to the remnants of classical civilisation, he produced a body of work there that compares with his best. Landscapes and beach scenes were obvious enough, but he also executed some exquisite drawings of mythological subjects, and paintings of colossal women, great sculptural nudes painted with a voluptuous delight for the female form. The last painting he completed before the outbreak of war was the sombre *Pêche de nuit à Antibes*, a gloomy metaphor for the forthcoming struggle: fishermen overshadowed by the old Grimaldi castle.

After the war in the early autumn of 1945, Picasso returned to the coast as soon as he could procure the petrol he needed for the drive. He visited Golfe-Juan and Cap d'Antibes. In the summer of 1946, he returned to Golfe-Juan. The Grimaldi castle was being used as a museum, and he was offered the top floor as a studio. Neither paper nor canvas was available, so he was forced to paint on plywood and even fibro-cement, to use house painters' brushes, and paint intended for boats. However, he discovered he had an inexhaustible supply of energy, and enjoyed a period of huge fertility. Perhaps the best of the paintings was *La Joie de vivre*. The maritime novelist Patrick O'Brian, one of Picasso's biographers, wrote, 'Among blue hills, with black to enhance them, goats with smiling human faces dance on a golden ground, with the piping of a centaur and an ambiguous blue creature that has climbed on to a purple eminence, while a sort of femme-fleur capers in the middle with the sun caught in her hair and a boat sails by on the high blue sea.' According to O'Brian, those months were possibly the happiest of Picasso's life.

Although Picasso returned to Paris for the winter, he visited Golfe-Juan regularly for the next few years. In 1948 he bought a small and notably ugly villa called La Galloise in Vallauris, two miles inland from Golfe-Juan. The following summer he acquired a disused scent factory in the immediate neighbourhood, and turned it into a studio. There, he carved, modelled and created structures out of junk.

Marc Chagall returned to the Côte d'Azur in 1949, like Picasso with boundless energy. He had found a home at St Jean, in the lee of Maugham's Cap Ferrat. His lover Virginia Haggard recorded:

> St Jean was still only a village when we went there in 1949 and our Pension de Famille, a yellow stucco home with a stairway leading sideways up to the door was a modest place: cool tiled floors and iron bedsteads, big white tables covered with fruit and flowers like a Bonnard painting. The children went to the peninsula and came back with sprigs of olive and mimosa ... these were memorable days, amongst our happiest. Marc settled down in a small bedroom overlooking the sea and brought out pots of gouache and sheets of paper. I have seldom seen him more euphoric. He set to work excitedly to render the dazzling visions that were taking shape in his mind. A

> store of treasures was suddenly released from his memory at the sight of the sea and palm trees, and came pouring out in sumptuous array. Never before had he worked his gouaches so richly.

Among the masterpieces he painted during this time were *The Fishes of St Jean* and *St Jean Cap Ferrat*. In 1950 he moved to the medieval hill town of Vence, where he stayed for the remainder of his long life.

Picasso celebrated his seventieth birthday in Vallauris in October 1951, by which time he had become a fixture on the coast – indeed, one of its many attractions. By now, though, it was apparent that fame, every bit as corrosive as power, had him in its thrall. One day he told his liveried chauffeur to drive him to St Jean. He encountered Chagall on the beach. Petrol was still rationed. 'How do you manage to get so much petrol for that great car?' Chagall asked. 'There are oceans of petrol for those who can afford it,' Picasso replied.

In addition to the villa at Vallauris, some friends of Picasso had rented a house in St Tropez for his use. One summer's morning when Picasso was there with his *maîtresse de la jour*, Geneviève Laporte, they were accosted by a young Austrian painter who asked the master to cast an eye over his work. The Austrian was clutching a bouquet of gladioli.

'Why the flowers?' asked Picasso.

'To paint them,' was the reply. 'They smell pleasant.'

'Are you married?'

'Yes.'

'Then bring me your wife and I will —— her. After that you can smell my —— and see if it is not better than your flowers.'

Patrick O'Brian commented that, by then, Picasso 'looked on few as completely human. Those who were unwilling to accept this view were compelled to do so.'

Another aspect of the return to normality was the inauguration of the Cannes film festival. 'The one vital art of the century', Evelyn

Waugh had called it. '*La photographie c'est la vérité: le cinéma la vérité vingt-quatre fois per seconde*,' claimed Jean-Luc Godard. 'The cinema,' announced Marcel Camus, 'has replaced the church, and people seek truth at the movies instead of at the Mass.' The coast's status as a cradle or the arts, and the quality and persistency of light that it shared with Hollywood, meant that the cinema and the Riviera were natural bedfellows. The Victorine studios has been established in Nice as early as 1911, and by 1927 thirty films had been shot from there under the auspices of the producer Rex Ingram – who had made his name by shooting Rudolph Valentino in *The Four Horsemen of the Apocalypse*.The future looked promising, but Nice was a city without conviction or work ethic: the stars of the day, Charlie Chaplin, Douglas Fairbanks, Mary Pickford and the Marx brothers, were happy enough to holiday on the coast but they worked elsewhere.

The Venice Film Festival had been inaugurated in 1932 by Mussolini, and had bolstered the city's then ailing tourist industry. French films, as Peter Churchill had suggested, were among the best, so it was a puzzle that they were overlooked by the judges mulling over the screenings at Florian's in St Mark's Square. It transpired later that only the Fascist productions of Italy and Nazi Germany were allowed to win. An alternative festival was needed to showcase French cinematic genius, and where better to hold it than on the French Riviera?

The intention was that the Cannes Film Festival should be inaugurated in September 1939. It would be graced by Norma Shearer (star of *Marie Antoinette*, and Irving Thalberg's wife) and Mae West (star of *Diamond Lil*, *I'm no Angel*, *My Little Chickadee*, and for a time the best-paid woman in the USA). The pair and their entourage duly boarded the liner *Normandie* in New York, and arrived on the Côte d'Azur just as Britain and France declared war on Germany. They re-embarked and returned to the US.

In September 1946 France's first film festival and post-war cultural event was launched at the Cannes casino, with films from various countries. The Americans were notable by their absence. The British – perhaps defensive about their own entry – sent aircraft-carrier *Colossus* to lend dignity to the scene, and the newly appointed British ambassador in Paris, Duff Cooper. The evergreen Jean Cocteau, now fifty-seven and still chasing boys, was among the festival's other leading lights. In 1947, there were entries from the USA, Russia, Poland, Argentina, Brazil, Bulgaria, Hungary, Mexico, Luxembourg and, of course, France. The French star Michèle Morgan was tactfully deemed Best Actress. There was no festival in 1948 – because, curiously, Hollywood claimed it had nothing suitable to screen. This provided the festival organisers with the opportunity to demolish the splendid old Cercle Nautique, erstwhile haunt of the Prince of Wales and Mrs Keppel, and to replace it with the Festival Palace, which was opened in 1949. That year the Best Film award went to Orson Welles's masterpiece, *The Third Man*.

The Cannes Film Festival had arrived, and was on its way to supplanting Venice as the doyenne of such extravaganzas.

3

Despite these successes, the clock on the coast could not simply be turned back to 1939. In 1942 Roosevelt's vice-president, Henry Wallace, had remarked, 'The century on which we are entering – the century which will come out of the war – can be and must be the century of the common man.' Desirable or not, this was certainly prescient. At first the coast welcomed its returning exiles – the Windsors, Picasso and Somerset Maugham – but then – briefly – it became a haven for the hard-faced Englishmen who had done well out of the war. Travel and currency restrictions had been imposed by Sir Stafford Cripps, chancellor in Clement Attlee's Labour government, which meant that the Côte d'Azur was beyond the means of those who had fought for their country. Nöel Coward, an occasional guest of the Windsors at La Croe before the war, returned in August 1946. 'The English people are beyond belief,' he wrote in his diary. 'They must all be black-market profiteers. Most of them are Cockney Jews.' Finally, at the end of the decade, the French working classes returned, partly as a result of the general democratisation brought about by the war, partly as a consequence of two forms of transport whose impact on the Riviera was just as profound as the railway.

Despite pre-war enterprises like the Monte Carlo Rally and the Grand Prix, the motor-car had yet to make a serious impact on the coast. In his 1928 guide to the coast Douglas Goldring attributed the problem with cars on the Riviera to little more than the nature of the roads and that the engines weren't properly silenced. At much the same time the Riviera photographer Jacques-Henri Lartigue could write, 'Having a motor car in this landscape is magical. The drive to Cannes, along the narrow deserted little road which follows the coastline via Golfe-Juan, is wonderful.' Between 1929 and 1938, the number of cars on French roads rose from 930,000 to just over 1.8 million – about a tenth of today's number. After 1945 the French economy recovered relatively rapidly, and one manifestation of prosperity was the popularity of the French equivalent to the German Volkswagen: the Renault 2CV. Motoring, hitherto effectively restricted in France as elsewhere to the middle and upper classes, was within the aspirations of just about everyone. Lartigue deplored the development on aesthetic grounds: before the war, he remembered, 'it was very amusing because each person had his special car made to his taste and each was different to the others. Today they all look like wheelbarrows.' When petrol was no longer rationed, motorists – mainly from France – flooded into the Riviera. By August 1953, 26,000 vehicles a day were crossing the Var – 200,000 a week, or a million a month. At one time the road had been the agent of civilisation. Now it seemed rather the reverse.

Before the war air travel had been as exclusive as motor transport had been at the turn of the century. It was extremely expensive – it cost around a thousand pounds to cross the Atlantic at a time when a small saloon car could be bought for a hundred. During the war military airstrips had been laid out all over Europe, and its aftermath saw a surplus of aircraft, some of which were turned into civilian airliners. The Lancastrian was a civilian version of the famous Lancaster bomber. The American DC3 and German Junkers JU-52 transports were similarly modified. The foundations for mass-market air travel were in place. Before the war Nice had a grass strip running along a stretch of the Var close to the western extremity of the Promenade des Anglais. The runway was extended and paved by the Allies a few weeks after liberation. On 12 June 1945 a service between Paris and Nice was inaugurated. It cost 2200 francs, less than twice the cost of the train, and the journey, five hours, took a quarter of the time. By the following year half a dozen flights came in every day, most originating within France. By 1950, the airport was handling almost a quarter of a million passengers each year.

By *belle-époque* standards, when fifty thousand visitors came in a good year, these figures were astounding. Even beside pre-war figures they were impressive. As early as 1947 numbers of visitors to the coast equalled its pre-war record. But the coast's hoteliers, as professionally pessimistic as farmers, shook their heads. It was not the numbers that worried them but the fact that by 1952 almost three-quarters of Nice's guests stayed in the most modest hotels – one or two stars by the now internationally recognised designation. A new class of visitor – French or otherwise – required a different sort of accommodation, and the coast had to adapt if it was to survive as a major holiday resort.

One of the first properties to be divided into apartments was Lord Brougham's Villa Eleonor. It was followed by Lord Cheylesmore's Villa St Priest, Lady Trent's Springlands, Prince Karageorgevick's Villa Fiorentina. The estates in which they stood were broken up into smaller units. Some of the great hotels suffered a similar fate. *Belle-époque* edifices with their monstrous public rooms and suites the size of tennis courts were ill-fitted to the democratic age. Nice's

Hôtel Splendid was demolished, more than half of the grounds in which it stood were sold, and an eight-storey block erected in its stead. Each room was supplied with a private bath, balcony and air-conditioning. Hair-dryers and sachets of shampoo soon followed. In the absence of urban planning, with local mayors controlling building permits (and taking bribes for doing so), there was a post-war property boom. In Antibes alone four hundred villas were built between liberation and 1950 – neither of a scale nor in a style that would have gratified Lord Brougham. Some were built as apartment blocks, to be let to visitors who – astonishingly – were capable of cooking for themselves. Most shocking of all was the provision of facilities for those who did not require a roof over their heads.

The Camping Club of Great Britain had been founded in 1907, with Robert Falcon Scott as its first president. After the First World War Sir Robert Baden-Powell, the founder of the Boy Scout movement, took over. Under his auspices, camping organisations sprang up all over western Europe. In 1932, this culminated in the establishment of the Fédération Internationale de Camping and Caravanning. At first the idea appealed to outdoor types, like Scott himself, and youthful adventurers, but immediately after the war, in the pinched economic circumstances of the time, it became an acceptable and indeed commonplace holiday for ordinary French families. Camping – cheap, Spartan, and free of social pretension – was the vogue in the early 1950s. By 1953 there were more than seven thousand campsites on the Riviera.

In the eyes of the local hoteliers, not only did these people litter the place with their 2CVs and their scrofulous infants, they spent scarcely any money. They also lowered the tone of the coast. It was the *congés payés* all over again, only worse. In *Royal Riviera*, Charles Graves wrote: 'French socialites claim that Cannes, Monte Carlo and other royal playgrounds are socially unsupportable in July and August. Certainly the growth of "camping", the transformation of villas into boarding houses and the nose-to-tail procession of motor-coaches, with all that connotes, from one end of the Corniche to the other, has popularised the Riviera in the most literal sense of the word.' A local fisherman, of a class – at least in France – ever sensitive to social nuance, put it even better: 'I even saw a tourist eating an aubergine *raw* in the street. Like a cannibal.' What would Lord Brougham have thought? Or given that he was dead, the Windsors? Before the war the coast had been the setting for their romance, their refuge from an England that had rejected them, and the perfect backdrop for two lives devoted to self-indulgence. The Windsors cultivated the new social landscape of the Riviera for two years. In 1949 they abandoned it. 'They were very fond of this house [La Croe],' wrote the Duke's biographer Frances Donaldson, 'but they found the Riviera too much changed.'

Some of this was down to snobbery and deserves no serious consideration other than as a sign of the times. Yet as the impact of large numbers of tourists on the coast became increasingly apparent, some more thoughtful analysis was made. The French historian and economist André Siegfried, a member of the Académie Française, gave a lecture on it in 1954. He objected less to tourism as such than to 'organised tourism, a mass-produced tourism which has become one of the most marked aspects of our century'. He saw it as a manifestation of the mechanisation of modern life, in which the adventure, individuality and imaginative stimulation of 'tourism's heroic age' had given way to the gods of efficiency. This was the packaging and emasculation of travel later to be satirised in Mel Stuart's film *If it's Tuesday, this must be Belgium*, in which a group of American innocents abroad reduce to a week the three-year Grand Tour of foreign places, customs, values, food and sex.

By no stretch of the imagination was this sort of experience the paradisal existence that Smollett had discovered two hundred years previously. Nor was it the deliverance that travellers only forty years earlier had experienced on drawing up the blind in the Blue Train.

12

Et Dieu Créa la Femme

'I married beneath me, all women do.'
Nancy Astor

1

In 1950, Rainier Louis Henri Maxence Bertrand de Grimaldi, otherwise His Serene Highness Prince Rainier III, acceded to the throne of Monaco. Born in 1923, he was educated at Stowe, in England, where he was persecuted for being the only foreigner and nicknamed 'Fatty Monaco'. When war broke out he was seventeen. He pursued his studies in Montpellier and Paris under the Vichy regime, which his father, Prince Louis, supported. In September 1944 he enlisted with de Gaulle's Free French forces, and saw action against the Nazis, eventually ending up as a colonel. After the war he returned to Monaco to live the life of a wealthy playboy, epitomising much of what defined the coast: the unbridled pursuit of pleasure. He dabbled in deep-sea diving, with fast cars, speedboats and the *gamine* French actress Gisèle Pascal. In short, as the beneficiary of a Monaco civil list income, he was spoilt. As Robert Lacey, one of Grace Kelly's biographers, put it, 'If there is anything more perverse and bloody-minded than a long-time bachelor, it is a royal bachelor.'

The death of his father and the dawning of the new decade impressed upon the young prince the necessity of embracing certain responsibilities, such as his principality. Transformed almost at a stroke by François Blanc's creation of Monte Carlo in the 1860s, the golden years had run on until the First World War. The disappearance of the Russians had threatened its existence in the early 1920s, but it had been rescued by the acumen and wizardry of the arms-dealer Basil Zaharoff. Then, in 1934, its monopoly of gambling on the coast had been broken by the legalisation of roulette in France, when Nice and Cannes established themselves as competitors in fleecing the rich. At much the same time the similar monopoly that Monaco had enjoyed as a base for the best professional courtesans was broken by the spread of mass amorality. Premarital sex and open marriages were hitherto something the upper classes had kept to themselves. Now all and sundry joined in. 'The professional,' noted a social historian of the Côte d'Azur disapprovingly, 'had been killed off by the amateur.' Once the Gestapo and the American GIs had disappeared after the war, Monaco and Prince Louis were obliged to look to their *belle-époque* laurels. The resort lacked the beaches that had been the making of Juan-les-Pins and the rest of the summer coast. The india-rubber bathing beach experiment, noted by Evelyn Waugh on his visit in 1929, had been a failure, and the principality seemed to have lost the cachet, glamour and *chic* that had once made it a draw for Queen Victoria's eldest son. When Prince Louis died the annual number of visitors had fallen to a quarter of pre-war levels, and the takings of the casino were just a tenth of those of the *belle époque*. Monaco and its new ruler were facing ruin.

It was widely believed, though, that Monaco confronted not merely penury but annihilation. One of the conditions on which the principality – an anomaly in an age of powers and super-powers – had been allowed to survive into the twentieth century as a French protectorate was that the Quai d'Orsay – the French Whitehall – should approve any marriage contracted by the prince on the grounds that it would affect the succession. It was also set out in the Franco-Monégasque agreement of 1918 that Monaco's autonomous status would be retained if the throne fell vacant in the absence of a successor. It was widely believed nevertheless that in the event of a prince dying without issue, Monaco would revert to France. People pointed to the story of Prince Louis himself, who had had an affair in Algiers with the daughter of his washerwoman. The child, born in 1898, was known as Princess Charlotte. There were lessons there for all. Accordingly, a male heir was the one desire of all right-thinking Monégasques. Given the divergent tax regimes of France and Monaco, this was understandable. Those in Monaco paid little; those in France's post-war Fourth Republic paid a great deal.

In 1952, as the Korean war continued to beset the real world, the dazzling figure of Aristotle Socrates Onassis appeared in Monaco. Born in 1900 to a Greek tobacco importer, he had shown little application at school. 'Great scholars do not make good businessmen,' his father supposedly commented, 'and are seldom rich.' In 1922 the young Onassis fled Smyrna after the Turkish defeat of Greek forces. He took ship from Naples for Argentina. 'That's when I first saw Monte Carlo,' he later claimed, 'from the deck of an immigrant ship taking me to a new life.' He ended up in Buenos Aires with sixty dollars to his name. There he made a fortune in his father's trade and, in the depths of the depression, began his career as a ship-owner. By the early 1950s he had created one of the world's largest independent merchant fleets and, with his super-tankers, had become a very wealthy man. He was the embodiment of the word 'tycoon', with all that that meant in terms of wealth, self-importance, power, whimsicality and excess. As for his home, he didn't want to live in Greece, which he considered *déclassé*: Monaco, at least by tradition, was a fitting location for the immensely – some might say newly – rich. The principality was also well placed for his shipping interests in Genoa, Marseille, Athens and London.

At first, following in the wake of J. P. Morgan and *Corsair*, Onassis settled his yacht *Christina* in the principality's harbour. A converted 320-foot Canadian frigate, she boasted a circular staircase with gold- and onyx-plated banisters, a swimming-pool that could be transformed into a dance-floor, a pink marble bathroom, solid gold hairbrushes, a cocktail bar with whales' tooth handles as hand-holds for the seasick, nine double staterooms, a dining room for twenty, and a crew of thirty including ten stewards. 'I don't think there is a man or woman on earth who would not be seduced by the sheer shameless narcissism of this boat,' commented the actor Richard Burton. Onassis replied, 'I've found that to be so.' There, he held parties that, according to the Hollywood mogul Darryl Zanuck, 'were as compulsive as Gatsby's'.

Onassis, though, craved more. In 1952 and early 1953, he gradually acquired a substantial holding of shares in Monaco's Société des Bains de Mer. By no means a gambler – in that sense – Onassis had his eye on the company's property, which included the casino, the yacht club, the *belle-époque* Hôtel de Paris, and about a third of the principality's 375 acres of land. At the annual general meeting in the summer of 1953 he effectively took control of the SBM. Within a week, his staff had set up the corporate headquarters of Onassis's Olympic Maritime in the old Winter Sporting Club in the Avenue d'Ostende. His purchase had given him rather more than a company. Once he had been just another rich Greek shipping magnate. Now, as the press kept saying, he was nothing less than the 'uncrowned King of Monte Carlo'. Like Basil Zaharoff before him, the poor boy from Smyrna thought this was a prize infinitely worth having.

Despite the gibes about the 'uncrowned King', Prince Rainier regarded Onassis as a source of new blood, new money and new life. Given the royal veto that existed over Société des Bains de Mer policy, the Greek could be supplanted if necessary. In the meantime, his skills and contacts seemed likely to be useful. It was true that 'Ari' was short, Greek, ugly, bumptious, ostentatious and painfully *arriviste* – certainly to the scion of the oldest ruling family in Europe – but one had to be practical. 'If he had not been quite so useful,' one of the prince's equerries commented, 'Onassis might have been the perfect person for the prince to cut dead.'

Perhaps not unreasonably, Onassis assumed that in acquiring a controlling share of the SBM he was acquiring precisely the same of the principality, and that he had become its *de facto* chancellor of the exchequer. If the corollary of this was that the prince assumed Onassis would restrict himself only to the narrowest definition of Monaco's business interests, he was wrong. By the time Rainier celebrated his thirtieth birthday, Onassis was already mulling over the delicate matter of the prince's heir. From Onassis's point of view, Monaco was badly in need of the stability provided by an heir and an infusion of chic in the form of a glamorous wife for the Prince; and he was prepared to procure her himself. 'A prince and movie queen,' he mused. 'It's pure fantasy . . .' But fantasy, as Onassis was sufficiently astute to appreciate, was the essence of Monaco in much the same way as it was of Las Vegas. The only question was, which actress?

Onassis, at the time married to Athina, daughter of fellow Greek shipping magnate Stavros Niarchos, took the general view of tycoons towards young women: most were at his beck and call and that all had their price. A number of leading ladies caught his eye. There were three, though, who seemed particularly alluring. The pouting adolescent Brigitte Bardot had featured on the cover of *Elle* in 1953 and subsequently celebrated her film début in *Le Trou Normand*. She was pretty, but French. Norma Jean Mortenson was now known as Marilyn Monroe, the empty-headed blonde idol of middle America, and the star of *Gentlemen Prefer Blondes*. For Monaco she would reopen the American market. So, too, would the pristine, sophisticated Grace Kelly, who had just made her name playing opposite Gary Cooper in *High Noon*. Onassis, without reference to Rainier, approached Monroe, perhaps because she had also just starred in *How to Marry a Millionaire*. She was nearing the zenith of her career as an international sex symbol, and her marriage to the baseball star Joe DiMaggio was collapsing. She was in the right state of mind to view the prospect of Rainier with some enthusiasm. Like the majority of Americans she had no idea where Monaco was, but she thought she was up to the job. 'Is he rich? Is he handsome? Give me two days alone with him and of course he'll want to marry me.'

There, for the present, the matter rested.

2

While Monaco found itself in limbo St Tropez, at the other end of the Riviera, was nearing seventh heaven. The harbour and its buildings, badly damaged by the Wehrmacht on the eve of the American-French invasion of August 1944, had been largely restored under the direction of Colette's committee. The result, by comparison with an increasingly urbanised eastern Riviera, was a community that still bore the appearances of the fishing-village it had once been. 'The streets,' according to one post-war account, 'are narrow, medieval and Spanish-looking, with high green shutters and old white-haired women in black sitting mending fishermen's nets.' There were also the beaches: while the port itself had next to nothing by way of sand, the whole of the peninsula – as the Allies had discovered when planning the invasion of August 1944 – was ringed with it from the Plage des Graniers just east of the town, right round to the Plage de la Briande – via Tahiti and the five-kilometre Pampelonne. For the French, there was no shivering behind windbreaks licking vanilla ice-cream in a light drizzle, applying embrocation as sun-tan oil and wondering when it would be time to go home. There were – or soon would be – bars, restaurants, sun-loungers and shops, not to mention endless sunshine. No wonder everyone came. The summer season had been pioneered by Bohemians, artists and intellectuals, and so was summer St Tropez – but there the French themselves did the pioneering: the port was the only one of the major Riviera resorts to be developed by them.

The fall of France, Vichy, the German occupation, liberation, *épuration* and the aftermath of the Second World War certainly gave French intellectuals something to think about. The result was the first genuine European cultural movement since the 1920s. It was focused on the Parisian Left Bank *quartier* St-Germain-des-Près, and had its own organ of opinion in *Les Temps Modernes*. This avant-garde quarterly had been founded jointly by the philosopher, dramatist and novelist Jean-Paul Sartre and his mistress Simone de Beauvoir. The latter had taught at the Sorbonne between 1941 and 1943, and in 1949 published *Le Deuxième Sexe*, which let the genie of feminism out of the bottle. With the likes of Juliette Greco, they formed the spearhead of the existentialist movement. In summer St Germain lacked charm so, like Paul Signac fifty years previously, Sartre and his entourage decamped from the capital for June, July, August and September to the coast. They were seen in Marseille, Porquerolles and Cap d'Ail. 'But above all,' wrote Eric Paul in *La Côte d'Azur des écrivains*, 'they were enchanted by Saint Tropez, by its relaxed lifestyle, its conviviality ... white wine, rosé. Life was a perpetual holiday.' The resort was still untouched by mass tourism, and possessed something of the Provençal authenticity that Juan-les-Pins, Cannes and Antibes had lost long ago. 'On the little *place*,' wrote Annabel Buffet, a follower of Sartre, 'there was a tiny grocer's where one found liquorice sticks, hair-pins and fish-bait. Albert and Margot Barbier ran their hotel-café-restaurant with the same generosity as Paul Boubal ran the Flore, and with perhaps more discretion. L'Escale, on the port, as select as Brasserie Lipp, received us more warmly than old man Cazes, who seemed alarmed by Existentialists ... Christian Maquard, Roger Vadim, Alexandre Autric and the rest of the group were already part of the scene.'

Roger Vadim – later the director of *Barbarella*, husband to Jane Fonda, and known as much for his feats in bed as behind the camera – was a good-looking, raven-haired teenage White Russian. He had been born Roger Vladimir Plemiannikov in Paris in 1928, brought up largely in the Bohemian St Germain-des-Près and claimed acquaintance with Sartre, Cocteau and Colette. Brigitte Bardot, on the front cover of *Elle* at the age of fourteen, attracted his attention. Vadim and the film director Marc Allegret inveigled her parents into agreeing that she should take a screen test, which was set up in a seventh-floor apartment in the rue Lord Byron. Vadim opened the door to her. Love followed. 'What bowled me over when I saw her naked,' he wrote candidly in his memoirs, 'was the extraordinary mixture of innocence and femininity, of immodesty and timidity.' They had to wait until Brigitte was eighteen before they could marry, by which time Vadim was twenty-four. In the meantime, he squeezed her into a series of minor films. Her fifth, *Act of Love*, starred Kirk Douglas, which meant it merited promotion at the Cannes Film Festival in 1955.

Vadim recognised this as the great opportunity it was. Doubtless mindful of the presence of the British aircraft carrier *Colossus* at the inaugural festival in 1946, the Americans sent the altogether grander 64,000-ton *Midway* as the setting of a photo-opportunity for the American film stars of the day: Douglas himself, Edward G. Robinson, Gary Cooper and Olivia de Havilland. The sun shone and the shutters clicked, but soon the photographers' attention drifted to Vadim's pony-tailed, pouting stowaway, dressed in a raincoat. She slipped it off to reveal an outfit worthy of Nabokov's Lolita. The following day photographs of her were across the world's newspapers. *Doctor at Sea*, in which she subsequently starred with the British actor Dirk Bogarde, established Bardot as an international star. And at this point, Vadim began to dream of a film of his own, set in St Tropez and starring his wife. It would be called *Et Dieu Créa la Femme*.

3

Brigitte was not the only girl on the block and neither, come to that, was Marilyn Monroe. Grace Kelly was the youngest daughter of a self-made Philadelphia businessman of Irish extraction, the son of a farm boy from County Mayo. Kelly's biographer Robert Lacey characterised her as a classic American beauty, distinguished by her wholesomeness: 'She epitomised a highly cherished element in American identity, particularly in the 1950s, the years of President Eisenhower. Grace went with country clubs, malted milk, *Readers' Digest* and a healthy ration of nice sex.'

She had been discovered by the director Alfred Hitchcock, and made her name in his classic thrillers *Dial M for Murder* and *Rear Window*. In the spring of 1954 she took the Blue Train to the Riviera to shoot another Hitchcock film with Cary Grant. This was the crime comedy *To Catch a Thief*. Grant played a retired jewel-thief who sets out to identify a cat burglar carrying out robberies using his trademark techniques. Grace was an heiress on holiday on the Riviera whose help he enlists. She was initially enchanted by the Riviera which was still, by today's standards, deserted; by its high mountain backdrop, unspoilt villages, dark-green cypresses and azure sea. Some of the film was shot in Monaco: from the heights of La Turbie, high above the principality, it still looked like Coleridge's Kubla Khan, 'Where blossomed many an incense-bearing tree'. 'Whose gardens are those?' she asked one day of the film's script-writer John Hayes. 'Prince Grimaldi's,' he replied, 'I hear he's a stuffy fellow.'

Stuffy or not, the pair met eleven months later when Grace returned to publicise the film at the Cannes Festival in late spring 1955. A photo-opportunity was set up in April for which, it transpired later, neither party had much relish. Hayes's comment had hardly been a recommendation to Grace, and Rainier had a low opinion of the New World. On the afternoon of 6 April 1955 Grace was driven over from Cannes. She was horrified by the Corniche, the old road clinging perilously to the high cliffs, the waves battering below. 'My Lord,' she exclaimed. 'I'd never drive this route. Forget it. I would go right over one side, I'm sure of it.'

Kept waiting at the palace for almost an hour, she was on her way out when Rainier appeared. He was small, maybe five feet six, slightly plump, but with pleasant regular features, sporting a well-tailored blue suit. At once she was struck by his faultless upper-class English accent and his old-world charm. Trailed by photographers, the couple toured the palace zoo and met Rainier's pet monkey. On parting, the prince mentioned that he was visiting the United States for the first time the following December to attend a charity ball. They might meet again. 'That would be wonderful,' said Grace, with genuine enthusiasm.

The prince's chaplain, Father Francis Tucker, had been appointed in 1950 to the chaplaincy by the Vatican. As the prince was a prominent Catholic, part of his brief was to ensure that Rainier made a suitable marriage. An Irish-American of the order of St Vincent de Paul, Tucker was one of those priests as familiar with a cocktail glass as he was with communion wine. Soon he wielded considerable influence in the principality, and his critics compared him with Rasputin. He made himself particularly unpopular by casting the ornamental Gisèle Pascal into the outer darkness – he thought her an unsuitable bride for the prince because she was not a virgin – although in fact he was in cahoots with Aristotle Onassis on the approach to Marilyn Monroe. By the time the prince met her, Tucker had broadened the search to include Natalie Wood (*Rebel without a Cause*), the British actress Deborah Kerr, and Princess Margaret. The latter's candidature was compromised by the assumption that the Queen would resist her sister's necessary conversion to Catholicism.

A few days after Rainier met Grace, he told Tucker, 'I may have found her, Father.'

'Well, who is it?' he asked excitedly.

'The American actress Grace Kelly.'

'Aha!'

Tucker was pleased. Grace was Catholic, apparently clean-living, and undoubtedly chic. The prince had chosen well. Tucker wrote to her, 'I want to thank you for showing the Prince what an American Catholic girl can be, and for the very deep impression this has left on him.' Then he was despatched to procure prints of *The Country Girl* and *To Catch a Thief* for Rainier to scrutinise her. Within days Tucker was off to Philadelphia to investigate her background.

4

Grace Kelly was not averse to the match. She had already been entangled with the film stars William Holden, Clark Gable and Ray Milland, and her lover at the time was the television actor Jean-Pierre Aumont, one of the relatively few French Jews to have survived the Holocaust. The relationship did not please her domineering father. 'I'd rather,' he told his daughter, 'you married a nigger than a Jew.'

Kelly had crowned her brief film career with an Oscar for *The Country Girl*, in which she had starred with Bing Crosby, who played a man fighting alcoholism. Now she aspired to marriage and motherhood, and was flattered by Rainier's interest. Like Wallis Simpson twenty years before her, she was entranced by his Old World trappings of ancestry, privilege, dignity and power. Which movie princess would turn down the chance to play a part in the real thing, however small? A long correspondence between her and Rainier followed their meeting in May. That November, in accordance with the Franco-Monégasque treaty, Tucker duly informed the Quai d'Orsay that the prince was looking for a bride in America. He said that several candidates had been identified. When the press got hold of the story, they presented it to a credulous public as a tale of the prince seeking not only an heir but the survival of the principality. It was the perfect story, blending the elements of quest, celebrity, romance, inheritance and sex.

On 23 December 1955, Rainier met the Kelly family at their home in the suburbs of Philadelphia, 3901 Henry Avenue. Father Tucker persuaded the republican Jack Kelly to address Rainier as 'Your Highness'. Grace's father somewhat spoiled the effect by adding, 'Royalty doesn't mean much to us.' Her mother, Margaret, was under the misapprehension that Rainier hailed from Morocco rather than Monaco. She was surprised both by the excellence of his English and the colour of his skin. Towards the end of the evening

Rainier and Grace went to the nearby home of Grace's sister Peggy where they all played cards. At some stage the couple withdrew to another room. They emerged looking dishevelled. A few days later, on 28 December 1955, the engagement was announced. It was, as Onassis himself pronounced, a fantasy, a fairytale, a dream come true. The press was thrilled. So was Jack Kelly: the last of his daughters was off his hands. At the engagement press conference on 5 January 1956 he remarked to his wife, 'Well, Mother, I guess now we're all sold out.' Unfortunately his daughter was within earshot, and was furious. She wrote to a friend: 'First I had to fight the Studio to avoid being a commodity. Now I find my own family trades me on the open market. Doesn't it ever end? When do I get to be just a person?' It was a good question, and one that she would have cause to ask again.

Marilyn Monroe, the also-ran, was not best pleased. Her note of congratulations to Grace supposedly read: 'So glad you found a way out of this business.'

But several obstacles to Grace's happiness had still to be overcome. In 1956 it went without saying that a princess should be a virgin when she married. Despite the nature of the world in which she worked – in which the use of the casting-couch was not unknown – and despite the men on whose arms she had occasionally been photographed, the public were prepared to give an icon the benefit of the doubt. An ice-maiden like Grace Kelly, with her slightly prim looks, was assumed innocent until marriage or caught *in flagrante delicto*. The prince and his entourage were more cautious: Grace was required to undergo a medical examination to demonstrate both virginity and fertility. She approached it with some trepidation, but all was pronounced satisfactory. Altogether less so, indeed grossly compromising, was a series of articles by Margaret Kelly that appeared in the American press under the title: 'My Daughter Grace Kelly: Her Life and Loves'. This confirmed Grace's view that her mother was trying to take credit for the match. At much the same time, a Chicago newspaper took up an altogether contrary line: 'He's not good enough for a Kelly. She is too well-bred a girl to marry the silent partner in a gambling parlour.' Both Grace and the prince found this vexing, the prince in particular the allusion to the supremacy of Onassis.

Despite the local difficulties, on 4 April 1956 Grace Kelly set sail on the USS *Constitution* for Monaco, marriage and a $500,000 wedding. Vast crowds turned out on the New York waterfront to wish her well. Eight days later, Rainier's diminutive royal yacht *Deo Juvante* sailed out of Monaco's harbour to bring his new bride to his arms. Or, as it turned out, into the arms of the world's press.

The couple were surprised to be greeted in the harbour by a battalion of six hundred photographers, but Grace was wearing a huge hat so they could not get the shot their editors had demanded of the almost-princess proudly entering her new domain. They were most annoyed, and this apparent carelessness on the couple's part set the tone for the whole event. The photographers were with a thousand reporters, and the total press corps numbered more than that which had covered the Second World War. They were further irritated when it began to rain – the reputation of the coast was such that they had not brought raincoats. They were delighted, though, when Father Tucker said in a sermon that Rainier's marriage was predicated by love for his people rather than for Grace. To a friend, the bride wrote, 'Those damn reporters. They're ruining everything. They've descended like locusts ... The whole damn world is waiting for me to get married.'

At the civil ceremony on 18 April, television cameras beamed the ceremony to what was then a huge audience of thirty million. Afterwards there was a press conference. Rainier had been induced to call his new father-in-law 'Pop', so Jack Kelly reciprocated when he responded to a question as to how he felt about his new son-in-law: 'Who, Ray? Well, he seems a nice boy. If he's half as nice as the other two we have, he'll be all right. We call him Ray, you know.' The following day, six hundred guests descended on the Romanesque cathedral of St Nicholas for what was then the most heavily publicised wedding of modern times. A French Raffles called Réné 'Swagger Stick' Gigier appeared in the guise of chauffeur to Princess Charlotte: 'I thought the air and sun would do him good,' she said, 'after his years in prison.' Unauthorised photographers disguised themselves as priests in an attempt to gain entry. They were detected and forcibly ejected. With everyone at the wedding the local thieves took the opportunity to stage a series of daring robberies, and got away with some rather fine Old Masters.

At five o'clock that evening, when Rainier and Grace were finally married, *Deo Juvante* weighed anchor and headed out into the azure seas, the ocean of Odysseus, the *mare nostrum*, the centre of the known world. Turning to her new husband, Princess Grace remarked, 'Thank you, darling, for such a sweet, intimate wedding.'

5

At just this time, Roger Vadim was putting the finishing touches to the script he had created for his wife, *Et Dieu Créa la Femme*. It was filmed in Nice, St Tropez and the Victorine studios, and released in France in November 1956.

The plot revolves around the newly married Juliette, who is not the sort of girl to let her vows stand in the way of pleasure, particularly of the variety depicted as freely available in St Tropez. She seduces her new brother-in-law, turns to drink, and – worst of all – dances with some black musicians. Finally she is corralled back into the fold by her husband. As one of the other characters in the film puts it, 'She does whatever she wants, whenever she wants.' The film also included what was claimed to be cinema's first real nude scene.

For a post-war audience, Brigitte Bardot was a revelation. In England, where David Lean's chaste *Brief Encounter* had been hailed as a masterpiece (which it was), a critic declared, 'Brigitte Bardot on screen is not simply the selfish delinquent. She has a freshness and charm ... she is irresponsible and immoral but not deliberately cruel. She does not fit into any of the previously accepted categories of film personality.' She was, in short, the portal to the permissive society, and intuitively taken up by the public as such with much gusto. As the film director Federico Fellini put it, 'If she didn't exist, we'd have to invent her.'

The film cost $600,000 to make and, in the United States alone, grossed $4 million. With the respect for high art that characterises the French, a government official announced, 'Mlle Bardot is making an important contribution to France's balance of payments.' It also did wonders for Vadim and Bardot's bank account – and much for the place where it was set. As one of Bardot's biographers, Jeffrey Robinson, succinctly noted, 'The names of St Tropez and Brigitte Bardot became inextricably linked and, almost immediately, nudity was thrown in for good measure. St Tropez became one of the most famous villages on earth because it was where she lived, and she was one of the most famous people on earth.'

At the same time Grace Kelly achieved almost precisely the same result in Monaco. The worldwide televising of her marriage restored Monaco's tarnished image among older cognoscenti, and introduced the principality to an entirely new generation, who had tired of the austerities of post-war Europe and wanted an infusion of the glamour that the South of France represented. As *The Times* remarked, 'After this famous romance, Monte Carlo will be found graven on every romantic's heart. More to the point, perhaps, it will be printed bold on the luggage labels of Americans bound for holiday in Europe.' Visitors poured into the casino and the hotels in the months after the wedding. During the difficult period after the war, the Société des Bains de Mer employees had had a month's pay deducted from their annual salary; now it was restored to them. Monaco's appeal to the likes of Onassis, based on minimal corporation and personal taxes, soared. Between 1950 and 1960 its business turnover quadrupled. 'Grace,' claimed Robert Lacey, 'was the principal reason why most of the world headed to Monaco, and she was the only reason why anyone, with the exception of the Grimaldi family, three thousand Monégasques and twenty-two thousand tax exiles could exist.' In 1958, having given birth to Princess Caroline in 1957, she produced a son and heir, Prince Albert. Rainier's cup was running over.

Both Brigitte Bardot and Grace Kelly had done wonders for their adopted homes, as Simone de Beauvoir would doubtless have agreed. And the Côte d'Azur had reinvented itself for the post-war world.

13
Dreams and Hopes in Concrete

'St Tropez is like Lourdes. Young people come here looking for spiritual fulfilment, and because they have faith they find it. They come with all their worries and yearnings, seeking to be healed by the new religion of glamour and stardom.'

Father Xavier Delange

1

'When I was serving in the Royal Navy in 1971, based at Toulon, I remember seeing a village being built near the port of St Tropez. I recall thinking how wonderful it was,' wrote Prince Charles, arbiter of modern architecture and future King of Great Britain. The village he had seen under construction north across the bay from St Tropez, in the shadow of the tenth-century Provençal village of Grimaud, is now known as Port Grimaud. As the Prince had recognised, it was a remarkable piece of work.

Port Grimaud was the brainchild of the French architect François Spoerry. Born in 1917 in Mulhouse, where France touches both Switzerland and Germany, he showed an early interest in architecture by producing a design for the family holiday home at Cavalaire. South across the peninsula from St Tropez, this was one of the most sheltered spots on the western stretch of the coast and scarcely touched by tourism. Before the war Spoerry studied architecture in Paris at the École des Beaux Arts. Once the resistance was established in France in 1942, he joined the *maquis* in Provence. In its ranks he gathered intelligence on the Wehrmacht forces established around the naval port of Toulon, and located safe-landing sites for British SOE agents, parachuted or couriered by tiny Lysander monoplanes into remote areas of coastal Provence. Spoerry, like so many of his compatriots, was betrayed. In 1943, he was sent to Buchenwald, the Weimar concentration camp where 56,000 died. Then, as he was young and fit, the Nazis despatched him to the huge natural caves at Dora in the Hartz mountains to assemble V2 rockets, and eventually to Dachau, the death camp on the fringes of Munich. 'My experience in the concentration camps,' he said in a review of his life's work, 'like those of so many others, showed me the true dimensions of the human condition, both in its greatness and its misery.'

After the war he set up as an architect in Mulhouse. A natural conservative, he was horrified by the modernist ethos in architecture epitomised by Le Corbusier, whose first building was started in 1945 in Marseille. It took the form of the now familiar residential tower block, with a series of similar modular units. 'My first step,' wrote Spoerry in his memoirs, 'was to rebel against the intellectual tyranny and the doctrines held by contemporary architects.' On the basis that actions and, in particular, buildings speak louder than words, Spoerry cast around for a suitable project to give expression to his own concept of architecture. An enthusiastic sailor, in the 1950s Spoerry kept his yacht in the harbour close to his parents' Cavalaire home: 'I found it dreary to have to get up in the middle of the night, if there was a storm, and go to the port to secure our boat's mooring.' His idea was for a village, loosely based on the model of Venice, where boats could be supervised by their owners in close proximity to their homes.

Given his association with the Côte d'Azur – and the 1950s building boom – it was the obvious place to try to find a site. In practical terms this meant a creek where houses could be built alongside the water. By then the Riviera had been undergoing the attentions of developers for more than a hundred and twenty years, and Spoerry, despite searching long and hard, began to despair. Eventually he convinced himself that a flat site by the water's edge could meet his brief equally well with the provision of a system of canals. Though sites of this nature were more plentiful than creeks, even this posed problems. Eventually he found a location that he conceded was one of the least attractive on the coast. On the northern side of the Golfe de St Tropez, by the mouth of the river Giscle, it was little more than an agglomeration of swamps and sandbanks, infested with mosquitoes. It was not a rival for Cannes or a harbour for Onassis's *Christina*. In 1962 Spoerry purchased thirty-five hectares of the site. Friends, colleagues and, in particular, the banks thought him mad. In 1963 he applied for planning permission. Three years later, after he had overcome innumerable objections from various government bodies, it was granted – on 14 June 1966.

His plan called for what he described as a lagoon town behind a natural shoreline, with what would eventually amount to seven kilometres of canals winding through it. That much was uncontroversial. The style of the buildings was not. Unlike the vast majority of architects working on the coast at the time, Spoerry had steeped himself in the vernacular architecture of the Mediterranean. Before the war he had discovered some of the wonderful local work on the Greek islands. Then he made an extensive study of comparable styles in Italy, Spain and Provence. The result, in Port Grimaud, was a series of small houses of traditional Provençal appearance with low-pitched terracotta-tiled roofs, laid out in narrow streets and squares beside the new canals. The façade of each house was different from its neighbour's, and the colours, chosen from a palette of fourteen, were carefully selected to contrast or blend together. Spoerry scavenged features like monumental doors and archways from older buildings. Access for cars was limited.

If this all sounded like a pastiche – which it was – it was a charge Spoerry was keen to rebut. 'I also wanted to make a clear and unequivocal statement that a return to traditional and regional architecture can produce an authentic creation and not ... merely an imitation of the real thing.' As he acknowledged, the scheme was reminiscent of, and inspired by, Clough Williams-Ellis's Portmeirion – the Italianate village in Snowdonia.

As the nature of the project became apparent, the fulfilment of Spoerry's 'dreams and hopes in concrete', his concept of architecture, his peers were outraged. The village and its creator were subjected to the most virulent criticism by the modernists. 'Port Grimaud is a permanent celebration of boring deception,' declared the authoritative *Guide d'architecture contemporaine en France*. 'There were times,' Spoerry wrote in his memoirs, 'when I wondered whether anyone at all in the world of architecture shared my views or had the slightest understanding why I had built Port Grimaud.' As a consequence, the whole project hung in the balance. Spoerry had only managed to find backing to the tune of three million francs, a sum he fairly described as 'meagre and ridiculous ... compared with the magnitude of the task'. He was obliged to proceed on a hand-to-mouth basis: the sale of the houses of each completed section funded the building of the next.

2

Spoerry described his style as '*architecture douce*' – 'gentle' or 'soft' architecture. Whatever its merits, in the 1960s that was not a term applicable to other developments along the coast.

If the creation of the Côte d'Azur had been begun by English wealthy enough to enjoy a better winter climate abroad, its summer season was largely inspired by Bohemian Americans escaping from the philistinism of the USA. Now the French public wanted some of that world-famous Côte d'Azur chic for themselves, and they were finally in a position to buy it. The French economy exploded in the 1950s – not least because of American aid in the form of the Marshall Plan. A five-year plan was drawn up, key industries nationalised, and a new generation of administrators produced by the foundation of the Ecole Nationale d'Administration. Between 1950 and 1958 industrial output increased by 85 per cent.

Such endeavours generate rewards. In 1950, Le Corbusier's high-rise in Marseille had just been completed. At that time, eight million French workers could afford to take an annual holiday. By the time Spoerry was finally given planning permission for Port Grimaud the figure had almost tripled to twenty million. In 1966, 610,000 of those holidaymakers came to the Côte d'Azur. By comparison there were just 171,000 foreign visitors: 77,000 Americans, 64,000 British and 30,000 Germans. The French had reclaimed their own backyard. The Riviera was a colony no more.

But the French had to reach their destination. As in England, the 1950s saw the beginnings of the French motorway system, based on Hitler's *autobahns*. A branch of the system, the A8 autoroute, was built over the Esterels and opened in 1961. A year later, Nice airport was handling a million passengers a year. The resort was now just a two-hour flight from Paris. While the Blue Train continued to run, the French were planning a high-speed rail network that would bring visitors to the coast even faster and in even greater numbers.

Once there, the holidaymakers had to be accommodated. The result, in the 1960s, was a building boom right along the coast. According to one of the leading contemporary guides, *Provence and the Riviera*, the Côte d'Azur, 'once the preserve of a rich few, is now in the grips of a fantastic capitalist boom, cashing in on the new values of mass tourism. It is a paradise for speculators – no season goes by without a fresh property scandal.' From Port Grimaud in the west to Menton in the east, apartment blocks, hotels, motels and condominiums shot up. As the guide recorded,

> Cannes today, with its casinos and yachts and palm trees, its vast blocks of luxury flats is an uneasy blend of the genuinely exclusive and the merely nouveau riche ... In winter it is still the haunt of the aristocracy, who come for the mild climate of its lovely sheltered bay. In high summer it is more of a madhouse than anywhere else on the

coast, impossible to drive through, inundated with trippers and with half the new-rich of Europe, who come to perch in their modish flats. Each year a new monster block erodes the hilly skyline.

In Nice, great apartment blocks erupted on the Baie des Anges, designed by the Greek architect André Minangoy. According to the guide,

> Nice is something more than the world's largest seaside resort. It is a busy industrial and residential centre, with an active life that goes on all the year round ... In summer the basic population of 300,000 swells to half a million ... At any time of year you may find yourself caught up in a Miss Europe contest, or a visit by the Beatles, or a world film première. There are few cultural sights, but it is worth strolling in the alleys of the old town and visiting the flower market, the Russian cathedral and the rich hillside suburb of Cimiez.

Menton now catered for 'new-style English summer visitors, cramming the hotels in organised groups. The hotels are mostly quiet and sedate, on the Eastbourne or Bournemouth pattern, and geared for middle-aged English taste'. High above Menton, in the Alpes Maritimes, a new skiing resort was planned, developed and built by the British entrepreneur Peter Boumphrey. Just fifty miles from Nice, this was Isola 2000.

Still, at least there was St Tropez, which was, according to the guide, still unspoiled:

> How satisfying it is to find a place that really does live up to its reputation! St Tropez in summer is intense and exciting – there is nowhere else like it in Europe. All day and half the night throngs of bizarrely dressed youth process up and down the little port, between the bright cafés and the rich yachts – searching – for what? A Dominican priest on a visit here gave the answer. 'St Tropez,' he said, 'is like Lourdes. Young people come here looking for spiritual fulfilment, and because they have faith they find it. They come with all their worries and yearnings, seeking to be healed by the new religion of glamour and stardom.'

Having found a bed for the designated seven or fourteen nights, the visitors then had to be entertained. The great tradition of yachting on the Riviera was ripe not only for expansion but democratisation. Until the 1930s, yachting had been largely a rich man's sport, famously likened by the Scottish magnate and America's Cup contender Sir Thomas Lipton to tearing up ten-pound notes under a shower. It was the world of the Prince of Wales's *Britannia*, J. P. Morgan's *Corsair* and, later, Aristotle Onassis's *Christina*. With post-war prosperity came the virtual creation of the leisure industry, one expression of which was yachting. The vast expansion of the world's navies between 1939 and 1945 introduced the challenge of the sea to a new and – socially – more broadly based market. At the same time new materials like marine plywood, aluminium, ferro-cement and, above all, fibreglass dramatically reduced the cost of yacht building.

In the early 1960s a new generation of yachtsmen and yachts was born. The yachtsmen were poorer, the boats were smaller, and there were far more of both. Twenty-five feet became an acceptable size for a small cruiser, regional English accents were heard – albeit infrequently – at the prestigious Royal Yacht Squadron. The attractions of the weather and the absence of difficult tidal conditions increased the acknowledged attractions of the Riviera. Silent as the wind and, to many eyes, intrinsically graceful, yachts were an adornment to the coast. The marinas they spawned were not. Virtually unknown before the war, these complexes of floating piers and jetties enabled large numbers of boats to be safely berthed in a small area. They were the nautical equivalent of multi-storey car-parks, and just about as attractive. On the Riviera they proved a lucrative investment and a significant source of employment. Soon there were 130, berthing 52,000 boats on a stretch of coastline that – between Menton and Marseille – is only 140 miles long.

It was perhaps symptomatic of the rapidity with which the coast was changing that one of its great historians, long neglected, was suddenly accorded recognition: the photographer Jacques-Henri Lartigue.

Born into a wealthy family in 1898, he was first taken to the Riviera at the age of six. He loved the *belle-époque* coast that he had explored as a child, and after the First World War set about recording its ambience in paint and on film. In *Inventing the French Riviera*, Mary Blume described his image of his first wife Bibi as 'the emblematic picture of the early twenties'. In a white dress with a wide-brimmed hat she sits at a restaurant table at Eden Roc, in the background a headland sloping down gently into the sea, an image of summer elegance, sophistication and pleasure. One of the first photographers to use colour film, the informal style Lartigue developed has been credited with elevating the snapshot into an art form. Forty years later two albums of his Riviera prints fell into the hands of John Szarkowski, director of photography at the Museum of Modern Art in New York. 'They seemed,' he wrote, 'like a fine athlete, to make their point with economy, elegance, and an easy precision. It seemed I might be looking at the early undiscovered work of Cartier-Bresson's papa.'

In 1963 the museum hosted Lartigue's first one-man show. It aroused enormous interest – his images of unspoiled elegance seemed particularly appropriate in an age inspired by Le Corbusier and his rather less thoughtful disciples. In his mid-sixties, Lartigue had been discovered. '*Life* magazine gave his early pictures twelve pages,' noted Mary Blume. 'It was one of the magazine's best-selling issues for the saddest of reasons: on the cover was John F. Kennedy, assassinated days before.'

3

In June 1966, Monte Carlo was *en fête* to celebrate its centenary and the principality hummed with galas, official receptions and parties: the Duke of Edinburgh was there as principal guest. It was a celebration of Monaco's glittering past, but Prince Rainier also intended it to be an affirmation of the prosperity of its future and took the opportunity to launch a ten-year plan. Having secured an heir, he now wished to be certain that Prince Albert, nearly nine, would have something appropriate to inherit. 'When I was young,' he once said, 'I got tired of hearing that the principality made its money from gambling losses. I remember seeing a cartoon showing people with "Monaco" labels stuck on their back, collecting money from unlucky gamblers who were throwing themselves out of hotel windows. That image made a big impact on me, it was why my goal during the first years of my reign was to make the rest of the world take me seriously. I didn't want to be a sovereign state that was caricatured in any way.'

The most obvious way to do this was to make the principality less dependent on – and synonymous with – gaming. Virtually since the creation of the gambling halls of Monte Carlo, Monégasques had enjoyed their attractive tax regime. It was this that had brought in the likes of Onassis, and it was something that the principality would benefit from indirectly in the provision of offices, accommodation and the other services that wealthy businessmen required. Accordingly, in 1960 Rainier had established MEDEC, the Monaco Economic Development Corporation. Soon, businesses in North America and Europe were receiving mail shots proclaiming the advantages of moving to the principality: the modest corporation tax, the absence of income tax, the centrality of the location to major European business centres and – courtesy of Princess Grace – its rejuvenated chic. The response, from the Americans, the British and the Germans, was overwhelming. With the old French colonial empire collapsing, it came, too, from French business exiles obliged to return from Indochina, Algeria and Morocco.

The Philadelphian Sam Cummings, founder and chairman of Intermarco – the International Armament Corporation – was typical of those who came to Monaco. He had been a US army sergeant in Korea. After the war he spotted an opportunity to trade captured weapons and by the early 1960s he was a multi-millionaire. His Ivy League-style clothes belied a sharp business mind, and soon

Intermarco, with a fine line in jets and turbo-props, light and heavy artillery, tanks, armoured cars and personnel carriers, was the largest independent arms-dealer in the world. Cummings's clients included the dictators Trujillo, Somoza, Sakarno, Tito and Gaddafi. 'They have a sense of order,' Cummings commented. 'And they pay their bills promptly.' He had a villa in Nice, hideaways in Washington, Switzerland and London. With its tax regime, Monaco was his logical next stop. There he established his headquarters.

From Rainier's point of view, the result of the influx of people like Cummings was a gratifying property boom. To accommodate the newcomers, *belle-époque* villas were demolished to make way for office buildings and apartment blocks, and a huge Italian labour force swarmed across the border with cranes, scaffolding, bulldozers and pneumatic drills. Soon, Rainier acquired his nickname *Le Prince Bâtisseur*, 'the builder prince'. Monaco began to look like Manhattan.

And it was causing rumblings in Paris. The Franco-Monégasque agreement of 1918 prevented the two states establishing competitive tax regimes. Although Monaco's had existed since well before the agreement was signed, the Quai d'Orsay had chosen to turn a blind eye. It became less sanguine when Rainier began more actively to exploit Monaco's arrangements with MEDEC. General de Gaulle, newly installed as head of the Fifth Republic, looked even further askance when Frenchmen joined the rush to the haven of Monaco. He was beside himself when he discovered that they included members of OAS, the Algerian terrorist network known to be planning his assassination. (The idea was dramatised by Frederick Forsyth in *The Day of the Jackal*.) The last straw came when Rainier suspended trading on the Paris Bourse of shares in a flourishing Monaco media concern in which the French government held a substantial stake, Radio Monte Carlo.

De Gaulle at once demanded that Rainier lift the suspension. Rainier refused. On 11 October 1962, the President announced that Rainier had six months to reform residential and corporate taxation, the proceeds of which would go to France. The following day, he instituted what became called the 'Siege of Monaco'. On a pitch-black night of heavy rain, French Customs officials set up barriers on the roads into Monaco. It was rumoured that de Gaulle would soon cut off its supplies of water and power. To a friend, Princess Grace wrote: 'They may enclose Monaco in barbed wire tomorrow.' Even better, it was said that de Gaulle was contemplating a naval barrage or an air-raid on the principality. 'The Monégasques,' reported *The Times*, on 13 October 1962, 'see the French demands as the ruin of the Principality's prosperity.'

The international press took up the story, and France's behaviour was not depicted in a particularly favourable light. The United States, momentarily neglecting the Cuban missile crisis, sided with Monaco. The affair dragged on for six months. The eventual outcome was a new agreement between the two states, signed on 15 May 1963. It ended MEDEC, and banned French citizens from the Monaco tax regime. Long-time businesses and all resident Monégasques were left untouched. That day, finance minister Valéry Giscard d'Estaing announced the lifting of Customs controls. According to *The Times*, the affair ended 'with all the look of a French victory of attrition'. Others saw it as something of a triumph for the builder prince.

4

De Gaulle, though, was only half the battle. For Rainier there was also Onassis.

It was curious not so much that the two men should have divergent views on the development of the principality, but that Rainier wanted to popularise the resort and Onassis to retain its Edwardian exclusivity. The shipping magnate who had pulled himself up by his own bootlaces felt that 'Monaco will always be prosperous so long as there are three hundred rich men in the world.' As one of them, it was perhaps understandable that he wished the principality to continue to cater for people like him. The prince, however, wanted to modernise Monaco, enlarge it by reclaiming land from the sea, running the railway underground and creating an artificial beach. He wanted to attract the middle classes as well as the super-rich. Holiday Inns, which supplied a formulaic and predictable hotel experience for moderate cost, was one of the success stories of the 1950s. Rainier studied the chain with care and decided that he would like a Holiday Inn: 'My own feeling is that the economic wealth of the principality would be greatly improved if we could start off with two thousand comfortable, modern hotel rooms, of the kind which Americans are so good at. Not super deluxe, but moderately equipped, comfortable and agreeable rooms with a maximum price of $15 a day.' Onassis was aghast: 'Rainier won't be satisfied until Monte Carlo is nothing but hotels, tourists and tax shelters from one end to the other.'

Rainier started with the railway. The steel ribbons that had been the key to the principality's early prosperity were unattractive and took up an appreciable acreage of land in so small a place. If the line went underground, the eyesore would be concealed, the land on which it had once run could be released for development, and the spoil from the excavations could be used to reclaim the seaboard margin of Monaco from the waves. Work on the project had started in April 1958. As is the way with such schemes, it was soon behind on timing and well ahead on budget. Within two years it looked as though it would cost three times the amount estimated. When the new station opened on 13 December 1964, it had exceeded even that.

Nevertheless, its completion enabled Rainier to start on the creation of the beach. On the Larvotto to the east of the principality an entirely artificial beach was to be built, sitting on spoil excavated from the railway tunnel. There would be a promenade with restaurants, bathing cabins and shops. Best of all, there would be a Holiday Inn, with three hundred rooms, a conference hall and a swimming-pool.

With the old villas and their gardens fast disappearing, the noise and dust of the principality being turned into a building site, Rainier found himself on the receiving end of some robust criticism. As early as the year of her marriage, Princess Grace had complained that Monaco was like 'taking all of the City of New York and squeezing it out on the head of a knitting needle'. Later she added, 'I'm not too keen on some of the modern buildings and their height.' She even blocked the destruction of the elegant old Hermitage hotel. Similarly, the democratisation of the principality's appeal and in particular the gaming rooms horrified the Duchess de Rochefoucauld, who represented Monaco's traditional visitors. When she arrived at the casino and discovered coachloads of common or garden tourists feeding slot machines, she declared, 'I can't bear to set foot in Monte Carlo casino. I have no objection to Italian maids and suchlike, but I cannot see why I should lose money in their presence.' Onassis took a similar view: the exclusivity he had bought was being compromised. Relations between him and the prince were further soured by Onassis's liaison with the soprano Maria Callas. Rainier agreed with the Vatican that unseemly newspaper coverage of the affair brought the principality into disrepute. While the United States and the Soviet Union slogged it out on the global stage, the two pocket Napoleons argued over which end to open a boiled egg.

In 1966 Rainier, emboldened by his contretemps with de Gaulle, decided to lance the boil. He had fully restored relations with the Quai d'Orsay by persuading de Gaulle to endorse his ten-year plan for the further commercial development of the principality. Now he needed freedom from the Greek to put it into action. Onassis remained the principal shareholder of the Société des Bains de Mer. In June Rainier persuaded the Monaco National Council to create 600,000 new shares in the SBM. At a stroke, Onassis's majority position was wiped out. The shipping magnate took his case to law. As he was obliged to plead to the Monégasque courts, he got short shrift. He was eventually bought off for $10 million.

Rainier could now plough ahead with all of his schemes, while

Onassis, tiring of Monaco and Callas, found solace in the arms of John F. Kennedy's widow, Jacqueline. The late president's brother Robert resisted the match, describing Onassis as 'a complete rogue on a grand scale', but the couple married on 20 October 1968.

5

It would be misleading to suggest that in the middle and late 1960s the Riviera was simply pillaged by the French. Apologists like Geoffrey Bocca in *Bikni Beach*, a lighthearted portrait of the coast, could still claim that the Côte d'Azur was 'the greatest holiday resort on earth'. The guidebook *Provence and the Riviera* commented, 'The new development is a good deal less vulgar than in many parts of Spain or Italy, and Nice is large and dignified enough to resist being spoilt.' Of Monaco itself, the ageing Evelyn Waugh wrote, 'I go often to Monte Carlo for simple love of the place. For one thing it has the best hotels in the world ... It was part of François Blanc's civilising mission to introduce classic French cooking to the frugal Italian Monégasques and to supplement the drab little wines.' At the same time, Waugh's old friend and fellow novelist Graham Greene found the coast still sufficiently attractive to settle in Antibes. In 1966 he took a modest flat in the Résidence des Fleurs, close to the old town. Like his English predecessors more than a century previously, he claimed that this would address a chest problem. He told the *Sunday Times* in January 1966, 'My doctor says that I should avoid the London smog.' In the great tradition of Riviera visitors, he left to pursue an affair with a married blonde who lived in Juan-les-Pins. Dirk Bogarde also settled on the Riviera. In 1969 he bought a house close to Vence, describing the experience in one of the volumes of his memoirs, *Snakes and Ladders*:

> In this gentle, undulating wooded land as yet almost untouched by the rotting fingers of property tycoons, I determined to seek and acquire my house. St Paul, once so sweet and calm and lost, except

to a fortunate few, when I first came to it in the forties, was slowly, inexorably turning itself into a kitschy ruin of faux art galleries, Provençal boutiques, Vietnamese restaurants, and tarty little shops selling postcards, hideous porcelain, olive-wood salad bowls and key-rings. Only the Colombe d'Or managed to stay aloof from this onslaught of quaintness, remaining a small bright island around which the flotsam and jetsam of package tours and coach trips ebbed hourly, red-skinned, hot, smelling of sun-tan oil and pommes frites.

As for Port Grimaud, whatever its aesthetic limitations, it was certainly better than the brutalism of much of the Riviera's post-war architecture, and eventually proved the commercial success that Spoerry had anticipated. He wrote in his memoirs, 'The undeniable success of the lagoon town caused some of its detractors to reverse their initial judgments and re-think their views on the art of building. This happened to the extent that I can now hope that Port Grimaud is seen to be one of the achievements produced in France … which may herald the genesis of a freer architecture, closer to the needs and the wishes of the public.' Prince Charles could hardly have put it better.

14
The Road from La Turbie

> 'Several questions remain unanswered about what happened when Princess Grace and her daughter, Stephanie, were driving back from the family holiday home, Roc Agel, at La Turbie in the South of France,'
>
> *The Times*, 16 September 1982

1

Monday, 13 September 1982 was one of those late summer days in the South of France that any visitor from a less balmy climate relishes. As the nights begin to draw in further north, the temperature plummets and equinoctial gales beckon, the Englishman thinks how wise he was to extend the summer by venturing south. But although the weather remained constant, in the early 1980s the Riviera seemed in decline.

For those who lived there, a cloudless day with a light sea breeze and a temperature of 25 °C was their birthright, and went unremarked. For Her Serene Highness Princess Grace of Monaco it also went unnoticed. That weekend the Grimaldis had retreated to their farmhouse at Roc Agel, in the shadow of the peak that dominated the principality. Now, on Monday morning, it was time to return. Princess Grace thought she would drive herself and her younger daughter Stephanie the three miles back into town. Shortly after nine thirty the chauffeur brought round her old metallic green Rover 3500. The Princess disliked driving, not least on the tortuous and precipitous roads around

Monaco. On this occasion, though, she was determined to take the wheel. As she pointed out to the chauffeur, she had some dresses on the back seat that needed returning to the palace. That meant that the car was effectively reduced to a two-seater. No matter, the chauffeur told her, he could return later for them. The Princess was insistent. She wanted a private word with Stephanie about her affair with Paul Belmondo, the ninteen-year-old son of the actor Jean Paul, with whom she had just spent a holiday in Antigua. With everyone around over the weekend, it had been impossible. Now was her chance. At about nine forty-five Princess Grace slipped into the car and slammed the door. Stephanie, who was just seventeen, did likewise. Neither bothered to do up their seatbelts. It was only ten minutes into town. Princess Grace nosed the car cautiously out of the gates.

Her twenty-fifth wedding anniversary the previous year had put the Princess in a reflective mood. That March she had met Lady Diana Spencer at the Royal Opera House in Covent Garden, undertaking her first public engagement as Prince Charles's fiancée. The marriage on which she was about to embark with the heir to the British throne had some obvious parallels with Grace's own. She too had been a young bride, largely unversed in the idiosyncrasies of royalty, marrying a bachelor in early middle age who was used to having his own way. Lady Diana, though, was only nineteen and Grace had been an Oscar-winning, worldly-wise twenty-seven when she married Prince Rainier. As she now appreciated, twenty-seven is not the height of maturity, she had not been gifted with prescience, and in some senses she had been one of Henry James's innocent Americans caught up in the wiles of a corrupt Old World. She had taken Prince Rainier at face value and paid the price. She had got exactly what she and her parents bargained for. She was a movie princess who became a princess in real life. She had a palace, servants at her beck and call, and the cars, speedboats, royal yachts, helicopters and planes that went with the job. She had perfect weather and a life to devote to pleasure. If that wasn't a recipe for living happily ever after, what was?

But she had failed to find happiness in Monaco. It was, perhaps, predictable that, coming from the wide-open spaces of the USA, she would eventually find the Riviera and Monaco claustrophobic. The physical constraints were evident, but it was a little time before she could appreciate the social and emotional ones. Philadelphia, where she had been brought up, was a bustling, booming city of four million, with opportunities to meet and mingle with a wide variety of people from different backgrounds. Much the same could be said of the movie world in which the she had triumphed. By comparison, she found the social life of Monaco narrow, stuffy and constricted. As the society columnist Taki once put it, 'In Monte Carlo, especially among the tax exiles, one does not choose one's friends. It's a bit like being in prison. You must talk to the people you are thrown in with.' The community of exiles, arms-dealers, professional gamblers, white-slave traders and foreign-exchange dealers were not to Grace's taste. She made friends among her erstwhile peers, like David Niven and his wife, who had a villa on Cap Ferrat, and with the racing driver Jackie Stewart and his wife. Ultimately, though, by her tenth wedding anniversary in 1966 she felt caged. To a friend she wrote of Rainier, 'He has me cornered. I can't move. I can't go anywhere. I have no freedom.'

There was not much to Rainier, she had discovered, beyond his palace and the playthings of the rich. Behind the charm he was an arrogant man who devoted his life to himself and his principality. When he missed a shot at golf, he took it out on his Labrador. If he lost at tennis, he threw his racquet at his son, who seemed to expect it. The Princess could muster little enthusiasm for her husband's transformation of Monaco into Manhattan-by-the-Mediterranean. If the Monégasques were materially better off under their builder prince, they had made moral sacrifices – not to mention aesthetic ones imposed by the efforts of Le Prince Bâtisseur. It was in her children that Grace took solace. Interviewed in 1966, she said, 'I've had happy moments in my life, but I don't think being happy is a perpetual state anyone can be in. Life isn't that way. But I have a certain peace of mind. My children give me a great deal of happiness, and my life here has given me many satisfactions in the last ten years.' When Rainier asked what she would like for a tenth wedding anniversary present, she snapped, 'A year off.' In 1969 when she celebrated her fortieth birthday, an age she regarded as of great significance for a woman, her marriage had become a matter of form, the rumour mill attributing affairs to both principals.

2

It was an indication of the way in which the Riviera was changing that in early 1970 the twenty-six-year-old Mick Jagger might have been seen leafing through a copy of the *Daily Telegraph*'s new guide to the coast. He was thinking less of a holiday, delightful though that might have been, than of exile.

The Rolling Stones had just discovered that they were grossly in debt to the Inland Revenue. Bill Wyman alone owed the then fabulous sum of £118,000 – more than a £1 million in today's money. With their composing royalties, Jagger himself and his song-writing partner Keith Richards probably owed three times that much. Wyman commented, 'Once you owe over £118,000 you *never* catch up. All the money you earn to pay that off you get taxed on as well. You're working for the government for ever.' That didn't appeal to him or the other Stones. The alternative, they were advised, was tax exile. 'The choice of France,' wrote the Stones' biographer Philip Norman, 'was an almost inevitable one in those days when tax exile still carried a cachet vaguely associated with W. Somerset Maugham ... There was sunshine, the food and the booze.'

Jagger, educated with Richards at Wentworth County Primary school in Dartford, was not of an age to know much about the Riviera. The coast had been falling out of the ken of the British middle classes since the 1930s and had never fully re-established itself after the war. True, the British consulate in Nice had reopened in

1962, but hardly in grandiose circumstances. It was on the first floor of an office block shared with a bank and a car-hire firm. The following year, when the Stones shot to fame with 'Money (That's What I Want)', the coast welcomed only 65,000 British visitors. In 1968, by which time the Stones were on to 'Sympathy For The Devil', the figure had halved to 32,000. The *Daily Telegraph*, Jagger found, was far from uncritical of the Côte d'Azur. 'The French Riviera today,' it announced, 'its extravagant villas razed to make way for motorways, supermarkets, apartment blocks and campsites, may seem like a sadly pale offspring of its effulgent past.' It singled out Monaco in particular: 'Scarred by rows of skyscraper apartment blocks thrown up in the tax-haven era, and choked with traffic eternally crawling in search of parking spaces, the scene is not what it once was. One-armed bandits have been installed in the Casino and, next to the Casino, a huge new American Holiday Inn is going up.' As befitted a promotional guide, though, the *Telegraph* still found a good deal to praise. Among the natural beauties were Port Grimaud, 'a brand new, carefully crafted copy of an old Provençal fishing port', and St Tropez, '... the new capital of the Côte d'Azur'. It boasted Le Byblos, 'a huddle of luxurious Provençal style cottages in the Avenue Paul Signac', where bed and breakfast could be had from around eleven pounds a night.

But what appealed above all to Jagger were the *Telegraph*'s tales of excess:

> The French Riviera was at its most fabulous during the nineteenth and early twentieth centuries, and the chronicles of the excesses and frivolities there make fascinating reading ... the Princess Souvaroff who, to celebrate a spectacular casino win, leased a sumptuous villa overnight for a party and then, when the guests had still not departed, bought the villa outright at seven the next morning and toasted the purchase with her friend with champagne drunk from their shoes.

Despite the depredations of time, chance, war and development, there were some splendid inheritors on the Riviera. They ranged from 'casually dressed aristocrats, millionaires and international cosmopolites, from starlets and flashy entrepreneurs to secretaries, clerks and ordinary families – a kaleidoscopic mélange of humanity that is unique'. For the Rolling Stones, then seen as the embodiment of self-indulgence and excess, it sounded like paradise.

A handpicked team from the Stones' substantial entourage set out from late autumnal England, where Edward Heath's new government was trying to resolve the labour and union issues that would culminate in the three-day week. They settled themselves in Cannes, and started scouting the coast for a series of properties in which to accommodate themselves. According to Philip Norman, it was said that the local estate agents 'had to find villas with bathrooms of sufficient size to accommodate "Roman style orgies"'. When the team visited Mougins, a charming hill-town just inland of Golfe-Juan – then home to Picasso and Prince Sihanouk – the Stones' reputation was such that the local mayor campaigned on the platform that he would forbid the group residence permits. Eventually, all except Jagger rented properties close to Cap Ferrat, between Villefranche and Beaulieu, the home of Somerset Maugham until his death in 1965. Jagger settled for the more fashionable ambience of St Tropez. On 5 April 1971, the Stones – in accordance with British tax law – officially began their exile.

Their focus soon took the form of Keith Richards's Villa Nellcote. This was a *belle-époque* structure of some extravagance, built by a retired English admiral who had eventually thrown himself off its roof. High above Villefranche, its terrace commanded views of the Alpes Maritimes to the north, the cape and the azure seas below. Richards, his lover Anita Pallenberg and their young son Marlon had soon turned it into a home from home. According to Philip Norman:

> The villa's airy elegant salons were transformed, like all Keith's previous habitations, into the environment Keith found most comfortable – the semblance of a motel room recently ransacked by the police ... album sleeves, wine bottles, discarded clothes, half-smoked

joints settled as usual on the grand piano and the marbled mantelpiece. Baby Marlon voyaged, nappyless, along brocaded sofa rims. Nellcote was the centre of the Stones' exile, its familiar squalor lending continuity – comfort even – for the others' more stilted expatriate lives.

Headquarters established, all that remained was to find something to do. Deprived of their familiar haunts and friends in London's grey suburbs – although Keith had a place in Chelsea's Cheyne Walk – the Stones resorted to the pursuits that the Riviera had in its gift. 'It is easy to be idle on the Riviera,' Somerset Maugham had written in *Strictly Personal* of his life there between the wars. 'Especially in summer, what with bathing, conversation, tennis and bridge, and parties, the days were full enough without work.' Maugham's successors as artists in residence on Cap Ferrat found things little altered. 'Mick got very into tennis when we were in France,' commented Richards later. 'He took it *very* seriously.' All the Stones liked to sunbathe, and swim. Soon, in the tradition of the Prince of Wales' *Britannia*, J. P. Morgan's *Corsair* and Aristotle Onassis' *Christina*, Richards had acquired his own yacht – called *Mandrax*, in an allusion to the drug.

There were also little lunch parties, catered for by the resident Nellcote chef. 'I can remember fifty people sitting down for lunch,' recalled Mick Taylor, the guitarist who had replaced the late Brian Jones. 'It was like a holiday camp.' In the evening the mood altered, lightened, even. The presence of the Stones was hardly a secret and, rather like earlier prosperous English visitors to the Riviera, they attracted their fair share of parasites. According to Norman, 'The waterfront cafés at Villefranche swarmed with drug pushers of every kind and complexion, avid to supply and – if they were fortunate – join the orgies rumoured to be taking place up at Nellcote. If rumour was to be believed, those orgies did not belong to ancient Rome so much as the wilder hillbilly regions of Kentucky. One English student, hoping to peddle his mite of hashish, found himself drawn into conversation. "Zat's right. *Les poules*. Zey do it with chickens."'

On 13 May 1971 Jagger married the Nicaraguan model Bianca Perez de Macias in St Tropez. The guests included Paul McCartney, Ringo Starr, Keith Moon of the Who, Eric Clapton, and the Queen's cousin Lord Lichfield. Of the Stones, only Keith was invited. Brigitte Bardot and her former husband Roger Vadim were there – the latter as an official witness. The morning began with a row between Jagger and Bianca over the pre-nuptial agreement. French law requires that the couple must declare whether their property will be jointly or separately held. Jagger wanted his bride to waive her claim to his property in the event of a divorce. The bride thought both the timing and the proposal itself in poor taste, but eventually she reluctantly agreed. Then came the civil ceremony, which was conducted by Mayor Marius Estezan in the council chamber of the Hôtel de Ville. Scores of reporters and photographers had squeezed themselves inside it, and Jagger refused to appear until the room was cleared of all but his guests. The mayor responded that the ceremony was open to the public and he had no powers to disperse the eyes of the world. 'In that case,' said Jagger, 'I'm not going through with it.'

At last, almost an hour late, he was persuaded to appear. Wearing a pale three-piece suit and floral shirt, he took his bride into the chamber. A fist-fight broke out among photographers squabbling for vantage-points, Keith Richards and Anita Pallenberg indulged in a noisy row, and Jagger tried to turn back. His publicist had to drag him into the mayor's presence. The religious ceremony that followed was held at the fisherman's chapel of St Anne. After the congregation had arrived the doors were locked behind them in an effort to exclude the press. It was some time before bride and groom made themselves heard and were admitted. Abbé Baud, Jagger's spiritual instructor, observed: 'You have told me that youth seeks happiness and certain ideals and faith. I think you are seeking it, and I hope it arrives with your marriage.' Lord Lichfield gave away the bride, who had insisted that the organist played the theme from *Love Story*. At the reception at a theatre next to the Café des Arts Bianca, in a sequined turban, managed to upstage even Bardot. The cabaret comprised an impromptu performance by Stephen Stills, approaching the height of his fame with Crosby, Stills, Nash and Young. Hopes that the Stones themselves would perform were dashed. Richards wore a Nazi uniform and drank himself into a stupor.

Rather like the Grimaldis', the Jaggers' marriage was only a qualified success. Later, Bianca would say that for her it effectively ended on the day it had started.

Despite the delights available to him on the Riviera, Keith Richards was soon fretting. Like Scott Fitzgerald before him, he was discovering a certain emptiness in the pursuit of pleasure offered by the coast. It was time to start work again. On 6 July 1971 the Stones began to put together their masterpiece. In an allusion to their status in France, it was called *Exile on Main Street.*

Given the circumstances in which it was recorded, its genius is all the more astonishing. Needless to say, the house-party atmosphere of the Villa Nellcote was something of a barrier to creativity, despite Pallenberg's attempts to bring some domestic order to the scene. She was also the only one who spoke French, and later claimed rashly, 'I was completely responsible for everything that was happening.' The band recorded the album in the villa's huge cellar, which was so dank and humid that the guitars were out of tune by the end of each number, the vocalists' voices likewise. 'That's when I got into Jack Daniels,' said Richards. 'Because you're trying to get the backing vocals on a track and the voice starts to go. This'll give it another half-hour. It's the fumes, man.' The electricity, never to be relied on in France, flickered and fluctuated. On 11 October recording was interrupted by Jade Jagger's birth at a Paris nursing-home. Jagger absented himself to delight in his child, leaving the band to record without their main vocalist. A break-in at the villa on 17 October resulted in the theft of Richards's valuable collection of vintage guitars, an incident that left him in tears. Finally, when the recordings were more or less complete in December, the whole band was arrested on drugs charges and whisked off to appear before the examining magistrate in Nice.

Doubtless inspired by the diligence of their British counterparts, it emerged that the Nice *gendarmerie* had had the whole band under surveillance since their arrival on the coast. Some had even infiltrated the exclusive social circle at the Villa Nellcote.

Jagger, Wyman, Watts and Taylor were cleared, but Richards and Pallenberg were indicted on the evidence of their chef. By the time the *gendarmerie* got round to issuing a warrant for their arrest, the pair had fled to the West Indies. Richards was relieved to leave France: 'I love England and it's my country. If you're forced to stay out too long and you go back, you feel like D. H. Lawrence. He said, "I feel more alien here than anywhere else."'

If that was the effective end of the Stones' exile in the South of France, it was not the end of the album inspired by their stay. 'Tumbling Dice' and 'Casino Boogie' owe a debt to Monte Carlo, but the whole record wonderfully captures the limbo at the end of the 1960s. Psychedelia, counter-culture and the Summer of Love had been followed by the Altamont tragedy, President Nixon and the Ohio shootings at Kent State University. *Exile on Main Street* is the epitaph to that innocent decade, and it was the perspective with which the Stones provided themselves in their Cap Ferrat exile. As Richards later put it proudly, 'While I was a junkie, I still learned to ski and made *Exile on Main Street.*' Afterwards they never made anything as good.

3

The man ultimately responsible for the *gendarmerie* surveillance and subsequent arrest of the Stones was the mayor of Nice, Jacques Médecin. Ironically 'Le Grand Jacques', as he was known, was as corrupt a mayor as France had ever seen. 'The Médecin phenomenon,' commented *The Times*, on his death in 1998, 'said a lot about the mentality and mores of Europe's largest coastal resort. In France, it is said, "there's Paris, there's the provinces, and there's

Nice." It was a very Italian kind of city-state that Médecin ruled, virtually as a private fief, where the writ of Paris scarcely ran.'

Tall, moustached, something of a Lothario, with an easy manner, Médecin had succeeded his father as mayor on the death of '*le roi* Jean' in 1965. He found Nice in better shape than his neighbour Prince Rainier had found Monaco, but with certain problems in common: a crumbling infrastructure, an elderly population that attracted elderly visitors, faded, dated and lacklustre hotels, an image located firmly in the past. Yes despite burgeoning competition from the fast-developing Spanish and Portuguese rivieras – not to mention destinations outside Europe – the Côte d'Azur still retained a certain cachet.

Trained as a lawyer, Médecin had worked as a journalist, and certainly brought talent, energy and publicity to the job of revitalising Nice. By the time of the Stones' exile he was making remarkable progress. He had recognised that Nice was overly dependent on tourism for its living, and spotted the opportunity to expand into the fast-expanding business of conferences. The Akropolis, a huge *palais des congrès*, was built half-way between the port and Cimiez. Médecin also realised that a seaside resort with frankly indifferent facilities needed other attractions. Marc Chagall's donation to France of some of his major works enabled Médecin to found the Musée Marc Chagall in Cimiez, which opened in 1972. It was followed later by the Musée Matisse. The mayor also encouraged industry, which had hitherto played a modest part in the city's economy, which resulted in the development of the coast's remarkable equivalent to Silicon Valley, the 6000-acre science park on the far side of the Var. Médecin also expanded the airport, making it the biggest outside Paris. By 1975 it was welcoming a million passengers a year.

Business visitors, *touristes d'affaires*, began coming to Nice all year round, which diminished the city's reliance on what was by now a tourist season largely restricted to the summer. Typically businessmen spent twice as much as normal tourists, and had little taste for the campsites that contributed so little to the local economy. Soon Nice was attracting three hundred conferences annually. The profile of visitors and residents changed, the new businesses and industry attracting new and younger people. High-rise apartments on the lower Var plain were built to accommodate them. Like neighbouring Monaco, Nice was changing with the times, adapting itself to the modern age. The *belle époque* was history, and by the tenth anniversary of Médecin's accession to power, Nice had a brash new image that reflected a brash new reality.

The old order changes, giving place to new, lest one good custom should corrupt the world. Or so some thought. Others differed. Two environmentalists, René Richard and Camille Bartoli, produced a polemic about the destruction of the coast, *La Côte d'Azur Assassinée*. The travel writer Richard Binns, who had seen the coast transformed since he had first known it in the 1950s, commented, 'Much of the coastal strip is appalling: concrete mutations litter the landscape, a grim memorial to the planners (aided by backhanders) who conceived and continue to extend this twentieth century nightmare: pollution in both sea and atmosphere is rampant; the sound of traffic is deafening, in an environment where cars seem to outnumber people.' So much for the rural Nice that Tobias Smollett had enjoyed two hundred years previously, 'a little town, hardly a mile in circumference, said to contain 12,000'.

Still, Médecin's enterprise made him the darling of the French Right. In 1976, President Giscard d'Estaing appointed him junior minister for tourism. It was quite an accolade, especially so given the criminal associations and dealings of 'le Grand Jacques'. A token example of his methods concerned his second wife Ilene, an American. Of modest background himself, Médecin explained his new-found wealth by passing off his wife as one of the heiresses of the cosmetics giant Max Factor. He counted as friends Albert Spaggiari, charged with bank robbery, and Dominge Fractori, implicated in corruption at the Ruhl casino. Soon it became apparent that the city was amassing huge debts, that Médecin was siphoning off considerable sums from the city for himself and his cronies, and that he was paying no tax. Graham Greene, still living in Antibes, warned in his pamphlet *J'Accuse*: 'Avoid the region of Nice – the preserve of some of the most criminal organisations in the South of France.' Of course, he added, 'Nice has its sunny side also, but I can leave it to the mayor of Nice, Jacques Médecin, to talk about that side of the city.' In an interview in *Rolling Stone* magazine to promote *Exile on Main Street*, Mick Jagger put it more simply: 'In Nice and Cannes all the French are thieves.'

At around this time Brigitte Bardot, on her third husband, her film career in ruins, her looks fast fading, was reaching the same conclusion about the human race. In 1976 she opened a campaign against the slaughter of baby seals in Canada, and launched the Brigitte Bardot Foundation for the Protection of Animals. She commented, 'People will betray your secrets, your friendship and your love … But animals will never deceive you. If you love them, they love you back.'

In 1978, Médecin was effectively dismissed as tourist minister by the diplomatic method: his post was abolished. Yet he survived as mayor for more than another decade. It took the return of a socialist regime to ferret him out. He was charged with tax arrears of twenty million francs and the criminal misuse of city funds. It was just at this time that the Blue Train was abandoned as an outdated service. For many it was the end of the Riviera, the breaking of the last link with the *belle époque*.

4

The road from Roc Agel winds easily down to La Turbie, which the princesses reached at about nine fifty. There it skirts the edge of the park where the trophy to the memory of Augustus stands. A century before Grace's marriage, C. B. Black had described the view lyrically: 'The whole coastline lies before us … as far as the hills above San Remo, headland after headland running out into blue water, white little towns nestling in the depths of sunny bays or clinging to the brown hillsides, villas peeping from the dark olive masses, sails gleaming against the purple sea.' In the quarter of a century since she had come to Monaco, the view had changed as much as it had in the previous hundred years. Across the steep, scrubby hillside wound two broad strips of concrete, the extension of the A8 motorway that had taken drivers straight from Paris to Nice. Now it stretched to Pisa and ultimately to Palermo in Sicily. At La Turbie the traffic was a constant background drone. Converging with and crossing the motorway at several places were lines of electricity pylons, the cables providing power from Nice to Monaco, Roquebrune, Cap Martin and Menton. Smoke billowed up from a refuse incinerator somewhere on the coast below. Grace looked down to Monaco where once, when filming *To Catch a Thief*, she had thought she glimpsed the gardens of Kubla Khan. Now she could see only high-rise apartments, office blocks and cranes.

To reach Monaco, you turn left across the stream of traffic on to the D37, which takes you down to the Moyenne Corniche. It is then an easy run into the principality. The D37, though, is a steep, winding, dangerous road. Augustus's monument stands at 1600 feet above sea level. Much of Monaco is little higher than the sea and it is a steep descent. Whether at this point in their drive the princesses had started discussing – or arguing about – Belmondo, we do not know, but witnesses have said that the Rover took the first part of the descent perfectly normally and slowed as it approached a hairpin bend, beside a track used to race model cars, a sharp left-hander, which the car negotiated. Then, about half a mile beyond the turn, the Rover began to veer and wander uncertainly over the road. Just as suddenly it straightened up as it approached the next hairpin. There, just where the brake-lights should have come on again, it suddenly accelerated. A lorry driver was following it: 'I said to myself, "My God! It's not going to make that bend!" The brake lights weren't showing. It just took off.'

The Rover flew through a low retaining wall, dropped down the mountain more than a hundred feet into a patch of trees, rolled over two or three times and came to rest on a pile of rocks, upside-down. It was nine fifty-four. The lorry driver who had witnessed the accident called the emergency services, who arrived quickly. So, too, did Prince Rainier, summoned from Roc Agel.

Given that she wasn't strapped in and had been thrown around the car as it fell, Princess Stephanie was in fairly good shape. She had cuts and bruises, and was in considerable pain from a dislocated shoulder and a fractured vertebra, but she might have been dead. Princess Grace's condition gave more immediate cause for concern: she had a broken thigh, a fractured knee and a fractured arm. More seriously, she had unspecified brain injuries.

She was taken to the hospital that bore her name. There, she was examined by doctors who confirmed the seriousness of her condition. They wanted to give her a brain scan. The hospital did not have the necessary equipment, and she was taken half a mile across the principality to the municipal hospital. The scan there revealed two brain lesions. The first was suggestive of a minor stroke – if it had occurred at Roc Agel, it might have caused her to black out for a couple of minutes. It was speculated that this might have caused the accident. The second lesion was much more severe, brought about when Grace's head hit the interior of the car as it flew down the mountainside. If it had been treated immediately after the accident, she might have survived, albeit paralysed on one side. As it was, there was no hope.

News of the accident had spread like the wildfire from which the coast increasingly suffered, first to Monaco, then Nice and the rest of the Côte d'Azur, then to the world. There was, predictably, an orgy of discussion on the cause of the accident. It was the Grimaldis' habit to let their children drive on their own property before they were old enough to do so on public roads. Accordingly some said Stephanie, rather than her mother, had been at the wheel. Then Princess Grace was rumoured to have had a drink problem, and this was tacitly attributed as the cause of the crash. The palace itself went so far as to suggest that the Rover's brakes had failed. The manufacturers at once sent a team out to investigate, but the engineers could find no sign of mechanical failure, either of the brakes or the steering. The palace was forced to withdraw the accusation. The engineers did discover, though, that the automatic was in Drive, for normal road conditions: a Mountain setting, for use on roads such as the D37, had not been selected. There was talk of sabotage, indeed of a conspiracy. None of these notions appears to have had any substance.

In consultation with his children, on the evening following the accident, Rainier took the decision that Grace's life support should be switched off. Her widowed mother and sisters were not consulted. At ten thirty p.m., on Tuesday 14 September 1982, Her Serene Highness Princess Grace of Monaco died. She was fifty-two.

The funeral was held the following Saturday, coinciding with celebrations in Britain for the safe return of the aircraft-carrier *Invincible* from the Falklands. The red and white Monégasque flag hung at half mast from the principality's buildings. The casino, many restaurants and shops were closed. Among those who attended the ceremony at the principality's Romanesque cathedral were Nancy Reagan, wife of the then President of the United States, and Madame François Mitterrand, wife of the French president, Mrs David Niven, Mr and Mrs Cary Grant, Mr and Mrs Mstislav Rostropovich, Mrs Arthur Rubenstein, Mrs Frank Sinatra, Mr Sam Spiegel, Mr and Mrs Jackie Stewart, the Queen of Spain, the former Empress Farah of Iran, the Prince and Princess of Liechtenstein, Prince Fuad of Egypt, the Grand Duchess of Luxembourg, Prince Albert of Belgium, and the former Queen Anne-Marie of Greece.

There was also Her Royal Highness the Princess of Wales, a little over a year after her own fairytale wedding to Prince Charles. Many in the congregation – including the young Princess – wept openly. Throughout the service, *The Times* noted, tears poured down the face of the fifty-nine-year-old Prince Rainier, 'slumped in a chair between his two eldest children, Princess Caroline and Prince Albert, on a dais, by the altar, under the television lights'.

The enchanting dream of happiness on the Riviera was over.

Epilogue:
The Secret of the Côte d'Azur

'When in that moment, so it came to pass,
Titania wak'd and straightway lov'd an ass.'
William Shakespeare, *A Midsummer Night's Dream*

In the last few days of August 1997, the eyes of the world turned on Diana, Princess of Wales, and Dodi Fayed, another golden couple trying to carve out their own patch of paradise on the Côte d'Azur. The paparazzi photographs, long-range, fuzzy, showed the couple disporting themselves on Dodi's father's yacht, moored off St Tropez's Pampelonne beach. Despite the graininess of the images, there was something almost iconic about them. It related to the couple (privileged), the nature of their relationship (romantic), and the setting (voluptuous), all of which combined in a curious harmony. Their death at the end of that holiday in a Paris underpass on 31 August 1997 lent the photographs a particular poignancy. They were virtually the last that were taken before the mob of photographers set off in pursuit of the Mercedes driven from the Ritz by Dodi's drunken chauffeur Henri Paul.

Since the death of Diana's friend Princess Grace almost exactly fifteen years previously, the coast had changed for the worse. There were more cars, more pollution of land, sea and air, more forest fires, more supermarkets and fast-food chains, more drugs, more crime and, of course, more people. Yet these had all existed in such profusion in 1982 that the difference was hardly noticeable. The

Riviera was a mess. The Riviera still is a mess. *Plus ça change, plus c'est la même chose.*

Writing exactly forty years ago, Geoffrey Bocca, the author of *Bikini Beach*, remarked that 'The principal sports of the Riviera are swimming, gambling, tennis and criticising the Riviera. The last is a game that has been played with unflagging ardour throughout the twentieth century.' He was wrong only in so far as criticism of the development of the coast dates back to the 1860s and the coming of that great agent of change, the railway. Yet visitors continue to appear on the coast in profusion: nine million every year, and rising. Even more remarkably, the Riviera retains its ability to attract celebrities who – if by no means any more discerning than the rest of us – can certainly afford to go elsewhere. Royalty, film stars, pop idols, manufacturing and media moguls, sporting heroes, notorious criminals: Madonna, Elton John, Bill Gates, the Saatchi brothers, Elizabeth Hurley, Gwyneth Paltrow, Britney Spears, the Beckhams, you name them and, come summer, they're there. Despite the remorseless degradation of the coast, its appeal seems timeless, immutable, undiminished, unassailable. Just what is it about the Côte d'Azur?

Writing at much the same time as Bocca, the former SOE agent Peter Churchill claimed, 'The important point is that the Riviera is not overrated. It cannot be. The antediluvian upheavals which threw up the mountains, carved out the coastline and drew the sea, plus the sun which has shone since then and is shining now, see to that.' He was certainly right in calling attention to the immutability of what have been called the region's icons, 'palm trees in the foreground, the arc of the shore, the blue of the sea, a village clinging to a precipice, and rising above the whole tableau, the alpine peaks'. As the ruins of Augustus's trophy at La Turbie so powerfully suggest, they are certainly less mutable than Sophia-Antipolis, Nice's Akropolis *palais de congrès*, the apartment blocks and condominiums, the railway and the airport, the motorways, the trunk roads and the other great achievements of Jacques Médecin, le

Prince Bâtisseur, and the post-war age. These have come. In due course they will go. The coast, the sun, the arc of the shore, headland after headland running out into the blue water, sails gleaming against the purple sea, these will remain.

Yet much more powerful than the reality of the Riviera is the whole idea of perpetual human happiness that it promises. For everyone from Tobias Smollett to the Rolling Stones, this has been its allure. As Christian Arthaud and Eric Paul say in *La Côte d'Azur des écrivains*, 'C'est L'Eldorado qui parait sans limite, ici c'est l'Hesperide, L'Arcadie, le jardin d'Eden.' Even though the reality of the Riviera seems daily to diverge ever more from the dream and the ideal, so powerful is this promise that the reality is ignored. Writers and artists, the first to celebrate the glories of the coast, noticed that the Emperor's clothes were getting threadbare more than seventy years ago. As D. H. Lawrence put it so trenchantly, 'This place no good.' And as F. Scott Fitzgerald remarked, not only was the place no good but the whole idea of earthly paradise was flawed, the quest for it as inevitably fruitless as that for the Holy Grail. The secret of the Côte d'Azur – the original holiday resort – is that so powerful is its alluring image that no one has noticed its deficiencies.

And perhaps they never will. Despite the way in which it has been developed and degraded, the Riviera will always be a place outside time, beyond sadness, illness, death and sorrow – not to mention bad weather – where the normal rules governing human existence are miraculously suspended. Whether it exists or not, it is the place, the promise and the dream everybody needs. Hidden from me when I first visited the coast a quarter of a century ago, this is something I now understand.

Select Bibliography

Place of publication London unless otherwise stated.

Acton, Harold, *Memoirs of an Aesthete* (1948)

Adleman, Robert, and George Walton, *The Champagne Campaign* (1973)

Alexander, Sidney, *Marc Chagall: a Biography* (1978)

Alford, Henry, *The Riviera* (1870)

Allen, Bernard M., *August Caesar* (1937)

Allen, Frank Lewis, *The Great Pierpont Morgan* (New York, 1949)

Allfrey, Anthony, *Man of Arms: The Life and Legend of Sir Basil Zaharoff* (1989)

Anderson, Alan, *The Blue Train* (Leicester, 1955)

Aronson, Theo, *The King in Love* (1988)

Arthaud, Christian, and Eric L. Paul, *La Côte d'Azur des écrivains* (1999)

Ash, John, and Louis Turner, *The Golden Hordes* (1975)

Baedeker, *South-Eastern France* (1898)

Baedeker, *Southern France* (1891)

Bagot, A. C., *Shooting and Yachting in the Mediterranean* (1887)

Balfour, Graham *The Life of Robert Louis Stevenson* (1901)

Baring-Gould, S., *Book of the Riviera* (1905)

Bartoli, Camille, and Réné Richard, *La Côte d'Azur Assassinée* (Paris, 1971)

Baughan, Rosa, *Winter Havens in the Sunny South* (1880)

Bedford, Sybille, *Aldous Huxley: a Biography* (1973)

Bennet, J. Henry, *Mentone, the Riviera, Corsica and Biarritz as Winter Climates* (1862)

Bernard, Paul, *The Rush to the Alps* (New York, 1978)

Binns, Richard, *French Leave Encore* (Leamington, 1992)

Black, C. B., *A Guide to the South of France, the Pyrenees and the North of Italy* (1873)

Blume, Mary, *Inventing the French Riviera* (New York, 1994)
Blume, Mary, *Lartigue's Riviera* (Paris, 1997)
Bocca, Geoffrey, *Bikini Beach* (1963)
Bockris, Victor, *Keith Richards* (1992)
Bogarde, Dirk, *An Orderly Man* (1983)
Bogarde, Dirk, *Snakes and Ladders* (1978)
Bonus, A. R., *The French Riviera* (1928)
Borel, Pierre, and Pierre Devoluy, *The French Riviera* (1924)
Bosker, Gideon, and Lena Lancek, *The Beach: the History of Paradise on Earth* (1998)
Braudel, Fernand, *The Mediterranean World in the Age of Philip II* (1986)
Brewster, Margaret Maria, *Letters from Cannes and Nice* (1857)
Brooke, John, *King George III* (1972)
Brougham, Henry, Lord, *The Life and Times of Lord Brougham* (1871)
Brown, Alexander, *Wintering at Menton* (1872)
Bury, J. P. T., *France 1914–1940* (1949)
Chambers, William, *Pen and Pencil Sketches of the Riviera* (1870)
Christie, Agatha, *The Mystery of the Blue Train* (1928)
Churchill, Peter, *All About the French Riviera* (1960)
Churchill, Peter, *Of Their Own Choice* (1952)
Clark, Kenneth, *Another Part of the Wood* (1974)
Cocteau, Jean, *Professional Secrets* (New York, 1976)
Collas, Philippe, and Eric Villeday, *Edith Wharton's French Riviera* (Paris, 2002)
Cook's Handbook to the Health Resorts of the Mediterranean (1878)
Cordell, Richard A., *Somerset Maugham: A Writer for All Seasons* (1969)
Corti, Count, *The Wizard of Homburg and Monte Carlo* (1934)
Cowles, Virginia, *Edward VII and his Circle* (1956)
Davenport, Giles, *Zaharoff: High Priest of War* (Boston, 1934)
Davis, John Bunnell, *The Ancient and Modern History of Nice* (1807)
Dodge, David, *A Rich Man's Guide to the Riviera* (1963)
Dolan, Brian, *Ladies of the Grand Tour* (2001)
Donaldson, Frances, *Edward VIII* (1974)
Drinkwater, J. F., *Roman Gaul* (1983)
Duff, David, *Victoria Travels. Journeys of Queen Victoria between 1830 and 1900* (1970)

Dulles, Foster Rhea, *Americans Abroad*, (Michigan, 1964)
Duncan, Isadora, *My Life* (1927)
Dupaty, Abbé, *Travels through Italy* (1785)
Eastlake, Lady (ed.), *Dr Rigby's Letters from France in 1789* (1880)
Ellman, Richard, *Oscar Wilde* (1987)
Englund, Steven, *Princess Grace* (1984)
Evans, Peter, *Ari: the Life, Times and Women of Aristotle Onassis* (1986)
Firth, John, *August Caesar* (1903)
Fitzgerald, F. Scott, *Tender Is the Night* (1934)
Fitzgerald, Zelda, *Save me the Waltz* (New York, 1932)
Fosca, François, *Renoir* (1961)
French, Sean, *Brigitte Bardot* (1994)
Fussell, Paul, *Abroad* (Oxford, 1980)
Garratt, G. T., *Lord Brougham* (1935)
Germond, Jean-Daniel le, *St Tropez: Le Temps Retrouvé* (St Tropez, 1993)
Gilbert, Martin, *Churchill, a Life* (1991)
Goldring, Douglas, *The French Riviera* (1928)
Gombrich, Ernst, *The Story of Art* (1950)
Goujon, Michael, *St Tropez et le Pays des Maures* (St Tropez, 2002)
Graves, Charles, *Royal Riviera* (1957)
Graves, Charles, *The Riviera Revisited* (1948)
Green, Martin, *Children of the Sun* (1976)
Greene, Graham, *A Sort of Life* (1971)
Greene, Graham, *Ways of Escape* (1980)
Haedrich, Marcel, *Coco Chanel: Her Life, Her Secrets* (1972)
Hagen, Victor von, *Roman Roads* (1967)
Hamnett, Nina, *Laughing Torso* (1932)
Hare, Augustus J. C., *The Rivieras* (1897)
Hare, Augustus J. C., *A Winter at Mentone* (1861)
Hare, Augustus J. C., *South-Eastern France* (1890)
Hastings, Selina, *Evelyn Waugh* (1994)
Heaton, Peter, *Yachting, a History* (1955)
Hessen, Robert, *Steel Titan, the Life of Charles M. Schwab* (Oxford, 1975)
Hibbert, Christopher, *Edward VII – A Portrait* (1976)
Hibbert, Christopher, *Queen Victoria's Letters and Journals* (1984)
Howarth, Patrick, *When the Riviera Was Ours* (1976)

Huxley, Aldous, *Eyeless in Gaza* (1936)
Isherwood, Christopher, *Prater Violet* (1945)
Jackson, Julian, *France: the Dark Years* (2001)
Jackson, Stanley, *Inside Monte Carlo* (1975)
Johnston, Shirley, *Villas of the Riviera* (1998)
Josephson, Matthew, *The Robber Barons* (New York, 1935)
Kanigel, Robert, *High Season* (2000)
Knight, Jeremy, *Roman France: An Archaeological Field Guide* (Stroud, 2001)
Kurth, Peter, *Isadora* (2001)
Lacey, Robert, *Grace* (1994)
Lartigue, Jacques-Henri, *Memoires sans Memoire* (Paris, 1975)
Leslie, Anita, *Edwardians in Love* (1972)
Leslie, Peter, *The Liberation of the French Riviera* (1981)
Liegeard, Stephen, *La Côte d'Azur* (Nice, 1982)
Littlewood, Ian, *Sultry Climates* (2001)
Longford, Elizabeth, *Victoria RI* (1964)
Lubbock, Percy, *A Portrait of Edith Wharton* (1947)
Macmillan, Hugh, *The Riviera* (1902)
Macmillan, James F., *Twentieth Century France* (1992)
Magnus, Philip, *King Edward the Seventh* (1964)
Mallet, Victor (ed.), *Life with Queen Victoria, Marie Mallet's Letters from Court 1887–1901* (1968)
Masden, Axel, *Coco Chanel* (1990)
Massie, Allan, *The Caesars* (1983)
Maugham, W. Somerset, *Strictly Personal* (1941)
Mayfield, Sara, *Exiles from Paradise: Zelda and Scott Fitzgerald* (New York, 1971)
McCormick, Donald, *Pedlar of Death: the Life and Death of Sir Basil Zaharoff* (1965)
Meadows, Matthew, *Pablo Picasso* (1996)
Monkswell, Lord, *A History of French Railways* (1911)
Mooney, W. W., *Travel Among the Ancient Romans* (1920)
Moore, Harry T., *The Priest of Love. A Life of D. H. Lawrence* (1974)
Morgan, Ted, *Somerset Maugham* (1981)
Murray's Handbook for Travellers in France (1847)
Murray's Handbook for the Riviera (1892)

Norman, Philip, *The Stones* (1984)
O'Brian, Patrick, *Picasso* (1976)
Ogilvie, F. W., *The Tourist Movement* (1945)
Ousby, Ian, *Occupation: the Ordeal of France 1940–1944* (1997)
Pearson, Hesketh, *The Life of Oscar Wilde* (1946)
Pemble, John, *The Mediterranean Passion* (Oxford, 1987)
Perrottet, Tony, *Route 66: On the Trail of Ancient Roman Tourists* (2002)
Pickering, Henry Thomas, *Monaco* (1882)
Pimlott, John, *The Englishman's Holiday* (1947)
Powell, Anthony, *To Keep the Ball Rolling, Vol. 2: Messengers of Day* (1978)
Powell, Anthony, *What's Become of Waring?* (1939)
Robinson, H., *A Geography of Tourism* (1976)
Robinson, Jeffrey, *Bardot: an Intimate Portrait* (1994)
Scott, Leader, *Tuscan Studies and Sketches* (1888)
Seroff, Victor, *The Real Isadora* (1972)
Shelden, Michael, *Graham Greene, the Man Within* (1994)
Sigaux, Gilbert, *A History of Tourism* (Geneva, 1966)
Smith, Adolphe, *The Garden of Hyères* (1880)
Smollett, Tobias, *Travels through France and Italy* (1766)
Spoerry, François, *A Gentle Architecture: from Port Grimaud to Port Liberté* (1991)
Standish, Robert, *The Prince of Storytellers. The Life of E. Phillips Oppenheim* (1957)
Stokes, Sewell, *Isadora Duncan* (1928)
Sullivan, Edward, *et al.*, *Yachting 1895* (1895)
Suetonius (trans. Robert Graves), *The Twelve Caesars* (1957)
Taraborrelli, J. Randy, *Once Upon a Time: the story of Princess Grace, Prince Rainier and their family* (2003)
Vot, André Le, *F. Scott Fitzgerald* (1983)
Watson, Alfred T., *King Edward as a Sportsman* (1911)
Waugh, Evelyn, *Labels: A Mediterranean Journal* (1930)
Weintraub, Stanley, *Victoria, An Intimate Biography* (New York, 1987)
Wharton, Edith, *A Backward Glance* (1934)
Wharton, Edith, *A Motor Flight Through France* (1908)
Wharton, Edith, *The Age of Innocence* (1920)

Wilt, Alan F., *The French Riviera Campaign of August 1944* (Carbondale, 1981)

Windsor, Duchess of, *The Heart Has Its Reasons* (1956)

Winkler, John Kennedy, *The Life of J. Pierpont Morgan 1837–1913* (1931)

Young, Arthur, *Travels in France During the Years 1787, 1788 and 1789* (Cambridge, 1950)

Young, George, *Tourism, Blessing or Blight?* (1973)

Index

Index

Picture Acknowledgements

The author and publisher would like to thank the following for permission to reproduce illustrations.

© Bettmann/CORBIS: Page 3 (above), Page 5 (above), Page 12 (below). Fonds photographique des éditions Gilletta. Nice-Matin: Page 12 (above). Hulton Archive: Page 2 (below), Page 3 (below), Page 4 (above), Page 4 (below), Page 5 (below), Page 6 (above left), Page 6 (above right), Page 6 (below), Page 8, Page 9, Page 10 (below), Page 11 (above), Page 11 (below), Page 13, Page 14, Page 15 (above), Page 15 (below), Page 16. © James Davis; Eye Ubiquitous/CORBIS: Page 2 (above). Mary Evans Picture Library: Page 1. Photos12.com – Oasis: Page 10 (above). © Swim Ink/CORBIS: Page 7.